W9-AFO-968
ILLINOIS CENTRAL COLLEGE
PN1992.94.L66 1990
STACKS
Getting into video :
A12901 062037

GETTING INTO VIDEO

Also by Mel London
Published by Ballantine Books

GETTING INTO FILM

GETTING INTO VIDEO

A Career Guide

Mel London

Ballantine Books • New York

 Published in the United States by Ballantine Books, a division of Random House, Inc., New York, and simultaneously in Canada by Random House of Canada Limited, Toronto.

Library of Congress Catalog Card Number: 89-90932

ISBN: 0-345-35648-9

Cover design by James R. Harris
Cover photograph by George Kerrigan

Manufactured in the United States of America

First Edition: August 1990

10 9 8 7 6 5 4 3 2 1

To my dear old friend
MARILYN LA SALANDRA,
for whom the dedication in a book
is the same thing as being remembered
in a will.

CONTENTS

Introduction 3
1. Videotape and Film 6
2. The Growing Video Marketplace 30
3. Broadcast Television and Cable 55
4. The Corporate World 75
5. Advertising and Public Relations 103
6. Government Video Production 120
7. Independent Production 137
8. Expanding Your Horizons 150
9. Postproduction 175
10. Home Video 187
11. Videotape and the Independent Artist 198
12. Festivals and Awards 218
13. Schools and Training 229
14. Getting a Job: Welcome to the Real World 252
15. The Future Is Behind Us 288
Selected Reading 297
Index 301

ACKNOWLEDGMENTS

I have learned my lesson well after ten books: there are really many ''authors'' in the writing of a career guide. No one person could ever do it alone, and this book is no exception. When I first began the project, I started to make a list of those who had helped, those who had given of their time and energies, their philosophy and advice. The list grew; it soon filled eight large index cards, with notes reminding me to thank everyone profusely and, above all, not to forget anyone's name. I soon realized this would not work out, and the listing would soon make a chapter of its own.

And yet, I am indebted to so many people, not only to friends who so willingly assisted, but also to new acquaintances made along the way, people who were generous in their contributions. Thus, with the few exceptions that follow, I have carefully placed each name in its proper place throughout the book; in this way I have given due credit to those who deserve my thanks and gratitude. In this way, too, I know that I have forgotten no one.

I am especially indebted to Sally Simmons, who in her ''real life'' is my production manager. Her research and unfailing good spirits did much to support my effort over these long months. If ever there was a ''without whom I could not have . . . ,'' it is my dear Sally.

Paul Kleyman of ITVA also deserves a special word of thanks, since much of the information on the nonbroadcast and corporate field came from his office in a constant and very impressive flow. And, of all the groups that contributed to the files of information and photographs about the cable field, Cablevision must certainly take a bow, as should Marie Gentile of West Glen; Bonnie Behar, who knows everyone in Connecticut; Sybil Lindenbaum, Ralph Katz, Dina Winokur, and Jim Sant'Andrea of Burson-Marsteller; Pat Kogan of 1125 Productions; and particularly the staff at Henninger Video for their reliability and cooperation.

Although I am an avid reader of what sometimes seems like too many trade papers and magazines, I would like to add a word of special thanks to *Back Stage* and *The Independent*, both of which were a constant source of information that might be passed on to you.

I have also learned over these years the value of an editor with whom an author can work closely yet be allowed the freedom to overwrite, make grammatical mistakes and egregious typographical errors, and forget to give examples. My very first editor ten books ago, Susan Petersen, firmly taught me that an author could not get away with making general statements without giving specifics to back them up. I have been blessed with another editor who also manages to keep me in line without making me feel constricted. Ginny Faber has been through the revision of *Getting into Film* with me, and I am fortunate enough to also have been involved with her on this book. I thank her for her thankless work.

Finally, I must give thanks to someone who has been here through all the books and who fully understands what it takes to go down into my womblike dungeon every morning and "give birth" to yet another page, another chapter. Since she, too, is an author, my wife, Sheryl, has been my most supportive friend when I become totally incommunicative while a new chapter gestates. She has been terribly important to me, and I give her my gratitude and my love.

Mel London
Fire Island, New York

GETTING INTO VIDEO

INTRODUCTION

The year was 1927. Harry M. Warner, then head of the company that bore his name, was told of a new invention that would allow a record player to run in synchronization with a motion picture. His reply was, ''Who in hell wants to hear the actors talk?''

For many of us, the idea of change, especially extreme change that might affect our lifestyle, can be disconcerting. The saga of the development of the ''horseless carriage'' has been told and retold in history books and in fiction. The advent of electricity was fought by a public fearful of its consequences. My wife tells the story of her father, who bought airline stocks in the mid-twenties but sold them quickly because ''the damned things would never fly.'' To the list of changes that have affected us all, we might well add the arrival of video technology. For the filmmaker, nourished on forty years of Eastman Kodak from nitrate to polyester stock, the past few years have been a time of reevaluation and extraordinary readjustment.

Back in 1976, I wrote a book called *Getting into Film* (Ballantine). It was revised and updated to reflect the remarkable technological changes in the field and also the evolving job market, especially in the burgeoning realm of video.

In just a few years video technology has created a niche for itself in business and industry—in communications, television, advertising, corporate training, the legal profession, and other areas. Its use is widespread and varied. In business, video enhances sales presentations and training programs. In marketing and advertising, it is used in local cable TV commercials and in place of retail catalogs. In education, video has become a new learning tool. In medicine, it is used to record surgical procedures for future reference. In law enforcement, it is used to record confessions and provide evidence.

The most startling change, however, is that video has become ubiquitous not only in professional areas but in the ''outside world'' as well. It has entered every aspect of our lives. Small portable video cameras have replaced 8mm film as the choice of proud parents who record every instant of the growth of their children. Boring, shaky tapes of vacations have replaced boring, shaky film reels and out-of-focus slides. Everything from weddings, birthdays, bar mitzvahs, even tributes to dearly departeds are being recorded on video.

Though video recently celebrated its thirtieth birthday with the anniversary of the development of the videotape recorder, it is only in the past ten years that the rate of change and development has escalated so rapidly, giving birth to a career potential that overshadows that of the motion picture industry. Many filmmakers have had to make a deliberate effort to learn the new technology, the terminology, and the processes in order to flourish and survive. For myself, even though I have been working in video since 1961, the growth has created a study situation akin to that of a doctor trying to keep up with the newest medical technology and changes.

During this same period, a generation of young adults has matured that is comfortable with video technology. Today young people have been brought up on television and weaned on personal computers. They are the proud owners of sophisticated videocassette recorders and portable video cameras, and are familiar with the complex, newly minted terminology of the field. It is not at all unusual to find people in their twenties or early thirties who are successful in their own video production businesses or who are playing a major role in the development, operation, and research of new video equipment or intricate digital editing systems.

In the editing rooms, both off- and on-line, in the postproduction houses that have proliferated across the country, behind the Quantel Paint Boxes and the Chyron Scribes, the Sony BVE-900 and all the other lettered/numbered pieces of equipment that make up this awesome technical arsenal, are the talented, comfortable, very efficient young people who have grown up with this technology.

Getting into Video is a book about jobs, about the career opportunities that now exist or that might appear in the future of a rapidly growing industry. I have tried to give an objective and balanced view—the potential as well as the problems. Vast markets for video exist in everything from entertainment to corporate communications, from police work to public access cable, from production to distribution. Throughout this book, I have tried to include examples of job opportunities that will give you an idea of the variety of career paths you might follow, taking advantage of the flexibility of the technology. If the creativity is there, the career paths are unlimited.

I have included interviews with many of the people who have chosen just such successful career paths: in television, cable, the corporate world, advertising, computer graphics, music video, government, and home video, as well as in the areas of education and employee training. Their words should be further guidance in helping you to choose at least a beginning direction.

In addition, I have added my own experience and the best advice that I can offer after so many years in both film and video.

I am constantly amazed at how rapidly things change and improve in this field. It is both part of the excitement of video and, occasionally, part of the problem. All of us who work in the field have a hard time keeping up with the electronic geniuses who have changed the communications world so dazzlingly in just a few short years. Indeed, the state of flux is so constant that even in the writing of a book such as this, the new technology has a tendency to date an author's bold statements before the typewriter even finishes a line.

But all of this is part of the excitement of which I speak. Because video is such a technological wonder, it will continue to change and grow through the next century. With the change and growth will come an important benefit: video will continue to provide an ever-expanding number of jobs for those of you who have been weaned on this technology. Besides your technical knowledge, your familiarity with the medium, and your creativity, you'll need to have initiative in finding those jobs. It still takes hard work—and it still requires at least a little bit of luck.

Given all of this—read on. A career lies waiting!

CHAPTER ONE

VIDEOTAPE AND FILM

Videotape and I first met in Rome in 1961. I had been hired by NBC to direct a fashion special that starred Celeste Holm and Domenico Medugno, and featured the most exquisite backgrounds in all of Europe as well as some of the most exquisite models to grace the continent. The job was to be surveyed in seven days, shot in three, then edited overnight in the new two-inch medium, put on an Alitalia jet, and aired in New York the following evening.

Celeste Holm (right) with model at the fountain in Piazza Navona during the author's first videotape production, "Fashion Is News," aired on NBC in 1961.

7

VIDEOTAPE AND FILM

The first part of the trip was heaven. Rome was (and is) a documentary filmmaker's dream, and I fell instantly in love with it, taking longer and longer lunches, while the NBC executives fumed at the slowing pace.

Finally, after scouting the city, I chose the ten locations that would be featured as backgrounds for the fashions and for the songs and patter of Celeste and Domenico, both of them delightful, professional, warm, and charming. The location permits were secured from RAI Television, the Italian network, and I prepared myself for the pleasure of taping in the Piazza Navona, Hadrian's Villa, the Campidoglio, and the Forum.

The film crew arrived on the seventh day, a melange of Europeans who made up an international tape production service based in Paris. They were mostly French, some British and Belgians, one technician from Yugoslavia, plus a token Italian. The production crew was made up of Americans and Italian personnel from RAI.

The filming was in fact like most other jobs, except for the tape van. I was fascinated. As a director who had been brought up in live television, followed by five years in documentary film, the van that carried the Ampex two-inch tape decks was a revelation.

The three days of shooting were mostly a delight. The control room van was set up exactly like its cousin back in the New York studios, albeit a bit more crowded. We used three cameras for each sequence, with their cable connections coming back to the van and the switching executed on the console, just as we would do it for a live TV show. The technical director was French, but luckily he spoke English. The assistant director sat beside me and preset the cameras. Directions were relayed by loudspeaker during rehearsals and then by a floor manager who used hand signals on the outdoor sets. Crowded behind us, shoulder to shoulder, were the NBC executives, client representatives, and other hangers-on, all with opinions.

We finished on time late Sunday afternoon. The show would be edited right in that van overnight, put on a plane next morning at DaVinci Airport, picked up at JFK Airport at 3 P.M. on Monday, rushed to NBC, and aired on Monday night.

It was the editing that drove me crazy! The previous ten days had been a director's dream. The ten hours of editing that followed were a director's nightmare. Although most of the show had been edited by selection via the control panel, there were still about eight to ten edits that had to be done in order to smooth out the show and eliminate what we considered to be slight flaws in the shooting or in the continuity. We also had to bring the show down to time, since we were about a minute and a half over.

Herein, then, lies the story. The editing of the original two-inch Ampex tape was the slowest, most tedious, exhausting, arduous, boring process then known to the human race. At each edit point, the tape was rolled back a minute or so and then stopped. The screen went black. There was no "Pause" button, no "Freeze" button. Just black. The tape was started up. There were lines and jiggles and more jiggles, and suddenly a picture. At the point that we wanted to edit out a flaw or make a change, someone called, "STOP!" The machine stopped. The screen went dark. There was no picture, no way to tell whether we had or had not reached the exact point at which we planned to make the change. The editor then took a sharp, new razor blade and made a cut, while all of us held our breaths. Then we "found" the next place for edit in exactly the same way, usually about fifteen or twenty minutes later, and the two raw edges of the videotape were laid edge to edge while the editor pulled a slender piece of aluminum tape across the wound. Now all we had to do was to see if it had worked.

The screen was dark. The tape was rewound. The only sounds in the room were the rolling tape and the silence of more breaths being held. Then the tape was started up again. Jiggles, lines, jiggles, then picture. At the edit, if all went well, the tape merely continued its journey. If, on the other hand, we saw horizontal jiggle lines across the picture, it meant that possibly some metal bits had come off the razor blade and onto the tape itself. The edit would have to be redone. If the picture jumped or if we had hit the wrong spot, we would have to start all over again.

This introduction to video was jarring. But, as with all things new and different, I soon became familiar with the technology. Today, I use both film and video.

Since those early days of video, the electronic geniuses of the field have been hard at work making things less complex, more sophisticated, expanding its capabilities, not the least of which was the move from glorious black and white (in which we shot the Rome fashion show) to glorious color.

Or—have they made it less complex, more sophisticated? In many ways, they have. At the same time, however, they have made the field even more complex, given us more choices, developed new and better equipment and computerized systems even while the "old" systems are not yet out of date. For the amateur, for the home viewer, this may not be so much of a problem. You have your VCR machine. You rent a videotape. You make sure it's compatible, and you play it, returning it in the morning to rent yet another.

If you are choosing video as your career, however, the very sophistication, the multitude of choices, the ever-changing technology are all things that must be considered almost on a daily basis. An understanding of the benefits of video—as well as the *limitations*—can and will affect your eventual efficiency in your chosen job. More important, perhaps, is the fact that this understanding can and will affect your financial stake in the field, from your potential advancement to the planning and execution of the budgets that will determine profit or loss on the production. The planning and the final selection of the proper system, the proper equipment, the most efficient postproduction processes—even the choice of whether or not to use videotape at all—are all decisions that must be considered by the professional. Making a living in the field becomes quite different from choosing a Camcorder for home use. This sounds logical, almost too simple to be stated. It is, unfortunately, too often not considered.

What follows is an outline of some of the factors to think about as you pursue your entry into video. There are a great many reasons why videotape has been and will continue to be a boon in the area of communicating ideas. On the other hand, there are some limitations to its use, and if improperly used, there are distinct disadvantages. You should be familiar with both sides of the coin.

THE ADVANTAGES OF VIDEOTAPE

INSTANT REPLAY. I might call this "instant gratification," but in the professional field, the fact that videotape can be seen even as it is recorded is probably one of the most beneficial of all the blessings inherent in the technology. (You will note that I also have included this feature in the section that deals with the disadvantages of videotape. But read on.)

Film has always presented a problem. In spite of all the care that is taken to ensure that the film is handled carefully, that it does not go through an airport X-ray machine, that it is tenderly put into the bath at the development laboratory, one still hears horror stories about mishaps, errors, and outright disasters. All of us who have been brought up in the film field live in dread of the midnight telephone call that says, "Call the lab as soon as possible!" It is with shaking hands that we return the call to find that two hundred feet of film were found rolling along the laboratory floor—"But we don't know *which* two hundred feet."

With videotape you know the results immediately. Once the tape is recorded, it can be played back instantly and decisions can be made as to whether or not the sequence, scene, incident, or interview should be redone. In addition, while the taping is actually going on, monitors show the progress of the shot or sequence for all to see. This means that the director can be much more secure about his or her work and about the impact of the sequence.

Of course, the benefits of instant replay have gone much further than the mundane need for a production unit to see its handiwork without a twenty-four-hour wait for the lab to report. The prime example of its current use is in the field of sports: in baseball, football, basketball, tennis, hockey, track, and every other contest in which the director chooses to replay an action or to make a specific point about a minor detail. Instant replay has been both a boon and a liability to the poor referee, umpire, or lineman who must now have his or her decision reviewed in a video room while the audience waits in suspense for the decision. Was he offside? Did she fault? Was the ball inside the foul line? The verdict is delivered on videotape.

For some years now, Francis Ford Coppola has been using videotape's instantaneous playback quality in yet another way. Beginning with *Cotton Club*,

"Everybody in! We have videotapes of the first hour of the party!"

(*Drawing by Stevenson* © *1987.* The New Yorker *Magazine, Inc.*)

VIDEOTAPE AND FILM

Coppola generally has directed his films from a sophisticated, state-of-the-art video van that shows him everything that is being filmed on the set. In that way, he claims, he can monitor the progress of the sequence, judge its composition, and study the reading of the lines of the actors and actresses.

In speaking to people who have been on the set during production of his films, I have gotten mixed reactions on this system. Some argue that the video monitors give the director nothing more than he can determine on the set, except for composition and line delivery. One of the criticisms has been that "everybody is gathered around the monitors making comments. Everybody gets involved." But for Coppola, even with the distance that he puts between himself and the set, the system seems to work. His *Tucker: The Man and His Dream*, which was shot in this manner, received mostly excellent reviews, especially for the "look" of the film. He must be doing something right!

In any case, instant replay has taken a great deal of the pressure off during the taping sessions for many productions. Most of us can now sleep better at night without worrying about the laboratory bath being the right temperature for our precious film stock.

EASE OF SCREENING. The introduction of the home videocassette recorder in 1975 ushered in what the Electronics Industry Association rightly calls the Video Era. Along with the sale of videocassette recorders to the home market, sales have increased substantially to every imaginable type of organization and location. With the television screen and a videocassette player/recorder, we suddenly have more than half of the entire country available to us and to our productions: schools—for teaching science or recording plays for future classes; hospitals—for doctor training and patient orientation; corporations—for employee training and stockholder reports and image presentations. Classrooms. Courtrooms. Police stations. Bus and airline waiting areas. And the home—for every conceivable type of promotion and entertainment. The estimate for the end of this decade: 85 million VCRs in homes all over the United States, plus uncounted millions in the professional/commercial areas.

All of this is exciting not only to the public, but also to the professional filmmaker/video producer. Before videotape, in order to screen one of my films or to distribute a subject around the country, it had to be assumed that each locale had available a 16mm sound projector plus an adequate screen on which to throw the image. I remember time after time when I had to present my work on yellow cards tacked to a wall with no curtains in the room to block the light. Today, most places can accommodate video. I no longer need an expensive screening room to work with my clients and editors in the final stages of production. With a videotape player, a thousand facilities exist, even a setup in my own living room.

OPTICAL EFFECTS. Tape can use a thousand tricks and use them well. Where optical effects on film, even down to a simple credit crawl at the end of a feature, might take ten days or more in planning and production, videotape and sophisticated computers allow optical effects to be created almost instantaneously—and, in most cases, more cheaply than film. It is wonderful to watch a character generator at work: It changes the typeface. It changes the spacing. It changes the size of the letters. Remove one letter. Put in another. Juggle them. Then put it all on the scene that you've chosen. And that's only the easy stuff.

If you love kaleidoscopic effects; if you love shapes that flip over and turn around, move upside down and change color right before your very eyes; if you like computer-generated images, trips through space or under water, spinning logotypes, spinning genies, spinning bottles, spinning anythings, then videotape is just the medium to offer you sheer delight.

In general, optical effects can be done more cheaply on video than through the tedious frame-by-frame process of film opticals. On the other hand, there are techniques used in videotape effects that can cost up to $3,000 a second (such as complex computer animation).

COMPLETION AND DUPLICATION. Although the first or off-line stage of videotape editing, in which sequences are put together, can take as long as the film editing process, the beauty of videotape comes in the last or on-line stage, when the completed tape is edited into its final form. Within just a few hours, video masters can be made and the tape duplicated. The proliferation of tape-duplicating facilities makes the price of the duplication nominal compared to film. Even then we are not done. For, if the need arises to make final changes, the advantages of videotape over film are quite remarkable.

Consider the difference. When film has reached a stage comparable to the on-line phase of videotape, that is, when the work print has been approved by all concerned, the finishing process then begins:

- The work print must be matched against the original negative of the film, a tedious process done by comparing the numbers along the edges of both copies. This procedure is time consuming, taking a week to ten days, and any mistake in cutting can ruin the negative.
- The original negative is sent to the laboratory, where an answer print is made. This stage may take up to a week.

- The answer print is screened and color corrections are made. A second answer print may have to be struck. If you're lucky and if the lab is not too busy with the networks, this step may take one or two days.
- When the answer print is approved, the lab strikes a printing negative and then an interpositive/internegative from the original. This can take another three days to a week.
- After the printing negative is completed, a check print is made, which is then color corrected if needed.
- Finally, release prints are made, adding another week or so to the finishing process.

With video, on the other hand, even with two tedious days in the on-line editing room, the tape is completed when the final edit is done. No further work is necessary.

QUALITY. There is a continuing debate about quality differences between film and videotape. When analyzed by experts, all video formats are inferior to film in terms of sharpness and color fidelity. But to casual viewers, that difference is barely perceptible. In terms of cassette reproduction, picture quality is a trade-off for extended playing time. The very narrow band of frequencies for video necessarily affects the quality of the image.

But even here, there have been improvements (such as the Sony Super-Beta system). However, the current standard television system in the United States has a resolution of only 525 lines, while a frame of 35mm color negative can record the equivalent of up to 2,200 lines of horizontal resolution. High-definition video recording, already on the market and being used experimentally even in feature films, offers a resolution of 1,125 lines, giving a dramatic improvement in video quality but not quite up to the level of film.

I must say, though, that most of the discussion about quality of videotape versus film image seems to be a rather unimportant one at this time, especially since videotape is not being used for feature film production, except on an experimental basis (see page 34). For video, the final terminal is the TV. And the final viewer—the consumer—doesn't care about the tape–film controversy.

Ray Salo, who heads his own production company in Shoreview, Minnesota, put it this way: "We're in what I call a 'convenience culture' and the consumer wants to get the job done faster and for less cost. He or she couldn't care less about resolution! Remember, when tape came in, our client orientation began to change, and it was the consumer who became important to us—and still *is* important."

Since the quality of videotape has been improving, there has been an increasing volume of origination on tape, yet another reason that the job market in video has opened up in the areas of camera, sound, engineering, and production management. Ray Salo thinks that this is the most profound change in the industry in the past twenty years. He says: "Tape origination has become very good. Betacam is good enough so that it takes an expert eye to tell the difference from 16mm film. And remember, productions are not made for the expert eye."

Salo says that "tape usage is taking over, not only in corporate showings on VCRs, but also in schools. It's no longer true that schools require 16mm film. They'll also accept videocassettes, and many actually prefer them to film." But the bonus for Salo is that "tape origination is faster. You finish your project faster. You get paid faster."

That last statement might be reason enough to chose tape over film.

COMBINING FILM AND TAPE. The union of film and tape technology seems to be getting stronger, now that the couple has begun to discover the attributes that each can bring to the marriage. One trend is to shoot on film

Veteran cameraman Joe Longo now shoots both in film and in videotape, a part of the growing trend in the "marriage" between both media.

and finish on tape, thereby making the best use of each medium's strengths.

Most directors today prefer to shoot on film for a variety of reasons: the "look" of film, the flexibility in sound mixing, their own training. Just about every TV sitcom today is shot on film, using Kodak's color negative. There are, of course, exceptions that favor tape production ("The Cosby Show" and "Kate & Allie," for example). However, in the postproduction stages, the film negative is transferred to videotape in order to close the cost gap for completion, utilizing the speed of postproduction in video plus the advantage of more rapid dubbing of copies.

There may be yet another reason to shoot on film, finish on tape. By shooting on film, producers take advantage of the "look" of the medium, then take advantage of the flexibility and generally lower costs of video postproduction. The original film negative can be stored in a refrigerated or air-conditioned vault, to be transferred again when a still higher definition video system comes into being ten or twenty years from now. This technique is most valuable in the area of feature films, for the "classics" can be reissued again and again as the technology improves and the market for videotape continues to grow. What is on VHS today will soon be on Super VHS, and will probably be reissued on Super-Duper VHS or HDTV tomorrow.

COST FACTORS. When used properly, tape can be cheaper. However, when deciding whether to use film or videotape, you'll need to consider the following: What type of project is it? Is it a complex studio shoot that might require three cameras (and crews)? How much stock is to be shot? If you are going to run the cameras for eight straight hours, tape is obviously the answer. Film stock would break the bank! Editing: How simple? How complex? How many special effects? Deadlines: Plenty of time or on the air tomorrow? There is no doubt, for example, that in a hidden camera shoot, using three cameras to record a sequence of five- to fifteen-minute interviews over a period of eight to ten hours and possibly through two or three days on location, the use of film would be a huge budget expense. Nat Eisenberg, head of NBE productions in New York, is an expert in the field of hidden camera techniques. Eisenberg says:

> *When it comes to hidden camera shoots, both for cost and ease of operation, the nod must go to videotape. . . . Figure the cost of a one-hour reel of tape versus the cost of purchasing, developing, and printing the film equivalent. Reloading the tape and cassette machines happens much less frequently, and even with a videotape feed attached to a film camera, you really don't see it all as it's really happening.*

In determining the cost factors, you also must consider the complexity of the production in both the original photography and the postproduction stage, including editing and sound requirements. There are many features today that will improve the quality of tape, and none of them has anything to do with technical developments. The most important barrier that tape must still overcome is its early reputation of being "quick and dirty." Today, producers have learned to use tape efficiently and economically while still utilizing their years of film experience to guide them. Director Annette Bachner says:

> *The image of [videotape being] 'quick and dirty' comes from the Dark Ages when you shot on Friday and were on the air on Saturday. This has no relation to most of the work we do today. I take as much time for set and light on tape as I do on film, and I work with actors just as long in rehearsal and blocking. When it comes to editing, I make as many rough cuts as I do on film. Anyone who tells me that tape is quick, fast, and cheap is not shooting the type of tape that most directors are shooting today!*

Tape requires the same personnel as film. It still requires writers, production people, set designers, home economists, wardrobe, makeup, props, and hair people, stylists, special effects experts, and a whole range of postproduction personnel. Bachner adds: "The caliber of their work doesn't change, whether we're recording on film, tape, or Band-Aids!"

There is one more important element that most directors have just begun to discover. If you spend as much time in lighting for videotape as you do for film, the quality gap begins to narrow dramatically, especially if the end screen is a television set. We must begin to look at videotape from a different point of view when it comes to cost. Properly selected as the medium of choice, properly used, properly planned for in both production and postproduction, the medium can be cheaper as well as more effective for its eventual audience and objective.

NEW AREAS OF EXPERIMENTATION. For the video artist, for the technical researcher and the engineer, for the communicator, the teacher, the trainer, and the independent producer, videotape has opened up a whole new realm of possibilities. The uses of video are limitless. Museums across the country are now devoting entire exhibitions to single- and multi-screen video art. The computer revolution has spawned still new ways to create images that have never been seen before. Possibly some of the *Star Wars* razzle-dazzle, quick-cut technology will even serve to keep students awake in class as they watch the new videos.

Interactive video has begun to take its place in the worlds of art, sales, and communication. In the area of marketing, the video boom has let imaginations run wild, and a whole new range of services and products, such as interactive shopping networks, has begun to be offered to a public that has the final terminal, the TV screen, in their living rooms (or bedrooms, kitchens, even bathrooms).

In the days of *Buck Rogers* and *Flash Gordon*, teleconferences were the works of "movie magic." Today teleconferencing is a flourishing business, providing instant seminar and executive meeting potential. Videotape and its technology have only just begun to have an impact on business. The possibilities are endless.

THE REALITIES OF VIDEOTAPE

Every medium has its limitations. The listing that follows is given as a guide, an outline of some of the factors that we must take into consideration in the choosing of the medium for our project and for the budget considerations that these limitations place upon us. So, let's put aside the wonderful and glorious benefits of videotape and look at some of the disadvantages. Once you are aware of them, you can make them work for you.

INCOMPATIBILITY. The problem of incompatibility is not new, nor is it confined to video. Video systems and equipment, tape formats and sizes, are all incompatible. There are no worldwide video technology standards. Despite the fact that we constantly read in technical magazines that solutions are on the way, the day is not yet here when we can put a videotape recorded in France into a high-tech VHS machine in the U.S. and see anything but horizontal lines.

Where film now reflects the success of worldwide standards in equipment and formats, and thus has become a software-intensive medium—any film sent to any country will find a standard projector on which it can be screened—tape is and will remain for many years a hardware-intensive technology. Film is, in a sense, future-proof. Videotape is not.

The variations in standards affecting videotape are numerous. To begin with, different countries have different voltage standards and can use either 50- or 60-cycle power sources. Television standards are also different: 525 lines in the United States, 625 lines in Europe. Our system scans at 30 frames per second, theirs at 25 frames. The differences become even more complex when we consider the development and marketing of the videotape systems that are attached to these noncompatible television screens.

Professional television producers began by using two-inch tape, and over the years they switched to one-inch videotape, while improving the quality of the mastering. The home market saw the introduction of Sony's Beta system at the same time that VHS technology was being offered to the public. It was the equivalent for the consumer of betting at the racetrack. If you bought a Sony system, would it be around for a year, ten years, forever? In any case, if you bet on Beta, you lost. Sony has gone out of the consumer business, leaving the field to VHS. Now we are being sold Super VHS, which is mostly incompatible with its parent. Kodak then came out with Super-8, incompatible with everything else.

The professional market, not to be outdone by the consumer industry, had its own engineers hard at work in the laboratories across the world. Two-inch tape was joined by a host of other formats, many of which are still around today, with more coming down the assembly lines each year. Currently, there are available 3/4-inch U-Matic, U-Matic SP, one-inch, Betacam and Betacam SP, and M-11, which—you guessed it—are mostly incompatible.

All of this covers only the United States, where the National Television Standards Committee (NTSC) has been around for forty years causing nothing but compatibility troubles. When we begin to speak of systems in other countries, we run into other obstacles. Not only are their electrical systems not compatible with ours, but their videotape formats carry different names and

Worldwide Standards for Videotape

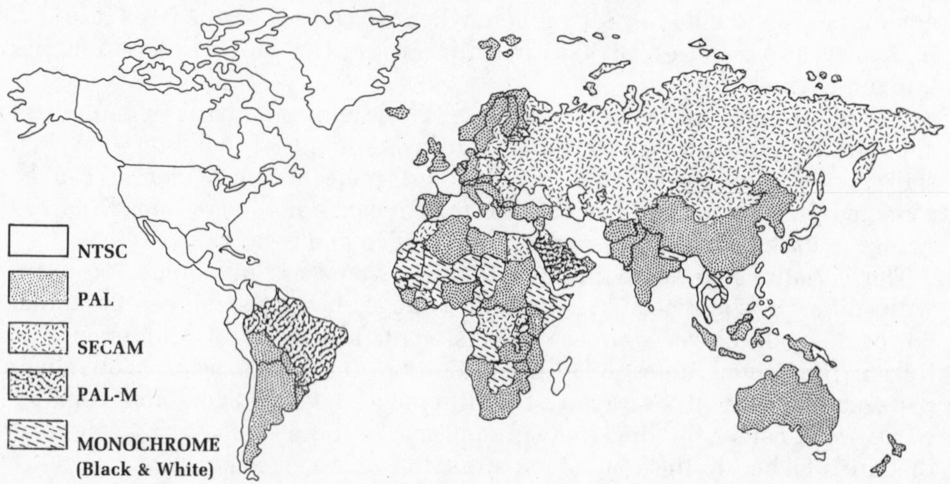

are not compatible among themselves. For instance, NTSC is not compatible with SECAM and both are incompatible with PAL.

Still, we continue to hear about the problems of standardization in an industry that has grown so tremendously over the last twenty years, just as we continue to read articles that complain of the chaos that this incompatibility has spawned. Equipment purchased at great cost today may well be obsolete within a year or two. For the producer, for the postproduction house, this can mean a terrible financial loss.

Worldwide Standards for Videotape

COUNTRY	B&W/COLOR	VOLTAGE (v)	FREQUENCY (Hz)
AFGHANISTAN	PAL.B	220	50
ALBANIA	D	220	50
ALGERIA	PAL	127–220	50
ARGENTINA	PAL.N	220	50
AUSTRALIA	PAL.B	240	50
AUSTRIA	PAL.B.G	220	50
BAHAMAS	NTSC.M	120	60
BANGLADESH	PAL.B		
BARBADOS	NTSC.M	120	50
BELGIUM	PAL.B.H	127–220	50
BERMUDA	NTSC.M	120	60
BOLIVIA	NTSC.N	115–230	50
BRAZIL	PAL.M	220	60
BULGARIA	SECAM.D.K	220	50
CAMEROON		127–220	50
CANADA	NTSC.M	110–240	60
CANARY IS.	PAL	127	50
CENTRAL AFRICAN REP.	K	220	50
SRI LANKA		230	50
CHAD		220	50
CHILE	NTSC.M	220	50
CHINA (PEOPLES REP.)	PAL.D	220	50
COLOMBIA	NTSC.M	110–220	60
CONGO (PEOPLES REP.)	SECAM.D	220	50
COSTA RICA	NTSC.M	110	60
CUBA	SECAM.D	120	60
CURACAO	NTSC	120	60
CYPRUS	SECAM.B.H.G	220	50
CZECHOSLOVAKIA	SECAM.D	220	50
BENIN		220	50
DENMARK	PAL.B.G	220	50

COUNTRY	B&W/COLOR	VOLTAGE (v)	FREQUENCY (Hz)
DOMINICAN REP.	NTSC.M	110	60
ECUADOR	NTSC.M	120	60
EGYPT	SECAM.B	220	50
EL SALVADOR	NTSC.M	110	60
ETHIOPIA	SECAM.B	127	50
FIJI		240	50
FINLAND	PAL.B.G	220	50
FRANCE	SECAM.E.L	115–230	50
GABON	SECAM	127–220	50
GAMBIA			
GERMANY (DEM. REP.)	SECAM.K.B.G	220	50
GERMANY (FED. REP.)	PAL.B.G	220	50
GHANA	PAL.B	230	50
GIBRALTAR	PAL.I	230	50
GREAT BRITAIN	PAL	237–220	50
GREECE	SECAM.B	110–220	50
GREENLAND		220	50
GUAM	NTSC	110	60
GUATEMALA	NTSC.M	110–220	60
GUINEA	B.K	127–220	50
GUYANA	SECAM	127	50
HAITI	NTSC.M	115–220	50
HAWAII	NTSC.M	117	60
HONDURAS	NTSC.M	110–220	60
HONG KONG	PAL.B.I	220	50
HUNGARY	SECAM.K	220	50
ICELAND	PAL.B.G	220	50
INDIA	PAL.B	230	50
INDONESIA	PAL.B	220	50
IRAN	SECAM.B	220	50
IRAQ	SECAM.B	220	50
IRELAND	PAL.A.I	220	50
ISRAEL	PAL.B.G	230	50
ITALY	PAL	127–220	50
IVORY COAST	SECAM.K	220	50
JAMAICA	NTSC.M	110	50, 60
JAPAN	NTSC.M	100–200	50, 60
JORDAN	PAL.B	220	50
KENYA	PAL.B	240	50
KOREA (SOUTH)	NTSC.M	100	60
KUWAIT	PAL.B	240	50
LEBANON	SECAM.B	110–190	50
LIBERIA	PAL.B	120	60

VIDEOTAPE AND FILM

COUNTRY	B&W/COLOR	VOLTAGE (v)	FREQUENCY (Hz)
LIBYA	PAL.B	120	50
LUXEMBOURG	PAL.SECAM	120–208	50
MALAGASY REP.		127–220	50
MALAWI		220	50
MALAYSIA	PAL.B	240	50
MALI		125	50
MALTA	PAL.B	240	50
MARTINIQUE	SECAM	125	50
MAURITANIA		220	50
MAURITIUS	SECAM	220	50
MEXICO	NTSC.M	127–220	50, 60
MONACO	SECAM	125	50
MONGOLIA	SECAM.D		
MOROCCO	SECAM.B	115	50
MOZAMBIQUE	PAL	220	50
NETHERLANDS	PAL.B.G	220	50
NETHERLANDS ANTILLES	NTSC.M	120–220	50, 60
NEW CALEDONIA	SECAM	220	50
NEW ZEALAND	PAL.B	230	50
NICARAGUA	NTSC.M	117	60
NIGER (REP.)	SECAM.K	220	50
NIGERIA	PAL.B	220	50
NORWAY	PAL.B.G	230	50
OMAN	PAL	220	50
PAKISTAN	PAL.B	220	50
PANAMA	NTSC.M	110	60
PARAGUAY	PAL.N	220	50
PERU	NTSC.M	220	60
PHILIPPINES	NTSC.M	115	60
POLAND	SECAM.D	220	50
PORTUGAL	PAL.B.G	110–220	50
PUERTO RICO	NTSC	120	60
ZIMBABWE	PAL	220	50
ROMANIA	SECAM.B.G	220	50
RWANDA		220	50
SAMOA	NTSC	120	60
SAUDI ARABIA	SECAM. PAL.B.M	120–230	50, 60
SENEGAL	SECAM.K	125	50
SIERRA LEONE	PAL.B	230	50
SINGAPORE	PAL.B	220	50
SOMALIA (REP. OF)		220	50

COUNTRY	B&W/COLOR	VOLTAGE (v)	FREQUENCY (Hz)
SOUTH AFRICA	PAL.I	220	50
SPAIN	PAL.B.G	127–220	50
WESTERN SAHARA			
ST. KITTS	NTSC	220	60
SUDAN	B	220	50
SURINAM	NTSC.M	115–127	50, 60
SWAZILAND	PAL.B.G		
SWEDEN	PAL.B.G	220	50
SWITZERLAND	PAL.B.G	220	50
SYRIA	B	115–220	50
TAHITI	SECAM		
TAIWAN	NTSC.M	100	60
TANZANIA	B	230	50
THAILAND	PAL.B.M	220	50
TOGOLESE REP.		127–220	50
TRINIDAD & TOBAGO	NTSC.M	117	60
TUNISIA	SECAM.B	117–220	50
TURKEY	PAL.B.G	110–220	50
UGANDA	PAL.B	220	50
UK	PAL.I.A		
BURKINA FASO		220	50
URUGUAY	PAL.N	220	50
U.S.A.	NTSC.M	110	60
U.S.S.R.	SECAM.D.I	220	50
VENEZUELA	NTSC.M	110–220	60
VIETNAM	B.M	120	50
VIRGIN IS.	NTSC	115	60
YEMEN	PAL.B.NTSC.B	220	50
YUGOSLAVIA	PAL.B.G	220	50
ZAIRE	SECAM.K		
ZAMBIA	PAL.B	230	50

This situation was described in an excellent article by C. Cecil Smith in the magazine *Video Manager*. Smith described the chaos in this way:

> *The . . . problem is one of basic VTR [videotape recorder] standards. Professional 3/4-inch recorders of PAL and SECAM operate in what is called a high band. Industrial and consumer 3/4-inch recorders of PAL and SECAM signals operate in the low band. High-band tapes cannot be played in low-band machines and vice-versa. A SECAM tape made on the PAL*

> *version of a Sony BVU professional machine will not play in the PAL version of a Sony Type V VTR. . . .*

If you are one of the many millions of VCR users, then much of what I have written will not come as news to you. On a professional level, as you progress in your career you'll need to consider the following:

- Be careful of formats. Choose the right one for your market.
- Make sure that any purchase of equipment for your production is chosen carefully and with an eye toward eventual obsolescence.
- You might consider renting equipment instead of making an investment in cameras and editing and recording equipment.

A word about HDTV (High-Definition Television). The last word with regard to equipment compatibility belongs to Phil Hage. He recently said to me in a telephone conversation from St. Paul:

> *You know, in consumer electronics and even more correctly in data recording, technologies change completely in five years. For example, at 3M, we recently introduced a new diskette that we warrant will withstand* 25 million passes *of the head. We call it a multi-generation diskette, because that's basically* 2,000 years *of day-to-day use. So, the* medium *is going to be there. The question is whether the* hardware *is going to be around. That's something else.*

This revolutionary new system, which promises to bring cinema quality image into every living room in the country, is currently the video industry's heavyweight contender. Japan recently made its first transmission using the new system. With receivers selling at about $60,000 per set, it is not yet commercially available, but it will be very soon. It will be compatible with all Japanese-made HDTV products: television sets, videocassette recorders, and video disk players. But it will *not* be compatible with the systems now being developed in the United States.

The Federal Communications Commission has issued guidelines that will protect U.S. television systems manufacturers by requiring that all HDTV signals be compatible with existing television sets. Since some TV systems work at 1,100 lines, some at 1,125 lines, and some at 1,160 lines, you can begin to see the problem! You will not have to buy a new TV set if you want to receive the signal, but it will not be high-definition television that you'll be seeing. In order to view HDTV, you'll have to buy an HDTV monitor, and projections make it substantially more expensive than the current Japanese imports of the standard sets. However, with the market now projected at more than $20 billion a year by 1997, you can understand why the FCC ruled as it did. On the other hand, the old monster of incompatibility will still be with us. There will be three totally incompatible HDTV systems: one in the United States, one in Europe, and one in Japan.

For the TV viewer, it matters not. For the professional, it is terribly important. Welcome to the year 2000!

COLOR RESPONSE. An engineer with whom I work once told me that the most disastrous color for videotape is red. As he put it, "You couldn't think of a more awful problem than giving us a shot of a model in a *red dress* sitting in a *red convertible* and sipping from a *red can* of Coca-Cola!" Unfortunately, on almost all video formats, the color red has a tendency to emanate halolike from its subject.

Certainly, the overall quality and color response of videotape continues to improve. I read the technical magazines and constantly find such quotes as "videotape will overtake 35mm film within ten years and soon you won't be able to tell the difference *on a television screen*." Well, actually, it's pretty hard to tell the difference now—on a television screen. Remember, the final adjustment is made by the person using the TV—and many times, it would make no difference if the blue were tinted green or yellow, so long as the image was in color. The instant success of colorization, with its sickly hues, has proven the point.

R. O. Blechman, who created and produced "A Soldier's Tale" for PBS, complains that his choice of a very special color (Parrish blue) for the production lost all of its luminosity in the transfer from film to tape. And, though everyone agrees that tape has a sharpness and raw immediacy, many producers are still choosing 35mm film in order to get gauzy, dreamlike, rich response. HBO's "Linda Ronstadt in Concert" was shot on film for that very reason.

There are other reasons why the color response of videotape is less than professionals would like. Virtually every format in use in the field has a different formula for the paint (the oxide coating that records the information). In addition, since each manufacturer has developed its own electronic mixing systems and parameters of compatibility, even the use of something like a Sony monitor with a JVC player can harm the final viewing stage, unless the tracking, color, and hue are delicately tuned. I have found that in such cases, switching to a Sony–Sony or a JVC–JVC combination can improve the image considerably.

EQUIPMENT BREAKDOWN. This is one of the realities that we live with when we produce videotape. There are as many horror stories for this medium (camera stops operating, recorder stops recording or puts jiggly lines across the picture) as there are for film (scratches in the lab, film lost on an airline), but many of the video stories come from the fact that we are dealing with a sensitive, highly technical, computer-driven medium. Human errors will always be the same, no matter what the medium. But equipment breakdown, especially in a distant, isolated area, can be disastrous to your budget (as well as to your good humor).

I thought for a while that I was the only producer to suffer a video camera breakdown during a blizzard, fifty miles from civilization on a Sunday. I thought that a dear friend of mine was the only producer to suffer a recorder breakdown on the island of Aruba on his first day of shooting, while using a format for which there was no substitute in that area. And then I found out why we take engineers with us as part of our crew. And why we frequently take backup equipment with us, even though it means lugging too many pounds up too steep a road on too high a mountain. The best advice I can give is this:

- Check out the equipment thoroughly before using it.
- Rent from a reliable supply house.
- Take a good engineer with you.
- If you are working in an isolated area, consult with your engineer in advance to determine which pieces of equipment should be taken as backup.

For the most part, you will not be filming in isolated areas. And today, with the absolutely incredible spread of the videotape industry, chances are that you'll be able to find a spare piece of equipment somewhere in the area, in almost any town or city. On that fateful Sunday I mentioned above, we contacted a production manager of the rental company and she drove a new camera out to us, ignoring the six inches of snow that had already fallen.

EDITING PITFALLS. Video editing and postproduction can be much cheaper than film editing and postproduction. Video editing and postproduction also can be much more expensive than film editing and postproduction. It all comes down, once again, to choosing the right medium and then planning far enough in advance to avoid the pitfalls of time and, thus, cost.

In many instances, tape editing is much quicker than the editing of film, especially with the newer electronic marvels such as the Montage system, where many pictures can be seen all at once and the selection made. On the other hand, don't be fooled by the publicity surrounding the editing and postproduction industries. Tape editing is divided into two major categories: "off-line" and "on-line." The first phase is the one in which scenes are selected by both picture and code number, and then put together in what is to become final continuity. Generally, the editorial rates and the rental of equipment are based on hourly or weekly use. The editing of a complex, sophisticated, effective product that requires the selection and computer placement of many short sequences or complicated montages can take weeks in the off-line phase, as well as adding expensive hours during the on-line production.

During the editing stages, the sound/music/effects track is put together. If the sound track is complicated, the tape edit can take two to five times longer than the typical film edit. Where a film edit deals with a piece of physical material that can be handled, cut, rewound, and played again, a tape edit involves mathematical input, shot by shot, number by number. As editor Ted Kanter puts it: "Editing tape is like pulling a locomotive. You find the edit. You program the edit. You rehearse the edit. You perform the edit. You review the edit. You make the edit."

Many editors are now editing pictures in videotape, and doing their tracks as they would in film, mixing them in a studio and then laying them in on the finished product. Either way, editing can be expensive. But the mind-boggling costs are yet to come.

The difficult time, when money can go down the drain, and the budget along with it, is in the on-line stage, when the final product is put onto a master tape. It is not unusual to spend somewhere around $400 an hour in the major markets. Add to that figure the use of sophisticated special effects equipment that makes videotape such a joy and your costs can go up to $1,000 an hour.

Steve Zahler, a freelance producer/director and a managing partner of The Electronic Cutting Room, an off-line editing suite in New York, puts it beautifully when he speaks of on-line editing:

> *Remember, this is the final edit. The taximeter in your head is ticking away the semiprecious minutes as your on-line editor types more time-code numbers into the computer, previews the effect, stops, trims off a few more frames, recues the audio track, previews the event again, stops, trims, recues, turns to you for approval, and you say in controlled anguish, "Let's do it!"*

Zahler warns that tape postproduction requires the same kind of skills and creativity as film production.

INSTANT REPLAY. This is both an advantage and a disadvantage of tape. Just be warned that when you take your place on your first set or location,

VIDEOTAPE AND FILM

Editor Herb Altman and client preview an insert edit during off-line session at the Electronic Cutting Room in New York. All edit decisions are stored in computer memory and transferred to 8″ floppy disc for "autoassembly" of the master in the on-line suite.

you'll see that everybody but *everybody* becomes a director, particularly when tape instant replay is available.

In film the director works closely with the DP (director of photography) or cinematographer. Only one eye goes to the camera eyepiece, and the results are seen the next day in the "dailies." If something must be reshot, it will be at great expense.

In videotape a reshoot can be done immediately if something goes wrong. However, all of the viewing is also done on the spot. The monitor is right there. The director now has a tendency to look at the monitor rather than at the set and the actors. The assistant director, the stage crew, the actors, the clients, the agency producers, the art directors, the hangers-on, the caterers, the mothers of the child stars, and anyone else who happens to be in the studio, including messengers and off-duty police officers, are now looking at the monitor. Instead of one director, we now have ten or more. And everyone has an opinion.

''What do you think?''
''I didn't like the way he sipped the drink.''
''He blinked, I think.''
''Run it back and let's look at it again.''
''He didn't blink.''
''But he didn't sip the drink with joy!''
''The engineer says the blue wasn't right.''
''I don't see anything wrong with the blue.''
''He says you don't see it on the screen. His sine wave is wrong.''
''Let's do another take.''

''Everyone back on set. Okay, everyone. Here we go. *Take Number 33.* Let's get it right this time.''

STORAGE. The field of videotape is so new—barely thirty years old—that we are just now beginning to see articles that deal with the storage of tape. After all, at the beginning of a new technology, who even dares to think about thirty years hence? Bruce Fellows, a technical service engineer with the 3M Memories Technology Group Labs in St. Paul, Minnesota, has written that the company gets at least one call a month from people who would like to store a videotape in a time capsule. The first question he asks them is whether they also plan to include a videotape *player*, since the format may well not be available a hundred years from now.

In film storage, we now know that the original negative must be stored in refrigeration, that some of the formats of years back have a tendency to fade (Eastman Color, for instance) while others look as good today as they did in the 1930s and '40s (Technicolor). With videotape, we are just learning that proper care and storage mean much in terms of what we will have available to us in years to come. Knowing this, the major videotape manufacturing companies, such as 3M, run a constant series of tests on their product to ensure that the tapes will withstand some of the handling given them by the consumer.

Fellows notes the following characteristics of tape that affect storage:

- Tape absorbs humidity. When it does, its playback characteristics will be affected.
- Temperatures above 120°F will create the possibility of layer-to-layer adhesion. As a result, 3M routinely runs 125° blocking tests to make sure that adhesion won't occur.

- Heat encourages the growth of fungi that feed on the organic material found in most tapes.
- Light changes the physical characteristics of plastic film, and although light discourages the growth of fungi, the polyester in the tape backing might become brittle.

Both Bruce Fellows and Phil Hage, who is with the 3M public relations department, recommend that those of us who are interested in storing tape for archival purposes do so by making several copies of the materials and storing them in different locations for safekeeping.

Having analyzed and dissected, complimented and criticized this comparatively new technology, let's take a closer look at the video marketplace.

CHAPTER TWO

THE GROWING VIDEO MARKETPLACE

The whole business has changed radically in the last ten years. Before videocassettes, I would never have been able to do Salvador *and Alex Cox would never have been able to do* Sid & Nancy *and David Lynch would never have been able to do* Blue Velvet. . . .

Oliver Stone, director

The statistics are staggering: More than 50 percent of all homes in the United States now have at least one VCR. There were half a million VCRs in 1979 and more than 30 million seven years later, an increase of 575 percent. By 1990, the figure was estimated at 85 million. This does not include video cameras, software, and television sets. But the most important fact for the potential job seeker or career changer, especially the communications graduate just getting out of college, is that none of this takes into consideration the areas where the most jobs are being developed and where the most openings now occur. The home market is important. It has spurred the growth of a new industry. But it is only a small part of the picture.

For communications school graduates, the ''glamour'' area seems to be in the television stations and the networks. I cannot fault graduates for wanting to get into this end of the business, having begun my own career in live television. However, it is only part of the potential job market.

If you look carefully at the video job marketplace, you will notice that there are only about 1,000 commercial TV stations in the country plus about 600 more in the noncommercial and low-power categories, a figure that is expected to increase dramatically in the next decade. On the other hand, there are currently about 50,000 nonbroadcast video users across the country, with a projection of over 80,000 by 1995. It is these organizations, corporations, government agencies, and service companies that offer the best opportunity for breaking into the field in production, management, and in creative areas. In addition, you should take into account production houses, postproduction facilities, and the vast freelance market that services both sides of the business: writers, engineers, consultants, camerapeople, directors, editors, and artists.

In order to choose the area of video that you are most interested in getting into, you need to consider the following:

- the range of markets in which you can work
- the choice of geographic areas in which you'd like to live (and work)
- the specific job you'd like to do

I will cover much of this in detail in later chapters, but for now I'd like to outline the many choices that are open to you in the burgeoning world of videotape.

MARKETS

> *The Department of the Interior, finding itself in the middle of a dispute over a proposal to erect a sprawling shopping mall next to the Manassas (Bull Run) National Battlefield Park, turned to the state-of-the-art technology to make its case: It made a videotape for the press . . . the first time the Interior Department has done something like this in the area of information policy. . . .*
>
> *The New York Times*
> Sept. 9, 1988

BROADCAST TELEVISION. This includes on-the-air systems such as the networks and their owned and operated (O&O) stations, local affiliates, independent and public service stations, and even a growing segment of local low-power television stations. It also includes the individuals and smaller organizations that feed broadcast television programming.

CABLE. What started out as a small industry whose only objective was to provide a means of improving poor-quality TV reception in rural areas has now become a giant that reaches almost 50 percent of all American households. As a result, the employment picture in this burgeoning industry has also grown, with over 50,000 people employed on a full-time basis in jobs that parallel those of the broadcast industry.

CORPORATE IN-HOUSE PRODUCTION. Although this might not seem quite as glamorous as broadcast or cable TV, corporate in-house production actually provides some of the best entry-level opportunities in video. Corporations, using in-house and freelance production staff, facilities, and audiovisual managers, are busily engaged in major communication areas:

- Employee training films
- Employee communications
- Corporate image productions
- Stockholder reports
- Point-of-sale videos

NONBROADCAST TELEVISION. This includes the corporate networks that communicate with distant locations via private television systems. Nonbroadcast television allows corporations to effectively train and contact their employees about policy changes, new regulations, and news items, and is a growing field. For example, the Taco Bell Corporation now has 1,400 sites in its network and plans to expand to 2,400 in the near future. The same uses listed in the Corporate In-House Production section are also a factor in the expansion of corporate networks. In addition, corporate networks allow for teleconferencing, for interactive programming (through both videotape and laser disc), and for satellite production of special events.

PRODUCTION AND POSTPRODUCTION COMPANIES. Independent video production companies provide many of the services needed by television stations and corporations. In postproduction (the editing and completion of the job) these outside service firms become even more important, for the investment in high-tech equipment at this stage is often out of the reach of many smaller organizations. Thus, production and postproduction companies become potential job sources for the beginner as well as for the experienced producer. There is frequently a crossover of jobs: many production and postproduction people are hired by corporate audiovisual departments, while many corporate people leave to form their own production companies. Their first clients are often their ex-employers!

ADVERTISING AGENCIES AND PUBLIC RELATIONS FIRMS. Ad agencies have begun to produce some of their own commercials in-house in addition to using videotape for interoffice communications, creating still more opportunities for staff producers, writers, videographers, and supervisors. Public relations companies, quick to find another service for their customers, have used videotape to great advantage to teach clients how to speak and to conduct themselves in television interviews or before the press. There's nothing better than seeing yourself on tape to realize that you do (or don't) make a believable impression when the questions are coming at you hard and fast. For the job seeker, in-house studios and production facilities have opened doors to new opportunities.

GOVERNMENT AGENCIES. Government agencies are beginning to find hundreds of uses for videotape. Every governmental group—federal, state, and city—has begun to use the medium. The Department of the Interior, the Federal Aviation Administration, and the Central Intelligence Agency all use it, as do police departments, district attorneys' offices, and state and city courts. Just read the newspapers:

- A New York City Corrections officer was arrested after he had been videotaped smuggling a gun to an inmate in the Rikers Island prison.
- Court aides working for a Surrogate Court were videotaped stealing from the dead as they entered the apartments of the deceased, none of whom had left wills.

These agencies use in-house videotape technicians and producers as well as independent production companies and freelancers.

UNIVERSITIES. Here again, we find a combination of job openings: production units located on campus that consist of both professionals and communications students, plus freelancers and independent production companies. The uses of videotape on the university level range from a video tour of the school for prospective students to training aids and educational adjuncts for almost every course.

EDUCATIONAL VIDEOTAPES. Closely tied to the universities category is the educational video market. But the potential use of video is much broader than for student bodies. These tapes are produced for home audiences, teaching everything from literature to zoology.

HOME VIDEOS. Besides feature films, this market includes how-to and self-improvement tapes, specialized documentaries and "shorts," foreign films, and classic TV show compilations—just go to your local video store to discover what's available. For the feature filmmaker, this market has been a bonanza (witness Oliver Stone's paean to VCRs at the opening of this chapter). A number of films that had been box office mediocrities or financial disasters have become cult videotapes. For the video professional, there are entry-level jobs here in production and distribution.

INFORMATION SYSTEMS. This is a natural outgrowth of the home video and education markets. Videotapes are everywhere: in department stores selling fashions, cosmetics, and point-of-sale items; in auto dealerships showing the features of the latest models; at conventions and sales conferences publicizing companies' images and products. Someone has to shoot, edit, produce, and distribute these tapes.

COMPUTER GRAPHICS. For people who are adept at computerese, mathematics, and/or art and graphics, this field has proven a golden opportunity for entry and development. Graphics are used in almost every category of the videotape industry: by advertising agencies, corporate in-house units, and independents.

INDEPENDENT PRODUCTION COMPANIES AND FREELANCERS. This includes production and postproduction personnel and such creative classifications as writers and designers. It also includes documentary video producers, a growing field since the television networks have cut back so drastically on their own production of documentaries and specialized programming.

FEATURE FILMS. At the time of this writing, only one feature (*Julia and Julia*) has been produced and distributed in theaters after shooting in HDTV, with another ("The Littlest Victims") appearing on television. Several others are now in production, but the total number is still small. Given the rapid advances being made in HDTV, there is no doubt in my mind that the number of feature films shot on high-definition videotape will increase substantially in the future. Newspapers and trade magazines are filled with the plans of producers to develop feature projects on videotape and then transfer them to 35mm film for screening in theaters. Thus, video-trained technicians and creative people will find that even this area of production will begin to open up to the new technology, with even more jobs available.

Remember that there are hundreds of crossover jobs in the industry. What I mean by that is simply that if you begin your career in commercials, you might well find yourself eventually working in documentaries, or moving to an advertising agency, or editing a soap opera for television. Certainly, the editors among us can be working on tapes that cover every market I've mentioned. This also holds true for the computer experts, artists, directors, and makeup people in the field.

GEOGRAPHIC AREAS

In a letter to me, Chip Dreamer described his background and his current position with Idaho Video:

> *I'm originally from Nebraska, but please don't hold that against me! I have a B.A. degree in journalism from the University of Nebraska and twenty-three years of experience in educational, broadcast, and corporate television. . . . I guess one of the most interesting things about [Idaho Video] is that the entire staff ended up in Idaho Falls at the same time. [The area's] not really a hotbed of video production . . . although we've already been involved in some pretty interesting projects.*

IDAHO VIDEO. . .
An Editor's Ideal Vacation

We're halfway between Sun Valley and Jackson Hole, half an inch wide and half as expensive.

Yes. Betacam is waiting for you in the mountains.

Call Chip Dreamer at IDAHO VIDEO (208) 522-2020.

P.O. Box 2148
Idaho Falls, Idaho 83403

Idaho's Premier Betacam/Interformat Post Production facility

Idaho Video is an example of the thousands of small video production companies scattered around the country. It is also an example of the state of flux in the business. A few months after he wrote the above, Chip corresponded with me again:

> *Ah! The problems of running a small business. It all sounds like the basis of a great soap opera!*

Chip's director/producer had quit and gone to Seattle. His cameraman quit soon after. Chip's wife decided that she didn't want to be his writer and went to Denver. Naturally, just as everybody left, the company became extremely busy. Fortunately, the summer intern graduated from college and joined Chip full time. Idaho Video went from a staff of five to a staff of two:

> *We're working fourteen to sixteen hours a day and we're back in production. . . . We're shooting projects for ESPN and Video Press Pac out of L.A. They put together commercials and short filler pieces for movie companies to promote their upcoming features. We've done two in Montana and one in Wyoming.*

Chip and his assistant taped a segment for ESPN's "Baseball Magazine," a two-day shoot with a fourteen-hour bus trip sandwiched in between:

> *We got four hours sleep in two days, one meal, and hit ten baseball players in the head with a sun gun while shooting on the bus. We were stopped at the Canadian border when one of the players was asked if he had anything to declare and he said, "Yes, war on Canada!" I'm getting too old for this kind of videotaping trip.*

Idaho Video also produced a tape for the Mountain Bike Championships in Sun Valley, a piece entitled "Snowmobiling the West," three commercials for the Eastern Idaho Regional Medical Center, and a promotional marketing tape for another medical center. Future projects included a promotional tape for the Blackfoot, Idaho, Chamber of Commerce and one for the Idaho Falls Chamber.

This should give you an idea of just what the range is, even for a small two-person company: commercials, promotional videos, sports. Small companies around the country provide production and videotaping services for a wide variety of clients.

The *Video Register and Teleconferencing Resources Directory* lists over 5,500 equipment manufacturers, teleconferencing resources, dealers of new and used equipment, video users, cable access facilities, program producers and distributors, and trade organizations. The *Back Stage TV Film and Tape Production Directory* lists approximately a thousand more agencies and production companies. If you add the 50,000-plus nonbroadcast video users in the U.S., the technical facilities that provide editing, postproduction, and dubbing services, then you begin to realize that there is no limit today in choosing the geographic area in which to work.

Many corporations, independent producers, and smaller companies find it inconvenient or too expensive to keep a large video production staff on hand, so there will always be a need for local technicians and equipment and production facilities. For example, one of my largest clients is Duke Power

Company in Charlotte, North Carolina. My sound man, Bill Shaver, lives in the area, and I rent my equipment from Carolina Productions. It saves me time and money to use local people and suppliers when doing work for Duke Power.

There's another reason why local video production is growing. It was summed up by Steve Zahler of the Electronic Cutting Room: "Clients just don't like to travel!"

In the past, film clients would accept the waiting, the time in the lab, the travel. But today, with video, clients do not need to wait. They want the results here and now. So the facilities and technicians need to be here and now.

As a job seeker in the video industry, you no longer need to confine your search to Los Angeles and New York. In fact, you may find that moving to a smaller market can be profitable.

Ray Salo, whom I mentioned earlier, started his career in video twenty years ago on the East Coast, then moved to Shoreview, Minnesota, a few years back because he preferred the pace of the Midwest. His company has been quite successful in the medium-sized Twin Cities market. His list of clients includes national *Fortune* 500 corporations, as well as local companies and social agencies. Salo has operated on the theory that you can be successful by basing and selling in a systematic way to a select market that can be easily serviced by a local operation.

Keep in mind that the proliferation of local video opportunities has also created a tremendous amount of competition in the field. Not every videotape company stays in business. Not every freelancer works fifty-two weeks a year.

When the time comes to pick an area in which you'd like to work, the trick is to exploit the local opportunities, to research and analyze the needs of the area in the field of video and communication. If you travel around the country, you find that the successful video companies in each area have done just that. My files are bulging with available production facilities, personnel, and equipment rental companies in almost every state.

Trade papers and magazines bear me out. If you eliminate the ever-present hype that dominates the communications and entertainment industry, you still come up with some interesting and amazing proof that the video boom is nationwide:

> "LOCAL PRODUCTION COMPANIES ARE NEW ENGLAND'S LATEST COTTAGE INDUSTRY"
>
> *EITV Magazine*

"FAIRFIELD COUNTY IS BECOMING A MECCA FOR VIDEO ENTREPRENEURS"

Fairfield (Conn.) *Advocate*

And from *Back Stage*, one of the industry's bibles:

"PRODUCTION BOOM IN MICHIGAN BUILDS CONFIDENCE"

"THE TWIN CITIES: BULLISH ON IN-TOWN POST"

"INDIANAPOLIS PRODUCTION: SOMETHING MORE THAN STATUS QUO"

So, there is a real video world out there, and you might even be able to stay in or near your own hometown and still make a career. Many production companies are one-person operations, while others use outside personnel. Corporations may have only one person on staff, or boast a unit of ten specialists.

State-of-the-art facilities can now be found all over the country. Robert Henninger founded his company barely six years ago. Henninger Video in Arlington, Virginia, now has a 10,000-square-foot facility, employs 28 full-time staff members, and has three on-line edit suites and two off-line suites, plus three computer graphics systems. (Photo: Katie Henninger)

- New York City has over 300 production and postproduction companies and videotape services, plus studios, dealers, equipment repair and maintenance companies, and recording and editing services.
- In Chicago there are more than seventy editing and postproduction facilities.
- Florida numbers about 150 videotape producers, with most of them in the Miami area, but others based in Clearwater, Pompano Beach, Tampa, and Orlando. In addition, Florida backs up these producers with 250 companies that offer services, supplies, and equipment.
- Maryland, New Jersey, and Delaware can supply complete production packages as well as equipment rental and postproduction facilities. Pennsylvania offers close to 100 producers from which a client can choose. Michigan, Texas, Iowa, Virginia, and the District of Columbia all boast extensive listings of video-related companies. Every state has its listings; every state has its videotape users, and thus a range of operating personnel.

Of course, in smaller communities the only game in town might well be a one-person production company or a cable or broadcast television outlet. Every so often, *Back Stage* publishes a state-by-state listing of production companies, agencies, equipment suppliers, and postproduction facilities. Check out this directory; it's a good way to become familiar with a particular area.

Before you pack your bags, you should consider whether there are any corporations that make their headquarters in that area. Many smaller cities are home to corporations, and many of those companies are actively engaged in videotape production.

If you look at a list of *Fortune* 500 companies, you will see that not every large corporation is based in New York or Chicago or Dallas. Dow Chemical, for instance, has been in Midland, Michigan, for all of its years. 3M is located in St. Paul, Minnesota, Eastman Kodak in Rochester, Armstrong World Industries in Lancaster, Pennsylvania, and Maytag in Newton, Iowa.

Further along this line, there are many subsidiaries of major corporations that do their own videotape production rather than relying on tape produced by corporate headquarters. In the areas of product videotapes, employee relations, and certain local considerations, such as community public relations, it is certainly more effective to allow the branch factory or office to do its own work. Thus, we constantly read of local companies who have produced videotapes for organizations such as ALCOA, W. R. Grace, and AT&T, while never setting foot near the corporate headquarters.

Part of the search for a place to locate is dependent upon your talents and what you will have to offer. For example, is there a specialty in an area that makes you particularly valuable to a production company, a television or cable station, or a corporation based there? Are you an expert downhill skier who can handle a camera while traveling at 75 miles per hour on the slopes? What about wildlife photography? Or stop-motion and special computer effects? I know of one video production company that offers expertise in the photography of thoroughbred horses. They are, naturally, located in the breeding country of Kentucky; even New York advertising agencies come to them for those sunset-backlit-beauty shots that end up in the commercials on your television screens.

JOBS

Although we tend to think of jobs in videotape in terms of specific titles (director or producer or editor), the "real" world for the most part is composed of the "hyphenate," a combination of jobs: director-producer or director-cameraperson or writer-editor or salesperson-writer-researcher-director-producer-editor. The latter descriptor may seem overblown, but keep in mind that it exactly defines the jobs in many small operations around the country, both in production companies and in corporate in-house facilities. Many of the people who work in nonbroadcast television—audiovisual supervisors and managers at large corporations, production company executives and staff, and postproduction experts—are hyphenates. The exceptions are generally larger union shops, network television stations, and parts of the freelance market that service those big business areas. In these markets, the jobs tend to remain specialized—a gaffer (electrician) is a gaffer. In smaller production units, someone will no doubt double as gaffer–something else.

When you enter the field, realize that you will probably end up doing several jobs along the way. And all of that experience, gained in difficult, long-hour work situations, will help you later on. As my grandmother used to say, "It couldn't hurt!"

As you read the job descriptions that follow, keep in mind that they are not set in concrete. Jobs change according to the needs of the production. Any combination of two or more jobs will make you a hyphenate. Although I list myself in the credits on my tapes and films as producer-director, I have also acted as lighting specialist, doubled as sound person–still cameraman, worked as the writer of treatments and scripts, acted as agent to sell project ideas to clients, and filled in as bookkeeper of my own small company. And so will you.

PRODUCTION

This, of course, is the area that deals directly with the actual making of the videotape. Essentially, whether for videotape or film, for television or corporate communications, the jobs remain about the same.

PRODUCER. We used to say that "anyone who calls himself (or herself) a producer *is* a producer." Generally, the producer is the person who is in overall supervisory control of the production, who oversees the budget and the subsequent expenditure of funds for technical and creative personnel (such as the writer and videographer), and who has the final say about the production and its content.

There are occasions, especially in network television and cable production, when the producer may be supervised by an *executive producer*, a person who may be involved in several productions all at the same time, or a member of management who supervises budget and content but without the day-to-day hands-on control. As you will no doubt find in your work, even these definitions are often changed to fit the situation. There have been times when I have assigned the title of executive producer to a client of mine, who was in charge for his or her company. It can be a vague credit, but so is everything else in the video field.

DIRECTOR. This is the person who is in control of the day-to-day progress of the production, supervising the creative elements (such as the writers, set designers, actor rehearsals), and who then is in charge on the set or the location as the video is shot. The director is often involved from concept and research through the editing and completion stages.

AUDIOVISUAL MANAGER. This title exists within the corporation. It is the job that most clearly approximates the role of producer-director in the outside production companies or in television and cable. The audiovisual manager, however, is also a middle-level or upper-level executive, very much like the vice president of any corporate division. Costs are his or her concern, and the hiring of staff personnel is also one of the functions of the job. Some audiovisual managers supervise large staffs, while others hire outside freelance personnel to produce the work. J. C. Penney and Georgia Pacific, for example, fall into the first category, while a company such as Anixter (see page 84) uses only two or three people and then hires outside talent for the projects. Essentially, the audiovisual manager is an administrator as well as a trained video producer.

WRITER. Whether in-house or freelance, the writer plays essentially the same role. Usually the job begins with the research needed for the video and continues on through the treatment (a narrative outline of what the project will contain) and then into the script phase of the production. The latter, by the way, is usually not a part of the documentary, since no one can determine just what someone will say in an interview. However, the script (or screenplay) is an integral part of the writer's job for a teleplay or feature or any production that uses actors.

For those of you who plan to follow this path, it is essential that you know the forms that are used for treatments and screenplays. There are several good books on the market in the "Film and Video" sections of your local bookstore.

There is one other factor about writing that I would like to discuss, which transcends the script phase of the job. I think that every reader should understand that there are other things that one should be able to write in order to become successful—good business letters, contracts, follow-up communications after interviews—all of them in addition to what is generally considered the activities of a writer. Of course, not everyone writes—or writes well—but those of you who can make the word processor or typewriter do tricks should find breaking into the field moderately easy, especially if you have a good sample to show.

In the corporate world, the writer is critical in the area of communications: scripts and collateral materials for employee training and orientation, technical video presentations for new products or sales information, even speeches for top executives. Some large companies have begun to put their entire catalogs on videotape, for distribution to salespeople and clients, and all of them are scripted by in-house writers.

In advertising agencies, the copywriter is the wordsmith who starts the process from idea to aired commercial. Client contact, product, and market and demographics research are all part of the writer's function. Then, locked in a small office with only the hum of traffic below, it is up to the copywriter to come up with the advertising line that is going to move his or her client's product from the bottom to the very top.

In television and cable, the newswriters collect, organize, and of course write the scripts that are used by the anchor people. Their words are transferred to a TelePrompTer located discreetly off camera, then read aloud by the star of the newscast. Behind every newscast—morning, noon, evening, and late night—there is a writer.

VIDEOGRAPHER. In video, the person who handles the camera performs exactly the same function as the brother or sister who is shooting on film. With more and more people knowing the workings of video cameras and with the proliferation of in-house production, the job market has opened considerably, whereas in film the top cinematographers are tightly unionized. However, handling a video camera is not the same as being familiar with a home Camcorder. Remember, the video industry today is as professional as any other, and you'll have to know about the equipment that is currently being used in both studio work and location shooting. The videographer is generally under the supervision of the director, but this is also an area in which we find many hyphenates.

SOUND PERSON. Sound is a critical part of any production and sound people today are responsible for very sophisticated equipment. In the field of news gathering and in many documentary situations, the videographer frequently doubles as the sound person. This has come about because of the development of technology that allows sound to be recorded at the same time as picture, both on the same tape deck. Many sound people work in both tape and film.

PRODUCTION ASSISTANT. This has always been tricky to define, since many of the jobs in this category carry different titles for people who perform exactly the same function. The simplest way to describe this is to say that a

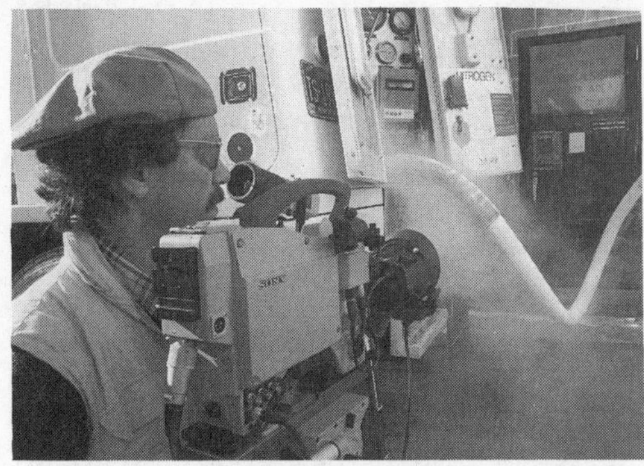

Videographer Ed Collins on location for a Union Carbide Safety Video on Nitrogen and Argon Gas. (Courtesy Scott Herde)

Video sets look exactly like their cousins in film. Lighting director Jim Nassetta adjusts a light for the Union Carbide Safety Video. (Courtesy Scott Herde)

production assistant aids the producer, the director, and/or the audiovisual manager. Job duties vary tremendously, and the job title can be imaginative: production manager, production secretary, assistant director, second assistant director, unit manager, production coordinator, and possibly one or two more that show up on the credits down near the bottom of the list. In many companies and for many television productions, production assistants are the backup, the support, and the workhorses for the supervisory production people. Many times it is they who determine whether the production will run efficiently or become an unmitigated disaster.

A great many preproduction details fall into this area of responsibility: telephone contacts for location approvals and permits, acquisition of permits and insurance coverage, booking of crews and scheduling personnel, script breakdown, making up shooting schedules, planning for inclement weather contingencies, travel arrangements, equipment rental, location scouting, acquisition of releases, and tracking of budgets.

During the actual production phase, the assistants are everywhere, and much of the efficiency of the job is the responsibility of these lower-level people. Duties can vary from getting the actors ready and on the set on time, to making changes in the script or the shooting schedule because of unforeseen circumstances (weather or an ill crew member), to ordering lunch (terribly important), to seeing to it that the video footage is given to the proper person at the end of the shooting day—and that it is all logged in properly. There is one other thing that *all* production assistants should be able to do: *drive a van or a car*. Without a driver's license, your value as an assistant decreases to practically nothing in this field.

On overseas jobs, the role becomes even more critical. It includes all of the above duties *plus* having a knowledge of currency exchange and requirements, brokerage for equipment, customs requirements here and abroad, bonding of equipment, registration forms, and the compatability of video equipment. And what happens if the equipment beaks down in the middle of Bangladesh?

For those of us who produce and direct, the hiring of a good production assistant is critical to our sanity. If you see me smiling, there is a good chance that I have a great backup on the production staff. Otherwise, I can become mean and nasty.

ENGINEER. On location or in the studio, the engineer is tied by an "umbilical cord" to the camera operator or videographer. He or she must see to it that the video signal is accurate, that the color balance is correct and within technical limitations, and that a signal is actually being recorded. He or she is also responsible for handling the playback when requested by a director or producer in order to check the quality and the composition of the image.

For news gathering and for other documentary situations, the development of small, self-contained units has eliminated the need for this job category. However, for most studio locations, and for the general requirements of location shooting in various formats, the engineer is a necessity. On long-distance or overseas locations, having a qualified engineer along is also an insurance policy against equipment breakdown, for the video systems have not been quite as reliable as the standard film cameras such as the Arriflex-SR.

Let's not forget all the other production people who go to make up the staff of a project. Certainly, not all of those who follow will be found on the set of every videotape project. Their inclusion depends upon the size, the scope, and certainly the budget of the job. If we are dealing with one of the few sitcoms to be originated on videotape or the production of an HDTV project, then there is a good chance that many, if not most, of the following people will be found on stage. On the other hand, with the proliferation in videotape of small, independent producers and in-house operations, many, if not most of the people listed below will not be found on set. Remember, too, that many of these production people move from film to tape in order to survive, and it is quite possible that you will also be moving from one medium to the other and back again if your entry level is in one of these categories.

ACTOR, MODEL, AND VOICE-OVER NARRATOR. I have always felt that these are the most difficult jobs in our field, mostly because of the constant rejection and the never-ending search for work through auditions and

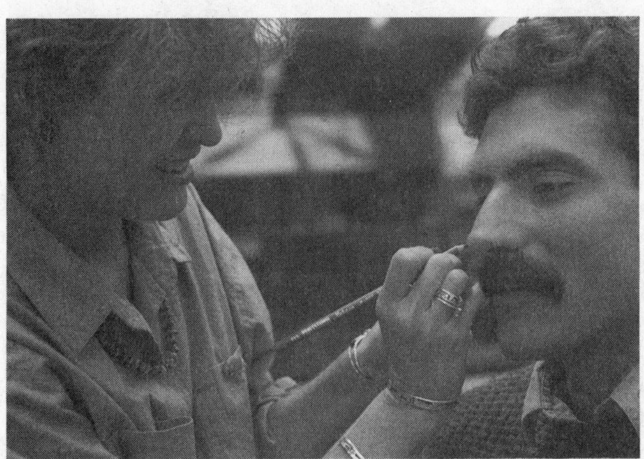

Among the crossover jobs in video is that of makeup artist. On the set of the Union Carbide shoot, Leslie Smith works her craft on Jim Nassetta. (Courtesy Scott Herde)

casting director interviews. Nevertheless, the videotape field is a lush one for these individuals in terms of commercial work, though the on-screen fame and fortune will never come close to that of the film feature field. New York, Los Angeles, and Chicago have provided an ever-expanding market in television (sitcoms, soap operas, commercials) and corporate in-house work, while almost every medium-sized city provides some work for actors in the latter category.

GAFFER, GRIP, PROP PERSON, AND CONSTRUCTION CREW MEMBER. These are the technicians who put the set together, who light the set for the videographer, who search out and gather the props needed for the production, and who push the dollies, run the cable, and generally keep the production flowing smoothly from scene to scene. On small location shoots, we generally do not find these stage crew members.

SCENIC DESIGNER, SET DECORATOR, PAINTER, AND ART DIRECTOR. The job titles are almost self-explanatory, in that these people are responsible for the "look" of the video. The best examples of their work are generally in music videos, for no expense is spared in the art direction of a Michael Jackson or a Madonna video. These professionals also work in commercials, sitcoms, and soap operas, but seldom in the documentary field. They are occasionally employed by corporations for major video presentations (such as new car introductions by Ford, General Motors, or Chrysler).

MAKEUP ARTIST AND HAIR STYLIST. I've noticed with admiration that some of my friends have taken their interest in these subjects and have successfully transferred them to the video field. Most makeup and hair artists that I've met and worked with started in exactly that way. Eventually, those in the upper reaches have managed to take the exams and enter the union, but much of the field in corporate work is still in the nonunion category. The field has grown so tremendously that there are even courses given in college continuing education programs that are specifically geared to video and film.

COSTUME, STYLING, AND WARDROBE PERSON. In this role, an individual can take his or her interest in fashion and turn it into a successful career. The look of the video is as much a function of this role as it is the art director's.

SCRIPT SUPERVISOR. This job category is critical to the efficiency of the scripted production, be it a corporate photoplay or a sitcom. The script supervisor must be able to break down the script into logical shooting sequences, since photoplays are never shot in order. More importantly, he or she (mostly she) must keep track of the props used and the clothing worn in scenes so that it will all match when the sequence is completed possibly several days or weeks later. When we were kids, we called the slipups "movie boners"—an actress picks up a glass with her right hand in one scene, then in the close-up is holding the glass in her left. Script supervisor foul-up!

COMPOSER. Original music is used in some videos, so composers are needed. The field also offers opportunities for arrangers, especially in the area of music videos. However, much of the work in video utilizes library scores, music provided by commercial music houses and paid for by license fee agreements. (See also page 52.)

Here are some other production people we seem to forget:

INTERN. An internship is an excellent entry-level position for television, cable, and the corporate world. Generally, the position is open to college students who want to spend their summers getting some experience. Though I personally think that interning is one of the most exploited areas of the industry, I also think that it is one of the most valuable ways for a young person to learn just what the industry is all about and what opportunities exist when college is over. Interns can have a variety of experiences—some actually get involved with production, while others spend their time in administration and in doing some of the most menial work that can be invented by senior managers.

GOFER. This term is used both in videotape and in film and it describes the very same job: "Go-fer coffee!" or "Go-fer another light." Sometimes the gofer is an intern; sometimes he or she has been hired just to run the errands, service the crew, and generally be there to make the director feel that he or she has someone at his or her beck and call to do the menial things. The job pays very little—if it pays at all. Is it any more exploitive than the job of intern? I can't really make a value judgment, since an awful lot of good production people started their careers as gofers and interns.

COMPUTER ANIMATION AND SPECIAL EFFECTS EXPERT. This is one of those crossover categories found in both production and postproduction (see page 5). The reason is quite simple: many of the projects on videotape today include the use of these techniques in the early planning and the production process itself. Thus, the design of a network logo or the complexity of a full-length video would bring the designers, computer and graphics experts, and animators into the scripting or storyboarding of the production.

I have probably left out a few job descriptors, for there are many jobs that lie hidden from the public, especially in the fields of television and cable;

for example: news directors, assignment editors, and reporters; field producers, floor managers, audio engineers, and videotape operators. There is, indeed, much more to video than the director and the producer!

But, even here, the specific and detailed breakdown of job categories is found only in the major markets and in the larger production units. Everywhere else, and in most videotape situations, we come back to the hyphenated group where everybody does everything. I just want you to be able to expand your thinking about job opportunities, moving past the obvious ones, since almost any one of them can be the start of a career that begins in one direction and ends in another. I began my own career as a sportscaster, disc jockey, and sometime engineer. When I found that I had begun to hate athletes, was bored with the Top 40, and had trouble getting the small radio station on the air at 6 A.M., I decided it was time to become a writer. Careers are made in strange and wonderful ways.

POSTPRODUCTION

The development and continuing sophistication of video have created a range of critical jobs for entry-level people as well as for experienced engineers and technicians. The following is a description of the main categories.

EDITOR. An effective video editor must have an understanding of composition, continuity, and structure, as well as a complete familiarity with the computer-driven systems and time coding of both off- and on-line editing.

The off-line editor is essentially responsible for putting the project to-

Paintbox artist Tom Leeser at the console of Editel/New York's new Digital Design Suite. The computer has opened up new vistas for the field of special effects. (Courtesy Ken Korsh)

Video editing systems look complicated, and they are. This is the on-line suite at West Glen with an announcer recording booth in the rear. (Courtesy West Glen)

The Montage Picture Processor System II, a video editing system designed specifically for feature films. It received the Scientific and Engineering Award at the 60th annual Oscar presentations. (Courtesy MONTAGE Group Ltd.)

gether, making it work as a storyline or a logical sequence of events. The on-line editor (who might be better considered an engineer) is responsible for transferring the edited material to the final form on a master tape. By the time the project reaches this point, the costs can mount considerably, so the on-line editor must work quickly from the time codes on the tape to make the transfers as quickly as possible.

With the development of montage systems, the job of off-line editing has become a less tedious chore and more like film editing, since the systems allow many pictures (and tracks) to be scanned at the same time. Nevertheless, the editor is still tied to the computer time codes, and much of the work includes logging (by hand or computer) those codes so that they can be transferred during the on-line phase.

In terms of the job market, these questions arise: Should a video editor learn film editing? Should a film editor learn videotape editing? The answer for both is simple: Yes.

The discipline of film editing can only help to sharpen a video editor's visual acuity, since the process of editing film is slower and more deliberate in the selection stage. Film is tactile. It can be held up to a light; it goes through an editing machine—the Moviola, the Kem, or the Steenbeck—at a controlled rate; it is cut, then spliced. As a result, film editors spend more time on the composition of shots, on the physical rearrangement of sequences.

In addition, the use of sound on film is more sophisticated and allows greater flexibility in the mix of music, voice, and effects. The reason is that tracks in film, unlike videotape, are separate and independent, and are cut physically rather than blended by computer. Many video editors are now using film technology in mixing their tracks and then laying them on to their videotape projects.

For the film editor, learning videotape editing has become a matter of survival. These days, if you don't know how to edit both film and videotape you find that half your clients have moved on and left you standing all alone at the Moviola.

ENGINEER. The field of video is filled with engineers, technicians, and computer geniuses. Engineers are found everywhere—in research and development departments, in private electronic companies, in television and cable stations, in postproduction facilities, even on the set during shooting. If you have a thorough grounding in the field of electronics, or if computers have been your hobby all these years, both operating and maintenance engineering might well be the path for you.

In television and cable and in postproduction houses, technicians and engineers are the people who keep the operation functioning. Titles vary. I have already mentioned the on-line editing staff. Here are some of the other jobs, all of them requiring some technical knowledge:

- Maintenance Engineer: Keeps the equipment in good operating condition, both in rental houses and at television studios and transmitters.
- Audio Engineer: Generally found in postproduction for the recording of narrators or the mixing of sound tracks. A good ear and a knowledge of music can only help.
- Transmitter Engineer: Generally the most knowledgeable of the group,

being thoroughly familiar with the most complex technologies and able to keep the station on the air during an emergency.

- Videotape Recording Engineer: Needed both in the studio and on location, responsible for the actual recording of the videotape. Also responsible for color quality and optimum playback potential.

Active in the cable industry are installers, service technicians, and trunk technicians, who work to correct any malfunctions in the main cable lines or the feeder lines to subscribers.

In postproduction service facilities, there are also technicians and engineers who supervise:

- tape-to-film transfers
- film-to-tape transfers
- conversions from one system to another, for example, VHS to PAL or SECAM
- quantity dubbing of distribution tapes from the original masters
- color correction

COMPUTER ANIMATION AND SPECIAL EFFECTS EXPERT. Animation and special effects are used in both production and postproduction stages. All of the wonderful effects, the flips and explosions, the titles that appear magically on the screen and twist and turn out of the azure sky, are done in postproduction. The Paintbox, the Harry, the Chyron, the ADO are used on most television commercials and music videos.

If you have a knowledge of computers, and are willing to work long and sometimes tedious hours, then the area of computer animation and special effects offers an opportunity to break into video. Jeff Kleiser, cofounder of Digital Effects, suggests the following requirements for someone interested in a career in computer graphics:

- a firm background in computers, either through a college degree program or on-the-job experience
- some training in art, graphics, or design
- a knowledge of several computer languages
- a knowledge of the internal structures of computers

The world of computer graphics and video special effects has come into its own as a direct result of the computer revolution. It has no parallel in the film industry, though much of what we have discussed until now is used in both film and tape. The specific jobs in this category can be broken down as follows:

- Operator: Learns by being everywhere and doing everything—taking the tape to the postproduction house, running errands, observing the senior technicians. A good starting position.
- Animator: Writes programs and generates computer graphics for a specific job. Must have a background in animation, art, or graphics.
- Software Specialist: Designs new graphics that will eventually be used by the animator.
- Director: Performs the same function as the director of live production—deals with clients such as agency art directors and supervises everyone else.

COMPOSER. Though I mentioned the composer briefly in the section on production, the music for a particular project is generally contracted for and completed as part of the postproduction process. For people with backgrounds in music, composition, and arrangement—or even a knowledge of several instruments—the field of music can be an exciting (albeit competitive) part of the videotape industry.

Original scores are generally used for commercials and features or high-budget documentaries. For most other projects, however, library music scores are used. These are musical scores composed for a library, which rents them out. Companies that produce these scores exist in all major cities. The producer or director chooses the music he or she wants to include in the videotape, usually with the help of an editor and/or a creative music librarian, then pays for the right to use that music. Usage fees vary. The libraries are very specialized, and the people who work there are generally versed not only in music but also in editing, since they must be able to match music to picture and vice versa.

SALES, FINANCE, AND PROMOTION

Blinded by the "glamour" of the industry, especially in television and cable, we sometimes forget that there are other areas for opportunities. The general business side of video provides entry-level and career-advancement positions.

Some of the people in sales or finance never wanted to be a part of the production mayhem and are quite happy in the executive offices. Others move from executive management to production of feature films (Jaffe-Lansing, for example). Sales or marketing experience can be used to gain entry into the more "creative" areas of video.

SALES REPRESENTATIVE. First of all, I'd like to mention that the best salespeople I've met in videotape and film are the producers themselves.

Before they even begin to produce a product, they have to sell it. Some producers hire representatives to do the job, but many of them are quite adept at selling both themselves and their product to the networks, clients, or sponsors. Others have become expert in selling themselves to foundations and public television stations in order to get funding for their projects.

Salespeople are needed in most industry-related businesses: television and cable stations and networks, production companies, video services suppliers, and postproduction facilities. Someone has to sell the product or the service. Someone has to make the calls on new and old customers. Someone has to open new accounts. I also have a theory that any darned good salesperson can probably talk his or her way right up the ladder to the next step in the career climb or into a management position. A former client of mine—the chief executive officer of a *Fortune* 500 aluminum company—began his career by selling zippers on the Lower East Side of New York!

Let's take a look at some of the areas in which a sales representative might work:

- Production companies: selling services to ad agencies, clients, corporations, or television stations.
- Postproduction companies: selling services such as editing or music to producers, ad agencies, television stations, etc.
- Broadcast television: selling commercial time.
- Cable: selling the service to subscribers. Salespeople in cable are also involved in promotion and advertising to expand the service into a community.
- Equipment manufacturers: selling both to the public and to the industry itself, an especially important part of the field since the technology changes and improves so rapidly. The salesperson who knows his or her product can be the "expert" to the customer.
- Syndication services: selling TV programs for local airing.

Most sales representatives work on a salary plus commission. Some work on a small "draw," a salary advance against future sales and commissions. The compensation varies from market to market, from company to company. At the very top level, in the role of national sales manager or general sales manager or marketing director, the renumeration can be substantial.

Sales provides one of the best entries into video. It also offers opportunities for making contacts—with executives, station managers, agency time buyers—for future moves.

I mentioned earlier that producers were some of the best salespeople I knew. But the best "unofficial" salesperson I've met was a woman who ran up to me one day as I was completing the shooting for a recent production. As we were packing our gear, she breathlessly approached, put a light blue business card in my hands, and said, "This is my son's card. He does videotape. He's got all the equipment you'll ever need. And he's very talented!" I laughed, thanked her, and actually filed the card. You never know when I'll need someone who does videotape, has all the equipment I'll ever need, and is very talented!

ACCOUNTANT OR FINANCIAL EXPERT. Production and postproduction companies, cable and television stations, and advertising agencies, desperate to cut costs, welcome anyone with a knowledge of finance. I began my college life as an accounting major because my father said to me, "Learn a trade. You'll never starve." This training didn't go to waste and even in budgeting productions today I find that my accounting background is of invaluable assistance in cutting and controlling costs.

Certainly, as with any job that seems far removed from the "glamour" of production, you might well wonder if the accounting or budget department will be a dead end. But keep in mind that you are looking to enter the field. Networking works everywhere. Meeting the right people inside the organization is better than exchanging business cards at a cocktail party.

PROMOTION AND PUBLIC RELATIONS SPECIALIST. These are umbrella titles that can cover anything from working on the printed collateral materials that accompany videotapes to promoting cable systems or specific television programs. In smaller corporations, public relations people might also write treatments or scripts for videotape presentations. In larger public relations agencies, their involvement might include planning a promotional campaign and supervising the videotape training of a client executive for a television appearance or press interview. Many public relations agencies build fully equipped videotape studios for just these purposes.

CHAPTER THREE

BROADCAST TELEVISION AND CABLE

Most of our cameramen who were formerly [in] film have now converted to tape. We're working out our last two film pieces now, and then we will be all tape.

Joe Illigasch
Director of Operations for
"60 Minutes"

BROADCAST TELEVISION

I love to tell the story of the telephone call that I received late one night from Wichita, Kansas. The caller was a former New Yorker who had moved to Wichita sixteen years before and was actively involved with a local television station as a production manager-producer-director for the shows that originated there. He was now thinking seriously about coming back to the New York market, and he wanted some advice. He was a delightful guy, well versed in television and production, and a potential asset to any network or station. However, I warned him, the television industry was cutting back, there were at least a hundred thousand qualified applicants for every position, and the *last* place I would suggest that he solicit would be the haughty New York–based networks.

About a week later, he telephoned again. Despite my "expert" advice he had gone to New York and had interviewed at NBC. *A week later*, he landed the job as an outside production manager for the network!

I suppose that the story proves that there *are* thousands of jobs being filled at the networks and the local television stations and that *someone* has to fill them. Nevertheless, I begin this chapter on video's "glamour" industry by saying that the networks are cutting back, having lost audience share to cable.

Furthermore, the new managements of these corporate giants have been slicing away at costs, reducing the size of everything from the news department to the production crew.

On the positive side, at least in terms of job opportunities, the biggest change has been in the move away from film and toward videotape—in news, special events, documentaries, even some sitcoms. Because of the switch in the technology, new job categories have opened up, most of them available to the younger generation of computer-weaned, video-trained technicians: editors, engineers, videographers, postproduction animators, and graphics designers, as well as sales and marketing personnel.

Many of the new shows, such as CBS's "48 Hours" and other magazine-format programs, have *never* used film, videotape being the medium of choice. But the big switch has come in news reporting. Whereas high-speed reversal film was once the preferred medium, videotape has suddenly become ubiquitous. This is especially true on local news shows, and with good reason. No longer do the local shows have to go to a laboratory to process the film. Video editing equipment is right in the studio. The footage can be shot, edited, and on the air within hours—and all of it done by in-house personnel.

Currently there are about a thousand television stations on the air. This figure includes commercial VHF and UHF stations, both owned and operated and independent local. In addition, there are another 300 noncommercial stations—PBS and local community-operated—and about the same number of low-power television stations, one of the fastest-growing segments of the broadcast industry.

The jobs in television fall into two categories: electronic field production (EFP) and electronic news gathering (ENG).*

EFP takes place in a studio or on location. The crew works from a script or treatment. Generally speaking, EFP is the same type of production that we find in film; it can range from just one person handling a video camera as a self-contained picture/sound unit to a five- or six-camera shoot all controlled by a mobile van with its own videotape equipment or a studio control room situation very much as we find in live television. Projects range from pre-taped talk or game shows to the taping of segments of the Olympic Games for rebroadcast at a later date. Location shooting or insert photography for sitcoms would also fall into this category.

The EFP personnel include producers, directors, script supervisors, vid-

*For more information see Norman Medhoff and Tom Tanguary. *Portable Video: ENG & EFP* (White Plains, NY: Knowledge Industries Publications, 1986). It provides an excellent in-depth description of EFP and ENG.

As the technology develops, the quality improves. This is the Ikegami HL-55, compact and lightweight, specially designed for electronic news gathering (ENG) for broadcast use with ½-inch on-board VCRs. (Courtesy Ikegami Electronics (USA), Inc.)

eographers, cable pullers, lighting technicians (gaffers), grips, prop people, makeup and hair experts, set designers, floor managers, production assistants, and engineers. On a really large location job, we might also find truck and limousine drivers, catering people, wardrobe personnel, special effects technicians, and actors. With all these people involved, the production tends to move slowly.

ENG is exactly what the name says—news gathering, generally for television news, special events, or magazine format shows and documentaries. Here, the quality of the finished product is less important than the event. Consider the camerawork and the image quality for an on-the-run interview with an important government official leaving the White House and rushing to a waiting limousine. Or the interview with the winning pitcher of the last game of the World Series. Time becomes the most important element. There is no time to set lights, no time to work out camera angles, no time to worry about balancing color.

The ENG personnel can range from one person performing the functions of writer, director, reporter, and script editor to several hundred technicians and specialists. The major networks employ full-time staffers and freelancers or "stringers."

ENG provides thousands of jobs for field producers, assignment editors, reporters, videographers, engineers, sound people, writers, and tape editors. Added to these are the unsung researchers who probe and make telephone calls and sometimes come up with the great story that the "stars" offer to the public and for which they reap the credit. It takes a lot of people to make it all work.

On the entry level, there are other areas from which people can break into the field. Besides researchers, there are the tape librarians who catalog the huge amount of materials that flow into the stations, either locally or from around the world. We see, over and over again, the words "FILE TAPE" on stories that hit the air. These reports come from the tiny offices of some hard-working moles, who spend their time glued to file cards and video monitors. And, finally, there are the interns active at television stations, from networks down to the local level.

These so-called lower-level jobs often lead to bigger and better things. A good case in point is Mimi Edmunds, a producer-associate producer-researcher for CBS's "60 Minutes." (On this show, a producer is the same thing as a director.) Edmunds began as a researcher in a news department. She freelanced for two years and was eventually rehired as a summer temp.

Edmunds's background was not in video—or even in communications. She says:

> *I was in graduate school [for] anthropology. I had had some journalism experience as an editor of a magazine in Africa and had degrees in anthropology, not in journalism. When I was hired, I would do specials and evening news and maybe an occasional "60 Minutes" story. I worked in a pool.*

AN INTERVIEW WITH JOE ILLIGASCH

Since "60 Minutes" is so well known, and is certainly a prime example of a successful operation from almost every point of view, I interviewed the show's director of operations, Joe Illigasch, whose quote opens this chapter. Illigasch offered some fresh insights into starting out in video.

Anyone starting out in video wants to know about the glamorous world of TV. Can you tell us something about jobs, about opportunities? What qualities do you look for in a new person?

"It's very difficult for a new person to break in; it's almost impossible. It's no reflection on your talent. I'm speaking of the bigger cities. For example, if you lived in New York . . . I had a guy call me yesterday and he had tremendous credentials and he said to me, realistically, what are the chances of working there. I said they just aren't very realistic. You see, it's the producers who select the [crew] . . . [they're] ultimately responsible for the segments. And over twenty years or so, they've worked with certain people, and everybody's got favorites."

Is there a better route?

"Sure. Let's say that we're going to Austin, Texas, to do an interview. We do all our interviews with two crews. We might fly in a key camera person from Los Angeles or San Francisco or Denver and then supplement that person with a local crew, because that second crew is really only going to do that shot of the correspondent asking the questions."

So that would be a way for someone in a smaller community to get involved?

"A young person just breaking in would have to get hold of the roster of the normal cameramen and let them know where they are. Sometimes we just pick up shots. We'll do a story and somebody'll say, 'You know what we need; we need a good shot of the bank and the activity and the tellers down in Podunk, Iowa.' Now, we're not going to go to the expense of flying a New York crew out there, so we'll take a chance with the local guy, and over the phone we'll tell him exactly what we want. Sometimes a guy comes in and does an outstanding job and one thing leads to another."

What about the unions?

"We're all union. Now, that doesn't mean that a cameraperson who is not in the union can't work for us. What it means is that he can work for us one time, and then he must, within thirty days, make application to the union. It's expensive . . . it could be a thousand dollars. So for a guy to work for a day's pay—for two or three hundred dollars—and then lay out a thousand dollars to join the union, and then never get another phone call from us, well, that's a losing proposition."

Do you have any thoughts about training—school or on-the-job experience?

"Certainly there are schools in all of the larger cities. But the most obvious thing is to begin at the local level, or at the nonunion places, local stations, smaller stations, where you're not limited by union restrictions."

And cable?

"That's the way to go. It's cable or local small-town nonunion [places] where you go and do everything—camera, sound, lighting. You have no restrictions at all."

Are you saying that you take any job to start?

"Absolutely. I would take any job. The lowest job here is better than taking a job in the law department or the accounting department. I would take any job in the newsroom, where you might end up working the midnight to 8 A.M. shift because you are low person on the desk, but all you need is one crisis to happen and you're one of the only people there and can demonstrate what you can do."

Can you move up the ladder?

"Some of our producers were film editors, some of them were cameramen. It gets a little slow in the summer, for example, and there's not a lot going on and our editors don't have much to do. So they've been given an opportunity over the past years to do a story or two. You can move up within the ranks. There are a number of people here who were receptionists who are now associate and assistant producers."

"60 Minutes" now uses tape almost exclusively. Is that also true for the other magazine-format shows?

"I don't think there's anything left in film. Not on a major scale. Soon, it will be all tape."

There are two major trends that anyone thinking of breaking into network television must consider. First,

> *The cable companies have begun to provide some of the strongest competition to the networks since their inception.*

Because of the rapid expansion of cable, satellites, and the home ownership of VCRs, the network viewing time of the average family has been cut considerably. The networks have been stunned by the drop in ratings for some of their top shows. And, since ratings translate into dollar income, a drop of even a few points can mean several million dollars in lost revenue. Thus, the networks have effected a severe retrenchment in their operating methods, hiring policies, production costs, and programming. This, in turn, is closely tied to the second trend:

> *The major networks are now owned by bottom line-oriented corporations and are being run by cost-conscious executives appalled by the bloated, overpopulated divisions staffed by what they feel are too many highly paid people.*

Television has become, for better or worse, a leaner, more efficient industry. Enforced early retirement has moved many of the highly paid people out of the networks, giving staff people, most of them younger and making many thousands of dollars less, a chance to move up to positions of authority, from receptionist to associate producer, from editor to producer. This, in turn, makes it more difficult for outside people to get a start.

Some examples of the changes: Formerly the networks would each send hundreds of people to cover special events like a space launch. Now they pool their crews and coverage, sending only their top experts from New York or Los Angeles and filling in the other spots with local people. At one time, if the president visited a foreign country, the networks would cover with hundreds of technicians. Today they might send a pool of fifty and share the satellite feed. The savings are enormous, and even if some of the cutbacks have affected quality things probably won't improve much in the near future. In fact, I would predict that it's going to get tighter . . . and tighter.

Why have I gone on for so long about the cutbacks at the networks and the difficulties of breaking in? If you want to work in the field of broadcast television you should be aware of the realities, understanding that there are exceptions like my friend from Wichita, Kansas, who moved into NBC in one week. The good news is that there are other areas of television that provide a gold mine of opportunities.

LOCAL TELEVISION MARKETS

Local television stations provide some of the best opportunities for the beginner. With O&O stations (owned and operated by the networks), network affiliates (independently owned but tied to a network for programming), and independent stations, the person looking to break into the broadcast television industry might do well to look first in their own hometowns or near the schools where they were trained.

The advantage of beginning your career in one of the smaller markets is that you end up trained to do just about every job imaginable around the station. In the production area, for instance, you might be the floor manager for one show and then a cameraperson for the next; a producer of your own morning segment, and Xerox operator for part of the day. Your "spare" time might be spent in soliciting the regional businesses to sell commercial time.

When it comes to learning the technology, the small station is often the ideal place to start. Most of the reporters, camerapeople, and producers end up doing the entire job, from shooting on location to editing back at the studio in time to make the six o'clock news to developing stories for local elections or community events. In addition, many small stations also function as the producer for local television commercials. Whatever your job, you can eventually end up with a number of sample tapes that will allow you to move to another city or state, if you so choose.

And that is what many people in the television industry do. Though some people are content to stay in their hometowns for their entire working lives, many do move on to larger markets, using the sample work they've collected along the way to show their talents and creativity. For example, I know one young woman who began her career in Dallas, then moved to a station in New Orleans and then up to Philadelphia, one of the larger secondary markets. When she and her husband decided to move back to Texas, she took her sample reporting/editing tapes with her, and currently is working in Houston.

LOW-POWER TELEVISION (LPTV)

This area of the broadcast industry has been growing quietly and steadily. In a very few years, about 1,000 low-power TV stations should be on the air, and Congressman Al Swift (D.-Washington) calls this "the best kept secret in broadcasting." Since the average station can be on the air for a total cost of about $250,000, it generally finds itself in the black within the first year, certainly a remarkable feat for any small business.

Basically, a low-power television station is limited in its power output (10 watts on VHF, 1,000 watts on UHF). Its coverage extends from ten to twenty miles. Since budgets are also limited and audiences confined to local communities or specific targeted groups, low-power TV relies heavily on locally produced shows, both live and videotaped. Advertising revenue is provided by local businesses and many commercials are produced in-house to save on costs. These community-oriented stations also transmit local sports, town hall meetings, and other special events.

In 1988, the FCC lifted a freeze on low-power television. Syndicated programs such as sitcoms and game shows are finally being sold to the stations after a long boycott by producers, and we're likely to see a new boom in the licensing and construction of new stations. Indeed, some columnists and trade magazine writers have predicted that LPTV will become a major force in the broadcasting industry.

One final word. As with any small, growing industry, salaries in LPTV are likely to be low by the standards set in the larger markets and at the VHF stations. Many people working in low-power (as in cable and local radio) are holding *two* jobs, with their television/tape career a secondary one for the present time. Many full-time lawyers, businesspeople, retirees, students, real estate agents, and housewives now produce, host, and tape their daily or weekly shows on the subjects of cooking, special events, or books. Some do it to be involved in the "glamorous" world of television, others to gain experience for a new career.

CABLE

Back in 1984, a series of articles appeared that brought to mind the story of the Dutch boy who held his finger in the dike to stop the flooding. The "boy" in this case was the networks and their fingers seemed to be crossed while they tried to hold back the impending flood of cable expansion throughout the country.

One article was headlined: "HAS THE FLIGHT OF THE NETWORKS' AUDIENCE HALTED?" (*New York Times*, Jan. 1, 1984). According to the networks, they had stemmed the tide of viewers who had deserted to the cable systems, wreaking havoc on ratings. According to the cable representatives, the network share of viewers would decline to about 60 percent by 1990, a steep drop from the incredible 91 percent in 1972 and the very substantial 78 percent as recently as 1982. If you have been reading the newspapers and magazines, then you know that the cable industry was right!

Today, about 50 percent of American homes with television sets are hooked up to a cable system. And that figure is projected to hit 70 percent within the next five years. Whereas in the past the public rebelled against paying for things that they used to get for free, such as their favorite major league baseball games or commercial-interrupted movies, the average family now pays its cable bill with little or no resistance.

Certainly, there are many reasons for this change, not the least of which is the constantly rising cost (now up to $7.50 for an hour and a half in some parts of the country) of seeing a motion picture at the local movie theater. Multiply this single-ticket price by two or three or four, and you soon begin to see why staying at home and watching a movie on pay TV is an attractive alternative. Add to this the variety of entertainment available over the cable systems—sporting events such as heavyweight boxing, baseball, and football; special programming that ranges from the erotic to the exotic, from the arts to twenty-four-hour news programs—and you begin to see other reasons that the networks have begun to lag so badly. Indeed, if you look at cable programming across the country, you soon find that the subject matter is as broad and diverse as the flavors in a jar of jelly beans:

Movie Classics	Financial News
Black Entertainment	Religion and Inspiration
Sports	Nostalgia
Country Music	Travel
Music Video	Weather

And all of this is but *part* of the cable story.

When we think of cable networks, perhaps the major players are the first ones that come to mind: HBO, Cinemax, CNN. But cable has begun to break out in other ways, with smaller cable networks that might provide service to as few as half a million homes rather than the multimillions that the multiple systems operators (MSOs) service.

A good example is local cable station News 12, in Woodbury, Long Island. Owned by Cablevision, it is the first twenty-four-hour regional news station in the country. News 12 broadcasts to two New York counties—Nassau and Suffolk—and serves about 540,000 homes as of this writing. (A "sister" station operates in Fairfield County, Connecticut.) The station covers local politics, and provides commentary and news coverage for each of the more than 100 communities in the area. News 12 is being watched closely, for if it succeeds, it may be the forerunner of many more regional news networks.

News 12 airs a mix of tape and live coverage. The current staff is about 100 people, including six anchors, eight reporters, and eight one-person camera crews. In addition, there are the studio production and postproduction people, such as editors, technicians, writers, and administrators. Entry-level jobs closely parallel those in every other part of the television industry.

Because of the boom in cable revenues, there has been an increase in the amount of programming done by the cable networks themselves. Made-for-TV movies, documentaries, and docudramas are originating on cable. This has led to an expansion of jobs in studio work and production.

In addition, over these past few years, cable has begun to open up even greater markets, some by satellite, some by basic cable feeder lines. Cable can provide interactive systems such as security for the home or office, health monitoring for chronically ill patients with tie-ins to central medical center

News 12's Tom Appleby, News Director, with reporter Carlie Centrella at "Care and Share" Day food collection in Norwalk. (Courtesy Cablevision)

At the Westport Country Playhouse with Smith, co-host Deborah Downs, and guest James McKenzie. Jeanne Vallerie is operating the camera. (Courtesy Cablevision)

observation control points; education through home college courses; shopping at home; even home banking services, in which the customer can make deposits, withdrawals, and transfers by television (though this area has not taken off like a rocket). For the job seeker, this means increased production, administrative, and technical opportunities.

The growth of cable has been so phenomenal in the last ten years or so, that now there is talk about regulating the industry, removing the control of rates and access by local authorities and bringing it under federal guidance. Needless to say, the networks would love to see this happen, while the cable industry has been fighting tooth and nail to maintain the status quo.

Some of the cable networks, such as CNN and Financial News Network, produce all of their programming in-house. The National Cable Television Association reports that the industry as a whole has been spending more money on production than ever before, and the opportunities for people in the creative and entertainment arts, as well as in the production area, are growing.

The major networks are notorious for not dipping their toes into untested waters, but once someone proves that it's okay to swim, we begin to see a proliferation of programs cut from the same mold. The cable networks, on the other hand, have been more innovative, not only in their programming, but also in their willingness to give new people a chance. Part of the reason is that most of them operate on very small budgets for personnel. In an interview in *Back Stage*, Marc Chalom, Vice President of Production and Operations for the Arts & Entertainment Network, commented, ". . . the people we're looking for should have more than one skill. They should be able to look at a show, write and create a 30-second promo, then edit it themselves—a kind of Renaissance promo producer." Again we come across the hyphenate.

Of course, it pays to investigate the type of programming as well as the extent of in-house production before contacting your local cable station or network for a job. Many cable stations and networks buy their major programming from outside sources, such as the BBC or Lorimar.

However, some cable stations and networks coproduce their own series in conjunction with independent companies. For example, the Arts & Entertainment Network coproduced a five-part documentary on the Civil War ("The Divided Union"), originally done by a British producer. However, for the American audience, the series was completely reedited, with a new sound track added and a new host, George Peppard, videotaped at West Point.

Almost all cable stations and networks produce promotional spots, using their own studios, equipment (camera and audio), artists and graphic design-

Many cable networks also produce their own shows. This is the studio set for "Fairfield Exchange," produced by Cablevision. Co-hosts David Smith (left) and Rebecca Surran (right) interview guest Lynn Hollyn. On cameras are Amy Wade and Steve Meyerson. (Courtesy Cablevision)

ers, and videotape facilities.

All of the jobs that exist in network television and in the local VHF and UHF stations have also opened up in the field of cable: engineering, operations managers, marketing and public relations specialists, and program development and production experts. Here, too, administrative jobs—in sales, data processing, personnel, and finance, as well as in installment and service of cable systems within the franchise area—can be stepping-stones in the right set of circumstances.

The cable companies have discovered yet another area of potential business that will create still more jobs in the future. Many companies are going into outside production, competing with independent producers to develop training videos, commercials, and corporate communications for the companies in their region who do not want to invest the large amounts of money it takes to buy camera, editing, and postproduction equipment.

It makes a lot of sense: Cable stations already have their cameras, their editing machines, their personnel, and their expertise. With low overhead, since their studios are already in operation, and with the availability of necessary equipment, they can compete easily with outside producers. In many markets they have already begun to sell their services. In Chicago, for example, Group W Cable recently opened its own in-house production facility. As with most cable stations, they do all their corporate and promotional production on videotape. For small or medium-sized corporations, using these facilities makes a lot of sense, especially since the purchase of any equipment these days brings with it the threat of instant obsolescence. Although larger advertising agencies seem to prefer outside producers, especially "star" directors, these in-house cable operations have begun to successfully solicit business.

There is yet another area, specific to cable, that provides an opportunity to the beginner or to the would-be producer of programming on videotape: public access.

PUBLIC ACCESS

Throughout the country, there are cable channels reserved for individual or group use. Generally, the cable company exercises no editorial censorship, except to demand that the tape is of usable quality and that it conforms to certain rules and regulations. (See the accompanying box.)

Public access is an excellent way to gain experience and credits. Bill Wright and Rachel Love direct their show from the Cablevision van on location in Greenwich, Connecticut. (Courtesy Cablevision)

PUBLIC ACCESS

Here are some typical rules that govern public access television. They may change in each area of the country, but they will help to guide you in your quest for air time.

1. The studio is available for use on a first come, first served basis.
2. Prior to studio usage, the following must be filed with the Cablevision Public Access Department:
   a. an application for facility use
   b. complete scripts and shooting schedule
   c. crew list for *all* crew positions
   d. lists of any props or other materials to be brought into the studio
3. Videotaping *must* start no later than one half hour after scheduled time. If taping does not begin, user may forfeit the time and must reapply for studio use.
4. All preproduction meetings and planning should take place outside studio and prior to day of shooting.
5. Only certified access users shall move or operate equipment in studio or control room.
6. Visitors should be kept to an absolute minimum and arrangements should be made to greet and escort guests as they arrive. No one but crew allowed in control room or editing area.
7. All props and equipment must be returned to original positions.

Courtesy: Cablevision of Connecticut

Many cable operators also require that applicants take a short but intensive course in equipment handling. Technical instruction is offered, generally free of charge. Cablevision of Connecticut, for example, offers a free four-part technical and production training course. To date, well over 500 people have qualified. Cablevision's "students" have produced shows on a wide range of topics, including art, architecture, religion, philosophy, sports, and community interests.

The expansion of public access has led to *educational access channels*, on which schools, universities, libraries, fire departments, and other institutions have offered instructional programs, both live and on tape. For example, the Norwalk, Connecticut, Fire Department has used an access channel to train fire personnel who must be at their stations and cannot attend a class at some other location.

Both public and educational access channels provide excellent opportunities, especially for beginners. You will gain experience and training—all of it free of charge. You'll work with professionals as you learn. In addition, the videotapes that you produce will become excellent samples to show to prospective employers as you begin knocking on doors and trying to convince everyone that you are the next great production genius in the field of television and video. Don't underestimate the value of a sample. And, certainly, don't underestimate the value of *any type* of experience that you garner as you make your way through the minefield of competition that now exists out there.

I mentioned budgets a while back (a subject that keeps cropping up, doesn't it?). Since staff budgets are small at the local cable outlets, there are generally more internships available in cable than in broadcast television. One of the best ways to get information on just what a cable station or MSO requires for internships is to write for two small booklets put out by the National Cable Television Association (1724 Massachusetts Avenue, N.W., Washington, DC 20036): *National Cable Network Directory* and *Top 50 MSO's.*

In addition, the National Federation of Local Cable Programmers (906 Pennsylvania Avenue, S.E., Washington, DC 20003) offers a number of publications that can tell you how public access is being used around the country.

There are currently about 7,800 cable systems in the United States. They vary in size, operating methods, number of subscribers, and number of full-time, part-time, and volunteer (internship) personnel. Just as even the smallest radio station has provided a stepping-stone for now well-established professionals, the cable industry seems to have the equivalent potential in television and videotape.

With the proliferation of VCRs, satellites, and expanding services, the power of the cable industry has become more evident to everyone, from stock analysts to the public itself. The signs seem to say that cable will play an ever more dominant role in the entertainment and information industries. For the career seeker, the future is promising!

A VISIT TO CABLEVISION OF CONNECTICUT

There is no "typical" cable system among the many thousands that service the various parts of the country. Depending upon the needs of the community and the market in which it operates, each cable franchise provides a broad range of programming.

If I were to pick a "state-of-the-art" cable operator, it would be Cablevision of Connecticut, which is owned by Cablevision Systems of Woodbury, New York. Started in 1982, the system serves almost 70,000 subscribers in Fairfield County. Cablevision offers a remarkable range of programming from which to choose:

- Area TV stations
- Local origination, including "News 12" and "The Fairfield Exchange," an interview show that features interesting personalities, both local and national
- Four access channels, including public access, town programming, and educational access
- Microwave and satellite programming, including ESPN, C-SPAN, Financial News Network, and Nickelodeon
- HBO, Bravo, MTV, The Disney Channel, Arts & Entertainment, The Movie Channel, Showtime, Cinemax, The Playboy Channel, Country Music Television, The Nashville Network, and The Weather Channel

There are others, but I think you get the general idea. Cablevision is certainly among the most advanced systems in the country. It not only provides service from the other cable originators listed above, but it produces its own programming and is expanding in that area using its own crew members and staff. Perhaps most important of all, its public access channels provide a wonderful opportunity for would-be producers to originate and videotape their own programs, thus providing samples for future work.

I recently visited Cablevision's operations. My guide was Maryce Cunningham, who is public relations director. She commented that the first phase of development for Cablevision (and this is true for most of the industry) was engineering-intensive. The primary commitment for any cable system is to provide every home with a good picture. Once that is done, the company can begin to concentrate on expansion and then on original programming. When Cablevision went on the air, it had a staff of 40. It now numbers about 200.

To give us an idea of how you are structured, how does the staff break down?

"At the present time, we have about forty in the news room, about ten on the program 'The Fairfield Exchange,' about fifteen in the production department, five or six in master control, eight to ten in administration, plus programming, advertising, customer relations, sales, repair, billing, accounting. It's not a small operation, but it's still tightly knit enough that our people can have access to a wide variety of [experiences] and learn about equipment, production, and the business end of the operation all in the same place."

What about entry-level jobs in cable? Where do we find them?

"We're always on the lookout for people and we generally have a lot of entry-level jobs open. Currently there are about forty positions available. Some of them are in the area of installation, some in advertising, sales, or customer service. Some are in production. And though we might require at least six months' experience for a production assistant, we have training programs for the installation crews, right down to basic instruction in pole climbing. The beauty of this type of operation is that we are more than willing to train people on the job."

Does that include interns?

"It does. We offer three-month internships for which the student gets academic credit. They're assigned to one of the shows or one of the departments within our organization, and that's where they work for the whole three-month period. But again, they get to see all aspects of the business. There's a great opportunity to walk across the hall and say, 'Oh, let me try this.' "

And then where do they go?

"Cablevision is often a first job for people in the industry, and though we don't like to think of ourselves as only a stepping-stone into other areas of the business, we do find that people go on into broadcasting and the corporate sector. They don't go right from here into CBS New York, but they might easily move to a small channel right here in our area or up to Boston. We've had people who have left here with enough experience so that they now have their own businesses; they've developed . . . a reputation, and can now live on what they can make as freelancers. We had one person who had no experience whatever when she started here, and now she's flying all over the country doing production for a local company up in Maine. She married a man who was a cameraperson here, and he's now working for a television station in that same city."

What about freelancers? Do you use them in your production?

"Yes, of course. First of all, we do a lot of work with the production houses in the area. And then, on programs such as 'Focus on Connecticut,' instead of taking a whole crew from here to Hartford, pulling them out from our own studio, we hire people from the Hartford area just for that one program."

Where else might you use freelancers?

"When we can't spare the people upstairs, like for the Christmas show. Or sporting events. We use a lot of freelancers for the Fairfield University basketball games—mainly camera operators, audio people, or floor managers. You wouldn't have to know the inside of Cablevision in order to be a floor manager."

What about women? For the most part, the communications industry has not been overly open on the higher levels.

"There are a lot of women in management positions here at Cablevision. Women were able to sort of get in on the ground floor in all areas. I think that cable is a great opportunity for women to get the experience they need in order to develop an excellent career for themselves."

Let's turn for a moment to public access. What fascinates me is that there is no equivalent in broadcast television, or in radio, for that matter—and certainly not in the film industry.

"Well, when we first began access, everyone said, 'Oh, you're crazy. You're going to be inundated.' Well, access got really exciting for a while, but then people realized that there's a lot of work that goes into making a television program. It's not just that someone says, 'Oh, I have a great idea for a television program,' and there it is! But, as of this date, [access is] not being utilized to its fullest. We have about a hundred hours of programming a week on access, so it is being used to a great extent, but I wouldn't say that we are being overwhelmed."

Do access producers use professional equipment?

"Yes. And right now, we have four complete sets of access equipment including some new Camcorders and tape decks. But the studio is still open several evenings a week and practically all weekend. It's just not being used to its fullest. They warned us that people would be coming out of the woodwork when they heard that we had all that equipment and open studio time. I'm not so sure now."

I've seen the rules for access (see page 69), so I assume that people just don't walk in and take a camera and videotape deck and make a program.

"Certainly not. There are two areas that come into play—training and testing. If you don't know how to use the equipment, we provide a course of instruction. Or you can take a test. We've had some people like a former cameraman from CBS and he has the most wonderful time mak-

ing access programs. He didn't have to take the course, but he had to pass the test."

And where does someone go from there?

"We've seen only about one percent of our access programmers complete the course and then go on to do something professionally. But that is exactly the purpose of the course—to let people find out what is involved in producing a program. Most of them find out that it's a great deal more work than they thought. We want to give people a realistic overview of what it takes, rather than have them come in, get halfway through and say, 'I didn't realize what I was getting into.' We'd rather have them know it up front. So, it's about one percent—and I've given the course about forty times. Maybe that's why our equipment remains underutilized!"

Could you sum up your attitudes toward cable?

"I'm very enthusiastic, because I see the cable industry as a medium of great potential growth. We haven't even talked about the possibility of data transfer, even hooking up libraries to cable so that people can call up on their cable systems and ask if they've got such and such a book and then reserve it without ever leaving home. Every day, a new technology comes along and somebody says, 'Oh, let's try that with cable!'

"Many communications school graduates have told us that they've gotten more hands-on experience in our access course than they did in their theory of communications courses in graduate school. Usually, they come out [of school] ready to produce Oscar-winning movies, and for a while they think that cable and videotape are different career paths. But this is not theory. This is hands on. This is the everyday. This is where the reality is!"

CHAPTER FOUR

THE CORPORATE WORLD

This is a growth industry. Basically, it's doubling every four years. Think of the things that you've heard about broadcasting lately. Every time you hear a story about the networks, it's [about] cutbacks. [Corporate] is so much better than broadcast. There are opportunities in big cities. It pays better starting salaries, has better hours than broadcast, better lifestyle. There's a lot of good news. The bad news is that this is a secret to some people.

Linda Lee Davis
University of Kansas
ITVA Conference,
Las Vegas (1988)

Corporate communications is currently the largest market for jobs in the entire communications industry. And the reason goes further than the basic ease of handling a videotape camera and seeing an image instantly.

With the development of satellite and microwave communications, and the expansion of a complex system of long-distance coaxial cables, corporations have not only gone into in-house videotape production, but have also begun to form their own private networks, competing in size and complexity with the largest broadcast television organizations.

With each passing day, with every issue of trade magazines, we hear of the development of new, sophisticated, easy-to-use systems and videotape equipment, bringing with them improvements in teleconferencing, interactive video, and innovation in production techniques. Just as ubiquitous are the articles heralding the introduction of a new corporate television network, from Domino's Pizza and Taco Bell to J. C. Penney and Merrill Lynch.

Corporations make videos on everything from employee training to stockholder reports. The end product need not have a television network for its distribution. In many cases, the tapes are sent out to individual terminals for viewing on VCRs with a television monitor.

This means huge savings for the corporations who no longer have to bear the expense of bringing seminar participants or company trainees to a central location. Though the use of private television networks can cost substantial amounts of money, the communications can be done in "real time," thus saving days of travel and disruption of work schedules.

The world of corporate communications today is larger, more complicated, more exciting, more innovative, and more rewarding than it has ever been, offering more job opportunities for writers, producers, directors, videographers, audiovisual managers, and entry-level career seekers than ever before.

PRIVATE TELEVISION

Private television is probably the fastest growing segment of the communications industry, with about $5 billion spent each year on production, equipment, and distribution through the latest technologies: satellite, fiber optics, digital video, and HDTV.

In fact, it was private television that pioneered laser videodiscs for computerized training, the use of the ½-inch videotape formats, high-speed and real-time voice and visual data transmission, and live two-way videoconferencing by satellite. And, whereas broadcasting outlets through commercial and public television stations now number about 1,600, with cable at 7,700 systems, private television has grown to about 8,500 user groups* as of this writing. If we include all users of video in the nonbroadcast world, the figure jumps to 49,000!**

Private television (or business television) operates in many of the same ways that the broadcast industry does. Most of the equipment is exactly the same as that used by the professionals who cover the news, sporting events, special events, and studio performances for NBC, CBS, ABC, and CNN, and often facilities and postproduction equipment exceed that of the networks. I remember visiting a major network affiliate in Chicago a few years back. The whole place looked quite seedy. To say the least, I was not terribly impressed. The next day, I was taken on a tour of the Standard Oil television/videotape operation in the same city, followed by another tour at Sears. The corporate

*The Brush Report (1986).

**Judy Stokes, *The Business of Nonbroadcast Television* (White Plains, NY: Knowledge Industries Publications, 1988).

setups made the network studios look like something out of the Dark Ages!

Some companies broadcast programs live, others use videotape. Some use both. Some have studios in the corporate headquarters, others maintain their facilities at a distant location, connected to headquarters by their own fiber optic links. Still others rent studios at the public television stations or even at the commercial stations in "down time."

There are companies that have both on-line and off-line editing facilities, while others go outside for postproduction work. The transmissions of the final product, whether live or on videotape, are exactly the same as those in the broadcast industry and on the cable networks, with the signals moving from the studio to a microwave station or a satellite station (called an uplink) or through ground cable systems to the satellite stations.

Some business programs are encrypted, so that corporate messages can be received only by stations that have a converter. Other signals are in the clear, so that anyone tuned to the proper satellite transponder can receive them. Some private networks are used for one-way corporate messages, such as a speech by the chief operating officer. Others produce hours of tape transmis-

A live satellite teleconference being transmitted from the studios of Georgia-Pacific Television in Atlanta. The client, Federal Express, now has its own facilities in Memphis, a part of the growing trend to in-house production. (Courtesy Georgia-Pacific)

sions such as news programs and training sessions. Still others use their networks as a primary tool for interactive programming by employees across the country, so that participants need not travel to a central meeting place.

Some private networks are small. Some are gigantic, with as many as 450 downlinks. Regardless of size, each network requires the services of a broad range of personnel from producers to writers to technicians.

> "Once in a while, a management idea comes along whose time is right. Business television has arrived. It promises to change the whole character of American business life. It is clearly the communications medium of choice for forward-thinking executives."
>
> G. William Miller
> Former Chairman, Textron

In her book *The Business of Nonbroadcast Television*, Judy Stokes projects that the 49,000 professional video users will grow over the next eight to ten years to about 83,000. She defines a video user as "an organization that has more than one playback location, that produces its own programs and/or has its own studio." As she breaks it down:

23,000 are in the business/industrial segment
11,000 are in education
8,000 in medical
5,000 in government
2,000 in nonprofit companies

By the mid-1990s, these video users will spend close to $13 billion, with about $4.6 billion going toward the purchase of equipment and the balance for production and staff. Though most units are staffed by just a few people, others employ large numbers of professionals in every capacity, from engineering through production, postproduction, and distribution. Many entry-level positions and internships are available. And many are doing some of the most exciting and innovative work in the area of corporate communications, using every technique seen on commercial television from music videos to roundtable seminars, from full-scale musical and dramatic programs to news roundups and regularly scheduled programming. Yes, and quiz shows!

- Some of the most diverse corporations in the country are now tied into their own networks: Eastman Kodak, K mart, Hewlett-Packard, Merrill Lynch, and Computerland.
- Almost every subject that comes to mind is now being broadcast to target audiences via satellite: real estate auctions, new Food and Drug Administration policies to pharmaceutical companies, client seminars in finance, and health network information on everything from Lyme disease to nutrition.
- IBM uses its network to reach customers, stock analysts, journalists, and sales, marketing, and technical personnel through its 220 downlinks or receiving terminals. Over 300 field offices are now tied into the network. In addition, the company operates two other networks, designed especially for employees in customer relations and new product information, their customers for promotion and the introduction of new technologies, and personnel in research and development laboratories.
- Domino's Pizza delivers one-way video and two-way audio on its network, with ten downlink satellites at its commissaries. Between 500 and 700 employees can be trained at each session. The network also serves as a vital link between the Domino franchise managers and headquarters in Ann Arbor, Michigan, allowing both sides to exchange ideas and to discuss current problems.
- Merrill Lynch was one of the pioneers in the field of private television, beginning its network in the early 1980s. Within seven years, the company opened its 450th downlink and now broadcasts nationwide for about fifteen to twenty hours a month, with programs sounding exactly like those on broadcast networks: ''Action Line'' (weekly sales meetings) and ''Fund for Tomorrow'' (new products).
- One of the most publicized of the business networks is that of the J.C. Penney Corporation. The network allows buyers around the country to pick and choose merchandise without having to travel. *The New York Times* called the J. C. Penney operation ''an example of business television at its best,'' and noted that buyers have been known to watch ''lengthy television shows starring nothing but shoes, followed by more shoes—and then stick around for the sock show.''
- The Food Business Network is designed exclusively for food industry professionals. It offers daily telecasts of business news, documentaries, interviews, employee training, and seminars, as well as conventions, management programs, and special events. In addition to programming, the network can send high-speed data.
- In the health care field the business networks now reach thousands of

professionals each year on every subject from surgery to new research on drugs. The number of hospitals now equipped to receive the programming is about 1,500. Although the American Hospital Association has grown from 50 viewing sites to well over 400 hospitals in four years, and has reached an audience of 75,000 professionals in a single year, not all of these health networks have succeeded. Baxter Travenol sold the assets of its television network to former employees after deciding that the network was underutilized and too expensive to run.

- The world's largest private television network is owned by A. L. Williams & Associates, based in Atlanta, Georgia. The company sells term life insurance and since most of its agents work at home, its network of 800 terminals reaches more than 140,000 sales agents. Since starting the network, the company has cut down on the cost of dubbing copies of over 3,000 videotapes as well as postage and printing expenses. Information in training, corporate philosophy, and contacts can now be broadcast over the network. The company's next project is to connect laser printers, so that agents will be able to print policies on site.

The next big leap in telecommunications should be the move into Europe via business television. Some American companies are looking to expand their businesses overseas. One of the pioneers has been Wang Laboratories, which installed both a domestic and international network in 1986, to allow its overseas sales force to get the Wang broadcasts from the United States.

Within a year, however, the network went dark, mostly because of costs. An hour of satellite time in Europe is about $2,400, compared to the U.S. rate of about $600. Cable transmissions to company locations cost as much as another $2,500 an hour. Wang has gone back to sending videotapes to Europe overnight by air. But the expansion of the medium into foreign locations is really only a matter of time. Despite the obstacles, the borders are bound to give way soon.

And so we continue to read in the business sections of our daily newspapers and in the columns of the trade magazines that Federal Express had 20,000 employees at its Family Briefing, over half the company; that Texas Instruments counted 65,000 viewers worldwide in its Third Artificial Intelligence Satellite Symposium; that universities are just beginning to discover the potential for using satellite video for reaching the ever-expanding continuing education market. Philip Swain, Director of Continuing Engineering Education at Purdue University, rightly called it "a high-tech approach to teaching high tech." With programming going specifically to companies in Indiana, the program at Purdue has awarded more than 400 master of science degrees in engineering over the past decade.

Whether for Ford Motor Company, AT&T, Prudential, or the Army, there is a tremendous expansion of the potential job market for young people and career changers who are interested in video and the field of nonbroadcast television.

AN INTERVIEW WITH JUDY STOKES

Judy Stokes is the former editor of *Video Manager*, an important trade magazine. Her book *The Business of Nonbroadcast Television* covers the professional television companies that use video for training, public relations, promotion, and point of purchase. It provides information about budgets, equipment, and programming, as well as case studies of corporations, nonprofit organizations, and government agencies. To write the book, Stokes researched 2,400 video users. I interviewed her recently.

I guess we both agree that there's no definitive career path in nonbroadcast.

"A lot of people who end up in video start in nonbroadcast. It's like the trade magazine market. When you're in journalism school, they never mention that there are thousands of trade magazines out there. They tell

Georgia-Pacific is only one of many corporations that now have videotape and television facilities for producing their own subjects and for rental to outside companies. This one is the set for "CableCo Chronicles," a career recruitment video for the Coopers and Lybrand Foundation. (Courtesy Georgia-Pacific)

you about People and Life and Time, but they never tell you that there are magazines for people who fix dishwashers, and magazines for writers. So there's a whole other market that's never explored, and when you get right down to it, that's where people start out.''

Is that what you find? That people start out in the corporate world and then move on to broadcast?

''Or they just stay there. It's something that is just beginning to be explored in the schools. They're just beginning to [offer courses] on nonbroadcast video, on corporate television. Until recently this area was the stepchild, like trade journalism was. So it really is a big market. It's a good place for somebody to get her foot in the door. A lot of nonbroadcast facilities are three-person shops, or two-person shops, so you end up being the producer, the writer, the director, and the prop person.''

I've always felt that beginners are taken too often by the so-called ''glamour'' aspect of our business. Do you agree?

''Sure, it's much more glamorous to go to work for CBS than it is to work for General Foods, but what you may find is that General Foods has a multi-million-dollar studio! Merrill Lynch has a very sophisticated satellite network. In my book, I have profiles of fourteen companies using video and how they're using it.''

We've talked about in-house production. How often do the corporations use outside production and postproduction houses?

''What we're finding is that a lot of them are increasingly going to postproduction houses because it's cheaper to do that than it is to hire two more people and cover their salaries and their benefits. They may have a one-person shop that uses three postproduction houses on a regular basis. So, it certainly is something that postproduction houses and production houses should be looking for as far as work goes.''

Has satellite network use been growing?

''Yes, substantially. Also, the potential for videodisc is great, though videodiscs got off to a terrible start because they were poorly marketed to the corporate sector.''

You mean interactive video?

''Interactive. Exactly. It was just marketed poorly, so that people jumped into it, got themselves way over their heads, and said, 'Never again!' But

the potential is there now that people are going more slowly with it. And I think that in another fifteen years, we'll probably see interactive as common as linear. If it's done right, people are realizing that you really can get your money's worth out of it.''

What about the future?

''I think there are certainly more opportunities in business, far more opportunities. All of the big corporations have private TV, the whole Fortune 500. Out at General Foods, it's amazing—they have a multi-million-dollar studio. So does AT&T, [which has] a real commitment to videodisc.''

I've been reading recently about some other applications.

''Video newsletters, video annual reports are really gaining acceptance by stockholders who can't attend meetings and by employees of the corporation. Another major application is in the health profession. Hospitals are networking so that physicians can consult on a case without traveling thousands of miles. You know, if Sloan Kettering is doing an operation, doctors in Boise, Idaho, can watch it. They also hire independent producers on the Hospital Satellite Network or they are given material from the pharmaceutical companies or the companies that make prostheses. It's just another aspect of the industry that a whole lot of people aren't thinking of.''

And the government?

''I have figures in my book on what the federal government spends each year on video and they're staggering. It's things like that that people just don't realize. You think of television, and you think of 'Kate & Allie.' That's not where most people are going to end up getting jobs. That's not the reality of the situation.''

CORPORATE VIDEO PRODUCTION

Over 40,000 corporations, using in-house as well as outside contract production, are busily producing tapes to be sent out to their employees, franchisers, and executives on a continuing basis. At some point, every company today must face the growing problem of communicating with outlying bases, with their customers, and with their stockholders, and video is quite simply the most efficient, cost-effective way of doing this.

I thought that it might be interesting to investigate just how and why a company begins to develop its own in-house production. Anixter Brothers Corporation in Skokie, Illinois, provides technical equipment to most of the electronics industry, including cable, satellite, and network. As the company has grown, it has encountered the same communications problems as any corporation boasting many regional sales offices and distribution outlets. A recent information bulletin read, in part:

> **ANIXTER FORMS VIDEO PRODUCTION SERVICES GROUP**
>
> We are pleased to announce the formation of a video production group within the Advertising Department. All Corporate Videos including training tapes and special presentations will be produced by this in-house group.

The bulletin went on to name the people who would be producing the videos, with Paula Janos heading up video production services, assisted by Marcia Anderson, and supervised by Julie Anixter. Here, then, was an op-

Julie Anixter (center), Director of Training for Anixter, Inc. of Skokie, Illinois, in a preproduction conference with Jodi Schallman (left) and Director of Production Paula Janos (on camera) during the taping of training videos for their widespread sales force.

portunity to find out just why—and how—a company begins an in-house operation.

ANIXTER: A TALK WITH JULIE ANIXTER AND PAULA JANOS

Why did you decide to go into your own production?

JULIE: "When we did our catalog last year, we used a local TV access studio for that production, so we had some initial experience outside and doing some things inside, bringing some outside people into our training studio to produce some tapes. Well, quality tends to create demand. We worked with many different suppliers, who gave us excellent tapes. And our executives said, 'Hey! This is a very cost-effective way to do training. Let's buy a VCR and a TV for every location.' "

How did you start?

JULIE: "We started out in probably the most straightforward and basic way, purchasing a camera to [tape] sales and product meetings and using the videos for speaker support—to help people with their presentations, to give them feedback. Well, we pretty quickly discovered how naive we were. We thought that if we put a camera in a room and taped meetings, we'd get some quality footage. You know, almost like a video stenographer with a VHS camera. And we quickly realized that it was going to be amateurish."

So you decided to find a professional?

JULIE: "We were lucky enough to have access to a local cable company with its own local access studio. Its program manager, Paula Janos, helped us make our first videotapes; when we'd hire an outside script writer and producer/director and they would work with Paula."

What were you looking for in that person?

JULIE: "We were looking for someone who understood video production and Paula's got that skill. I mean, she's a director and producer, editor, a writer. She has lots of production experience, as is typical of people in cable. We wanted somebody who knows the process, and we wanted somebody who was a good communicator. You know, in a corporate environment you have to be able to talk to all kinds of people and to make some sense out of different kinds of products, technologies, and markets. You need somebody who has some degree of sophistication, not just somebody who is technically outstanding. If someone is going to work in a visual medium, we think that person should also be familiar with art and design and able to do some writing.''

What kind of videos have you and Paula produced?

JULIE: ''We have about eighty locations, and last year we made a videotape that was a takeoff on ''Superbowl Shuffle''—to kick off our new million-dollar catalog project. We called it ''The Anixter Shuffle.'' Paula directed it, I wrote the lyrics for it. We hired musicians and did some original music and we got about forty product managers doing the shuffle. It was really a blast, very funny. Kicked it off by having all our locations show it on a given evening and AT&T helped us hook up the eighty locations. It was very exciting and I think it gave the message to everyone that videotape was a great medium, not only for training but for a certain type of corporate communication. We wanted to do more of it, but video production, as I've recently learned, is very complex and you really need someone to guide it, who has it as a focus. At that point, we realized that we didn't have someone in-house and that we were really not able to produce the quality and the number of tapes that we wanted for the field, so we talked to Paula about coming in.''

Why the move from cable to the corporate world?

PAULA: ''I definitely enjoyed the entertainment aspect of cable television production. But some of it can be very community-oriented and very low budget, low quality if you will, though some of it can be pretty spiffy. It was fun to be involved with a variety of programming, from news to sports to talk shows. You name it. I wasn't contemplating corporate communications. I had always thought that the next path for me would be broadcast television, and so I had to do a lot of soul-searching.''

How is the product different?

PAULA: ''Well, the problem that Anixter was having by going outside to freelance people had to do with the nature of their 'product'—training. We're not selling hamburgers. We're selling highly sophisticated communications gear and it's extremely technical—and dry. I've had to do a lot on data communications and voice communications along the technical lines, so that I can finally write something entertaining about it. It's not like writing about hamburgers.''

Are you happy with the move?

PAULA: ''It's the place to be. Just as I got into local cable television as it was an infant, I feel that I'm in on the infancy or the toddler stage of corporate communications. I'm doing what I learned to do in cable television, and I decided that this field was a better option. It's a good opportunity. It's a growing field.''

In a sense, Anixter is quite typical. Every corporation that has gone into its own videotape production has had to begin somewhere. The process starts with outside producers and freelance personnel, followed by tentative in-house production, and then a plunge into full-out video production. Generally, one person is placed in charge (or inherits the job), or someone new is hired from the outside to run the new and exciting department.

The majority of companies do not have a private business network. Instead, they simply produce videotapes in-house, or with outside production or post-production help, then distribute the tapes to outlying terminals across the country. Sometimes those VCRs are located in branch offices, sometimes right

The author during the videotaping of a series of sales training tapes for a major chain of clothing stores. (Photo: Peg Schumann)

in the homes of the sales staff, sometimes in the shipping rooms of a chain store or franchise location.

Videotapes are produced on almost every subject, for almost every type of company, service organization, and government agency:

- The Avon Video Communications Center sends monthly news updates and product information videos to 500,000 sales representatives and has over 18,000 VHS machines in the field. Avon produces about 70 shows a year and plans to expand that number to 100 programs in the near future.
- Brooks Brothers, the national clothing chain, produces all of its product-orientation tapes, training materials, and employee benefits guides on video and distributes the tapes to its stores, where local managers run the programs for employees, usually before the stores open for the day. Other retail chains, such as Joseph Banks of Baltimore, are following suit.
- City Market is a thirty-nine-store grocery chain located in Colorado, Wyoming, Utah, and New Mexico. Even with a work force of under 3,000 people, City Market has made a commitment to videotape for its employee training. Formerly the company used slides and audiotape, but it found that the cost of videotape and the quick distribution made it a less expensive medium for an industry where markups and profits are very small.
- Prudential Insurance Company produces about twenty new video titles annually for more than 1,300 field offices. Its inventory at this point is over 80,000 cassettes. Although company officials have been considering a satellite distribution network (such as the one run by a sister company, Prudential-Bache), as of this writing they are distributing via videotape to the individual locations. Through these tapes employees are trained in policy writing, customer relations, and company benefits, and are given news updates regularly.
- With a staff of only two people, the video production unit of the Dallas-based Neiman-Marcus department store chain serves the needs of the company's twenty-two stores. Everything from training to product tapes is made, including cosponsored in-store promotion pieces such as the one done with Omega Watches.

There are other practical reasons for the use of videotape by the corporate sector, over and above the lower costs of tape duplication. In a recent interview with *Back Stage*, Mark Chernichaw, executive producer of audiovisual communications at Avon, said: "We're living in a print-illiterate society.

Most people want their information spoon-fed. So instead of the memo in the mail, which two out of ten people will read, everybody's interested in electronic media.''

And so, in-house studios have burgeoned, more and more sophisticated and state-of-the-art equipment has been purchased for production and post-production, and staffs have increased in all areas of the audiovisual departments. In fact, some corporations are so well equipped that they are now offering their services to other companies for teleconferencing and videotape production, and are making their private television networks available.

- J. C. Penney has opened its studios, and is offering its expertise, its equipment, and its personnel to other users. General Motors held a twelve-city press conference using the Penney facilities. Procter & Gamble, Pizza Hut, Pampers, Squibb, and IBM are among its clients.
- American Express, with two studios, editing facilities, and a master control room, has begun to provide services to outside customers through what it calls Blue Box Productions.
- Georgia Pacific, based in Atlanta, opened its own production facility in 1983, and has since offered its services to other companies. The outside revenues have enabled GP to expand its technical services and to hire some of the most talented people in the area. The production department develops about 120 shows each year, for internal and external use. As Don Blank, head of TV and photography at Georgia Pacific, puts it: ''You can't attract really top-notch creative talent to do sixty shows about plywood. The writers, producers, the artists on the graphics systems, the camera and lighting people can only do so many corporate shows for their own company before they get bored.''* GP has done commercials for Ford, live broadcasts for IBM and Federal Express, and shows for Standard Oil and Coca-Cola. The staff members at Georgia Pacific are obviously never bored!
- One of the most interesting developments in this area has been the entry of NBC. The network, sensing that corporate video production and private network development was, indeed, the wave of the future, acquired the Cleveland-based corporate communications firm of Judd Hambrick Company. Working from that base, NBC plans to develop a network of regional offices to serve the business community in the production of everything from corporate image tapes to TV commercials.

*An interview with Don Blank is on page 230.

When they begin their operations, most companies have the same basic objective in mind: to communicate a message to their target audience—customers, employees, stockholders, or franchisers. Sales training is one of the great beneficiaries of the medium. Video can add life to a sales meeting or provide visual impact at a distant location. For a new CEO, it is much easier to reach a network of employees on videotape than to try to visit 150 offices in the space of two weeks. Customers will be more receptive to a tape presentation than to the spiel of a salesperson who has done it at least ten thousand times before and who may have had a bad night, thus lousing up the sales pitch. If a sales tape is strong to begin with, it remains strong, showing after showing after showing.

The use of video is now so widespread that corporations have found new and ingenious ways to use the medium. An international airline posted a large sign in its ticket office window. If I would but drop in they would lend me (for ten days) a videotape of the location that I might choose to visit. As an old travel film producer, I am well aware of the fact that a video may or may not cover some of the ''warts'' of a place, but after all, isn't watching a gorgeous travel film better than merely listening to someone describe the scenery, the street life, and the food?

There are other examples, and probably you can add twenty or thirty more to the list:

- American Express offers a twenty-minute videotape called ''Cash Management for Small Business Owners,'' which promises to teach you all about forecasting profit and loss, leveraging, and improving relations with your banker—all for $39!
- Schlott Realtors, the second-largest private real estate broker in the country, produces programs featuring million-dollar-plus homes, with tours of more than twenty or more homes that are currently for sale. The company plans to begin offering tapes on investing in real estate and on refurbishing a home.
- The cosmetics industry uses videotape to help stem the tide of counterfeit products that come to this country from overseas. The Cosmetics, Toiletries and Fragrance Association produced the program at the request of the U.S. Customs Department for use as a training vehicle for officers stationed at airports and ship terminals.
- Just walk through your local department store and you'll notice another growing use of video. Designers and manufacturers such as Liz Claiborne and Calvin Klein are now presenting their latest creations on television screens placed carefully around the buying floor. The videos have begun

to flow into the cosmetics and housewares departments. Point-of-sale video is here to stay.

- The pharmaceuticals industry is now using video to introduce new products to doctors and hospitals. Though titles such as ''Bacterial Translocation'' might not draw a huge audience to the local cinema, they can be effective tools for describing a drug, more so than an ad in a trade magazine or a visit from a salesperson. Video is totally visual. It allows us to demonstrate actual case histories, interview patients and doctors, and tell the story in a very short period of time.
- Along the same lines, videotapes are being produced to explain medical processes or to educate patients about a particular disease. For example, Alcon Laboratories of Fort Worth now distributes a videotape called ''Glaucoma and You,'' which explains the condition and the treatment to patients. The tape uses animation and live actors who portray patients.
- The world of cooking and food has gone beyond the shows hosted by such luminaries as Julia Child. Corporations involved in food processing have been producing promotional point-of-sale material for everything from citrus to chickens. A company called Young 'N Tender has placed a nine-minute video in Publix and Winn Dixie supermarkets in Florida to promote the health and economy benefits of chicken.
- Corporate meetings have begun to feature videos in a variety of ways, from visual reports on profit-loss projections to show openers and sleep stoppers (to be blunt). Merrill Lynch, for example, did a music video featuring its own managers. Following the trend, The Muppets are now in corporate video. The Henson organization recently started its own company (called Ha!) for the purpose of producing Muppet Meeting Films. The tapes, with such titles as ''Coffee Break'' and ''Breakaway'' and featuring the Corporate Muppets, Leo and Grump, are designed to introduce meeting topics, rest breaks, or key speakers in an entertaining and unusual way. They are currently produced on film, but are distributed on videotape.
- One of the most effective presentations for trade shows and exhibitions has been a multi monitor ''video wall,'' a fast-paced product presentation designed to catch the eye of the passerby. Though media artists such as Nam June Paik have been using such displays for years, the corporate sector is only beginning to discover their commercial value.

Tapes on employee morale and quality control; tapes for quarterly reports, news releases, financial reports, and stockholder reports; tapes for the American Kennel Club on Rottweilers and German shepherds; videotapes from food companies on how to cook bouillabaisse; tapes on how to recruit personnel, on alcohol awareness; video catalogs on lighting fixtures and Christmas goodies. The latest to come through the mail to me is a videotape about a company that makes dubs of videotapes!

All of this means but one important thing: Somebody has to write, shoot, produce, edit, score, and distribute these tapes. Someone has to sell the original idea and then market the results. Someone has to supervise, manage, and keep an ever-expanding marketplace supplied with videotape product. The jobs are out there!

INTERACTIVE VIDEO: FUN AND GAMES

A few years ago, I was asked to be a consultant for the Discovery Place Museum in Charlotte, North Carolina. With eight others from various disciplines, I helped to design and develop science programs for young people. The main objective of the project was to excite teenagers with the potential of careers in science, from chemistry to physics, from computer programming to geology. All of the presentations were to be live.

The most successful program was ''The Great Intergalactic TV Quiz Show.'' It featured an elfin master of ceremonies and a clever robot, Quarksie Quasar, who outsmarted him at every turn. The audience, raised on a diet of TV quiz shows, loved the fact that they were a part of the performance, as participants in the questions and contests. It was, in the purest sense, an interactive experience.

Over the years, laser disc technology has moved many of these live performances onto the TV screen. Our popular quiz show would probably be programmed as a video show: the participant reads the question, then touches the screen to ''play'' the game with the computer.

Computers are ingenious in ''answering'' questions. Machines never tire, as live actors do; they may break down occasionally, but they give information or sell a product in the most painless way possible. Corporations have found that sales have actually increased when they have placed interactive systems in retail outlets. Florsheim, for example, reported a 12 percent increase in sales in stores that were equipped with interactive video kiosks.

Perhaps 75 percent or more of interactive video systems are designed for training purposes, since computers can be programmed for stop-and-start teaching and reactive questioning. However, point-of-purchase use has been growing rapidly, and while it is not quite up to the figures for training, it will probably equal them in a very few years. There are about 75,000 interactive systems now being used for training, while the number of point-of-purchase systems is up to about 10,000. SK&A Research, a leading market research group, estimated that the interactive video industry now totals about $850 million in production costs, and that about 3,000 programs are being developed each year.

For the career seeker, these developments have opened up still more opportunities, and the indications are that the medium will continue to expand. Consider these uses:

- Levi-Strauss developed a point-of-purchase interactive video called "Touch Me" that provides product information in a music video format. Each member of a rock group is wearing one of the Levi products. When a viewer touches any one of the players on the screen, he sees a short vignette about that band member and then some product information about the Levi clothing.
- At the "Infoquest" display in AT&T's New York headquarters, almost every exhibit is an interactive video installation. The game-playing visitor comes away with communications information that he or she has asked to see and hear.
- Interactive video is now being used to sell insurance at selected airports nationwide. In Aurora, Colorado, supermarket shoppers can get insurance quotes through an interactive video kiosk provided by the Travelers Insurance Company and their local agency. The menu includes quotes on auto insurance, term or universal life insurance, and home replacement cost estimates.
- Hewlett-Packard has developed a management training course based on dramatized case studies. Sales trainees can access any one of many vignettes in order to interact with the problem.
- Du Pont's Textile Fiber Department is testing a system that allows customers to scan and select over 400 different patterns for knitting or crocheting. Consumers view each pattern in full color on sweaters, afghans, or infant wear.
- Auctions are now being conducted on interactive video systems. Kennedy-Wilson, a Santa Monica real estate company, sold $16 million of Hawaiian property, including 65 condominiums and 152 undeveloped lots on Maui, over a two-day period using such a system.
- The pharmaceuticals industry has become one of the largest users of interactive video. Programs have been designed to inform and alert physicians to the dangers of such things as cholesterol and exposure to ultraviolet rays from the sun. Drug companies also use the video technology to develop and market their own products. Merck, Sharp & Dohme International, for example, has produced English and foreign-language

versions of a three-level interactive program called "Lipo-Touch" for use at medical conventions around the world.

Whatever its use, interactive video thrives on audience participation, for audience involvement practically guarantees that what is being taught is also being learned—and remembered.

Whatever your interest in video production, it is quite possible that you will be working in the area of interactive video at some point in your career. With two-way teleconferencing, satellite network training, and information programming, you can begin to see that the industry is growing faster and in a shorter space of time than almost any other medium. Along with that expansion, an interesting and amusing problem has arisen: What do we call the interactive video experts?

As a technology changes and grows, new terms and new designations must be coined. We now have programmers and software engineers, Paintbox artists, systems analysts, and colorists—all terms that were unknown twenty years ago. The trade magazine *Educational and Industrial Television* suggests that we call these new experts "knowledge engineers," people who have the skills of teachers, technical writers, and training experts, as well as the talents of audiovisual managers. So, along with the other job titles in the industry—director, editor, sound person, video technician—we add knowledge engineer.

JOBS IN THE CORPORATE WORLD

> *Commercial Directors Turn to Corporate Work in a Period of Spot Uncertainty.*
>
> Back Stage *Headline*

Videotape production in business is not confined to the corporation. Though some companies, such as Georgia Pacific and J. C. Penney, boast substantial and well-rounded staffs, many corporate audiovisual departments consist of only one person, with every project going outside to freelancers and independents.

The jobs in the corporate world break down into several categories, all of which offer opportunity to the beginner as well as to the experienced production person:

- Within the corporation itself are audiovisual managers, technicians, studio engineers, and control room personnel, as well as in-house writers, producers, and videotape supervisors.

- Outside personnel who provide technical services, especially for teleconferencing, include mobile unit operators, satellite engineers, studio technicians, videotape operators, and coordination and technical production managers.
- Staff in independent production companies who are hired on a per-job or contract basis for a specific project, sometimes to produce the complete package and other times for just a single segment.

Georgia-Pacific's state-of-the-art, custom-built mobile truck is designed for multi-camera location production. (Courtesy Georgia-Pacific)

Ron Richardson of AMAX Coal is dwarfed by the giant 3270 dragline at Ayrshire Mine in Warrick County, Indiana. AMAX is one of thousands of corporations that now boast their own in-house facilities for videotape. (Photo: Jeff Weber)

- Freelance production people or creative staff, including writers, directors, videographers, production managers, and on- and off-line editors. There seems to be a trend within the industry to greater use of this pool of talent, as corporations begin what they euphemistically call "downsizing." Though the amount of programming has remained fairly constant, many corporations are adopting a "wait and see" attitude about capital expenditures, as well as salaries for full-time employees in service-related areas. Thus, the market for the freelancer has continued to grow.
- Staff positions at independent postproduction facilities. Since many companies find this phase of videotape production too expensive to do in-house, much of the work goes to outside companies that offer editing (both off- and on-line), computer graphics, and duplication services. Since these facilities must invest in equipment that becomes obsolete rapidly, outside postproduction is not cheap by any standard. It is, however, one of the largest job-growth areas.

An organization that has evolved to service specific needs of business is the International Television Association (ITVA). The organization's market analyses and services have been invaluable to many people who are now employed in corporate videotape production. (See the accompanying ITVA job description guidelines.)

Begun in 1975 with just 800 members in the professional nonbroadcast industry, ITVA now boasts over 9,000 members in the United States alone,

Many corporations are equipped for full postproduction work as well as having production equipment and facilities. Ron Richardson develops computer graphics for the AMAX Coal videotapes. (Photo: Jeff Weber)

representing everyone from the *Fortune* 500 companies to independent producers. In addition to regular meetings, workshops, newsletters, and the magazine *Corporate Television*, ITVA sponsors a job hotline and an annual video festival.*

At the ITVA conference in Las Vegas in 1988, one of the seminars on the corporate video world was led by Linda Lee Davis. Davis, whose background includes five years as the director of a public relations firm and public television, teaches broadcast and corporate television at the University of Kansas.

*For more information, write to ITVA, 6311 N. O'Connor Road, LB-51, Irving, TX 75039, or call (214) 869-1112.

ITVA JOB DESCRIPTION GUIDELINES

Manager

- Responsible for planning, organizing, coordinating, budgeting, staffing, and overall administration of an audiovisual department
- Develops, recommends, and coordinates policies, plans, and programs for application of existing and new audiovisual technology on a corporatewide basis
- Approves or recommends staff and salary changes, and expense accounts
- Coordinates scheduling of audiovisual productions
- Directs all company media programs either directly or indirectly through delegation to a qualified staff member
- Recommends annual operational and/or capital budgets
- Develops department or section objectives
- Recommends staff and salary changes

Supervisor

- Supervises a media department or section
- Works with users in planning maximum utilization of audiovisual media
- Advises users on most effective uses of media including content and organization of a given program

One-Person Operation

- Department consists of just you, and you perform most of the duties listed under all of the other job descriptions

Producer/Media Director

- Evaluates and interprets user needs
- Analyzes the user audience and determines the program objectives

ITVA JOB DESCRIPTION GUIDELINES

Producer/Media Director

- Writes a proposed treatment
- Establishes budget
- Assigns writer and/or writes
- Assigns director and/or directs
- Responsible for the program being completed on time, within budget, and to the user's satisfaction
- Coordinates all aspects of assigned videotape productions. This includes developing information from content specialists; working with assigned writer, graphic designer, studio crew, and participants in the production
- Directs the actual production, including making decisions on placement for sets, props, lighting, staging, audio timing, technical direction of cameras, and editing
- Directs the activities performed by the assigned teleproduction crew, either on location or in the studio
- Evaluates program results

Director

- Directs the actual production, including making decisions on placement of props, lighting, staging, audio timing, technical direction of cameras, and editing
- Directs the activities performed by the assigned teleproduction crew, either on location or in the studio
- Selects and directs the talent for the video productions

Professor/Instructor

- Teaches full-time at a university, college, or in a school system

Writer

- Evaluates and interprets user needs
- Takes suggested program ideas on an assignment basis and develops visualized scripts for television or any other medium
- Researches source materials and interviews subject material experts including participating script outlines for approval
- Writes the actual shooting script for the production
- Evaluates program results

Media Specialist

- Analyzes media problems and determines the best medium to use
- Sets up media programs
- Troubleshoots media equipment problems
- An overall specialist in *all* media and their uses, operation, and setup
- This description is used for the *smaller* operation where you have

ITVA JOB DESCRIPTION GUIDELINES

Media Specialist

to perform many of the functions listed under other job descriptions

Production Assistant

- Assists in the production, serves as grip, gaffer, camera person, script person, gofer, etc.

Engineer

- Evaluates and recommends audiovisual and teleproduction equipment
- Assumes responsibility for technical performance of videotape recording systems, switching equipment, distribution, audio recording and distribution equipment, associated controls, installation, preventive maintenance, repair, fabrication, and design of audiovisual systems as required
- Trains other personnel in proper use of systems and electronic equipment
- Directs setup of special equipment, remote installations, and ensures that the operations meet the objectives
- Continually reviews new developments in equipment and techniques

Technician

- Operates all common types of electronic equipment and instruments (such as cameras, audio recorder, video recorders, projectors)
- Serves as a technical member of an audio, video, or film crew
- Performs minor maintenance and troubleshoots electronic equipment
- Sets and arranges studios, conference and training rooms

Sales

- Responsible for sales and services of products

Videographer

- Responsible for the recording of images on videotape
- Handles camera selection, setup lighting and shot composition
- Produces and edits small-format video

I was so impressed with the seminar and with the subjects that Davis covered that I began this chapter with a quote from that meeting in Las Vegas. Much of what she covered is what many professionals in the industry have felt for a long time—that corporate communications offers the best possible path for many new graduates and, indeed, for many career changers. Here are some other quotes from the conference, given to you with the permission of ITVA and the seminar leader herself.

LINDA LEE DAVIS: THE WORLD OF CORPORATE VIDEO

How does corporate television compare with broadcasting?

"Students these days have grown up with broadcasting and that's the first kind of television they think of. Broadcasting is pervasive; broadcast has a tradition of over fifty years. Corporate television, maybe fifteen. How does corporate television compare to broadcasting? The answer is: favorably."

How do broadcast and corporate compare financially?

"Starting salaries are better in corporate. In broadcasting, a large market is everything. If you're working in a large market, you make more money than if you're working in a small market. Market size dictates everything. Corporate television pays just as well in a small market as in a large one. Corporate pays just as well in Gilroy [California] as it does in San Francisco."

What are some of the other advantages?

"Hours. The hours in broadcasting are notoriously horrible, just horrible. Holidays in broadcasting are things that other people celebrate and you cover . . . if you're working the local news. In corporate television, you stand a better chance of a seminormal lifestyle. Most managers told me that their staffs work between forty and forty-four hours a week. No one reported more than fifty-two hours a week."

What about job stability?

"Corporate video tends to offer a lot more stability than broadcasting does. The average corporate video employee has been at one company—maybe at different jobs but at one company—for about five years. A little bit more for managers. In broadcasting, you wake up in the morning and you can't remember if you're in Des Moines or Cleveland because you've worked in so many markets. With broadcast reporters, there's a rule of

thumb. It's sort of the 'eighteen-month rule.' A reporter stays in one market for eighteen months before he or she moves on, generally not even to another station in the same market but an entirely different market. So, there's a lot of crazy movement.''

What about the corporate ''home''?

''Corporate video offers the advantages of a corporate home. There are both real and psychological advantages to this. The real advantages would include, for example, salary or stock option plans. Or travel. There is a tendency on the part of corporate managers to treat their employees a little more humanely than broadcasters. And for people who want more creative freedom, corporate television is very attractive. You turn out packages with different looks to them and you often serve a number of different clients. Corporate television is going to be a more comfortable place for you than broadcasting. There's a lot of false glamour attached to broadcasting.''

Are there any disadvantages?

''The one area where corporate video falls down compared to broadcasting? Women and minorities. Particularly blacks and minorities. If you look at broadcast, about a third of the jobs in the newsroom are occupied by women. About 13 percent of the newsroom jobs have gone to blacks and minorities, which is roughly equivalent to the population. The FCC licensing renewal process has helped. Look at corporate video figures. Less than a quarter are women, and minorities and blacks: less than one tenth of one percent! The comparison is staggering, is it not? I will say that broadcasting has not distinguished itself for the last few years in getting women, blacks, and minorities from middle management into upper management. You don't see a whole lot of your news directors or your general managers coming from the ranks of women and minorities.''

How are corporate hiring policies?

''I think we might want to consider the question: Is there opportunity for college graduates in corporate television? The managers that I talked to—the majority of them—said that they were willing to hire college graduates. Now, this is shocking if you come out of the broadcast perspective. Broadcasters don't like college graduates coming to work at their stations. There's just sort of a tradition in broadcasting that you want people with station experience, who go to work in market 210, and move up

to market 176, and then move up to market 153, and then fifty years later you're in the top fifty markets. So, this is really a sign of open-mindedness on the part of corporate television managers.''

What are the chances of working in your market of choice?

''There is equal opportunity in big cities in corporate television. I talked to fifty managers across the country, twenty-four of whom were in what broadcasters call the top television markets: New York, L.A., Dallas, Washington. And, there was no difference between St. Paul's manager and a top ten manager. My question was: Are the big towns as willing to hire as the small towns? And the answer was: Yes.''

CHAPTER FIVE

ADVERTISING AND PUBLIC RELATIONS

"Y&R 'EXPLORING' POSSIBILITY OF IN-HOUSE PRODUCTION UNIT"*

Back Stage
June 12, 1987

*"OMNICOM,** Y&R GO FORWARD WITH IN-HOUSE PRODUCTION UNITS"*

Back Stage
Jan. 22, 1988

It is not stretching things too much to say that the fields of advertising and public relations are closely tied to the corporate world. Almost all American corporations have public relations departments and a few mid-size companies do at least some of their advertising in-house. The in-house units are generally small, however. As corporations grow, as their needs become more complex, it has been traditional for them to go outside for the work they need.

This has led to a growth in advertising agencies, which are responsible for the creation, production, placement, and supervision of print ads and television commercials. The trend lately has been the conglomeration of ad agencies (Saatchi & Saatchi, for one), but there are still numerous small local firms.

There has also been tremendous growth in the number and size of public relations companies, which counsel clients on the best ways to communicate

*Young & Rubicam
**Omnicom, a part of BBDO and DDB Needham

their messages to the general public. Such international giants as Hill & Knowlton and Burson-Marsteller offer a range of services far beyond the normal umbrella of PR. Scattered throughout the country are smaller shops that offer the same thing: executive training, video production and postproduction, and multimedia extravaganzas.

The important issue here, of course, is that advertising agencies, public relations companies, and their corporate clients are all committed to the use of video. This means increased opportunities in videotape production as well as in teleconferencing and business network programming.

ADVERTISING

Up to about fifteen years ago, advertising agencies gave almost all of their commercial television work to independent production companies through a process in which storyboards (the art director's sketched outline of the commercial, frame by frame) were issued to several companies and bids were submitted to the agency. Though low bid did not always win the job, the process gave the agencies and their clients an idea of what the cost range should be. It was exactly in this area of cost control that the advertising agencies began to take a good, hard look at their soaring budgets for a twenty- or thirty-second commercial.

In order to justify their fees, the agencies had a tendency to assign too many people to a job and to nitpick the finished product until costs began to rise through the roof. But there are other factors that came into play. In addition, a very special ''star'' system began to develop. Commercial directors, usually part-owners or partners or contracted to independent production companies, began to ask for (and get) huge fees for their work. These fees sometimes reached as much as $15,000 a day of shooting, with that fee or a percentage of it being paid through preproduction (planning) and postproduction (editorial supervision).

Throw in the need for complete union crews, usually the same size as those used on a feature, and astronomical fees paid to ''name'' actors and actresses, and you can see why the cost of producing a simple thirty-second spot soared to somewhere around $250,000. Many commercials went over a million dollars (the Pepsi–Michael Jackson campaign, for instance), though in all fairness, I should also report that many, if not most, small production companies are working for figures that are one quarter of that or less.

With budgets rising as much as 29 percent a year, the advertising industry has from time to time appointed its own committees to examine the reasons for the increase in costs. Among their findings:

- The time it takes to produce a commercial has increased substantially. This is reflected in overtime costs, with crew and talent being paid as much as 150 percent to 200 percent of straight time rates.
- Costs for shooting crew labor, location expenses, and sets have gone up steadily.
- Commercials are becoming more complex in order to generate what the agencies call "quality advertising." Some are becoming mini-Broadway musicals. Computer animation also has added costs of thousands of dollars per second.
- Editorial costs are rising. Despite the fact that everyone thinks of videotape editing as cheaper than film, it is not. On-line costs—especially when agency personnel make changes at that point—can be mind-boggling, with the clock running on a per-hour basis of $400 to $1,000 or more.
- The cost of original music has risen, and as "music video mania" has taken hold in the commercial world, it has become a substantial part of the budget.
- The cost of travel and per diem is higher than it has ever been. It is not at all unusual, at this writing, to find hotel charges in major cities at up to $200 a day. Add to that the cost of meals. Multiply by the number of people who *must* be there and you begin to find that your calculator always answers in the thousands. Whereas documentary video producers travel with a crew of from three to five, agencies can send staffs numbering up to seventeen or twenty—creative, writers, account execs, clients. And if the location happens to be a glamour spot like Paris or Rome, watch out! Somehow, the group begins to resemble a tour sponsored by the local church in Waxahatchie, Texas.

Under pressure from their clients to lower costs, and faced with declining revenues, ad agencies decided to bring production in-house. This move has changed the industry.

In the mid '70s, Ogilvy & Mather formed its own in-house production unit called Eyepatch. Although the company began by using outside directors, it eventually went back to its own staff people. Other agencies followed. JBM/Creamer-Boston started up an in-house unit called Whitewater Productions. Young and Rubicam dubbed their new unit COP (Cost of Production) Group. Leo Burnett-Chicago set up a production unit called Starlight Productions;

in its first year, it produced fifty commercials with a projected savings of from 10 to 30 percent.

Has in-house production been successful? The jury is still out. There are no hard-and-fast rules as to how these units are run:

- Some are in direct competition with outside production houses. Clients and in-house supervisors may still choose an outside service on the basis of price.
- Outside "star" directors, many of whom now work discreetly for the in-house agency, still demand very high fees.
- Many in-house units are beginning to learn just how important cash flow is. It is quite easy to underestimate a budget, especially on a "problem" commercial. For example, some production companies that went out to California some years back in order to get good weather found that Santa Monica pier had been washed out to sea by some of the worst storms to hit the coast in over 50 years!

As we used to say, "the jury is still out" and some units are beginning to find that the production world is no picnic. If they operate as a union shop, if DGA (Director's Guild) members are paid scale or above, if insurance costs continue to rise, and if the agencies follow their usual practice of putting too many people on the job and redoing the spots for the usual reasons of insecurity or incompetence, then they may find that it was all a wonderful exercise in learning the trade.

Advertising agencies are involved in videotape in other areas as well. The in-house production units are developing their own casting files on video, as actors and actresses show their range by submitting tapes of their work. In addition, agency casting calls are also recorded on videotape for future playback. This, in turn, has created an entirely new industry outside the advertising agencies as independent casting directors now record the work of their clients for preliminary selection by the agency prior to a live casting call for finalists. The videotape work is generally well done and very professional.

A group called The Casting Company in Brookline, Massachusetts, has recently moved into a 3,000-square-foot facility that houses two complete video studios with both ½-inch and ¾-inch capabilities, plus a school that offers commercial classes all year long. In addition to casting for television sitcoms, they cast actors and actresses for ad agencies that handle both local and national accounts.

In Miami, a company called The Casting Directors Inc. not only has found the casts for thirty-nine feature films and sixty-one episodes of "Miami Vice," but it has also screened and auditioned actors and actresses for over 2,500 commercials. More and more often, ad agencies have turned to outside casting companies, like The Casting Directors, to save time and money. In fact, casting agencies have become such a force in the industry that they have begun to get their own credits on feature films.

Remember that not all casting sessions are for an episode of "Miami Vice" or for a commercial starring Michael Jackson. Don Case, a partner in Kelly & Case Casting, tells the story of one session where he had to find an actor who would be chosen to sell "The Woodpecker," a small plastic, brightly colored bird with a suction cup on the bottom. When the bird was wound, it would peck away. The actor Case needed was a baldheaded thirty-five-year-old man who had to read thirty seconds of copy while the bird was pecking away at his scalp. So much for glamour!

Video is now being used for location scouting. Ad agencies are using their own in-house people as well as location scouting services to produce videotapes of possible locations for commercials. State and local film/tape commissions send both still photographs and videotapes of their best locations to the agencies that request them. Florida, which receives production revenues of up to $200 million a year, offers a library of more than one thousand videotapes of different locations in the state. The state government currently employs eight people as full-time location scouts, with twenty-nine regional offices to help find the locations.

An interesting postscript: Some people are getting into video by renting their locations—houses, farms, boats—to producing companies and ad agencies. It might not be a steady job in the industry, but it can get you on television, if you look quickly!

Ad agencies usually ask for bids for outside producers by distributing storyboards for the purpose of budgeting the job. The storyboard also offers a clearer explanation of what the client and the art director have in mind for the commercial. There are now companies (such as Video Animatic in New York) that translate those boards to videotape, using manual or stop-motion animation, special effects such as chroma keys, dissolves, wipes—plus pans, tilts, and zooms—to make the storyboard come alive.

Advertising agencies provide a training ground that is quite unlike any other in the field:

In order to tell a complete story within thirty seconds, every shot, every move, every edit must count. In its own way, the TV spot is a classic lesson in the economy of video technique. You have a limited period in which to move your audience and convince them to buy a product. For people who have been trained in commercials, the move into video documentaries or features or training tapes has always carried with it the invaluable experience

DRUGS DON'T WORK ON THE JOB

American Association of Nurse Anesthetists

:30 TV Public Service Announcement

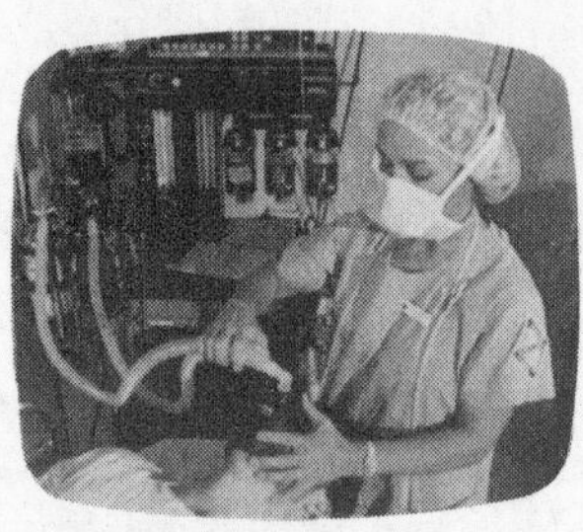

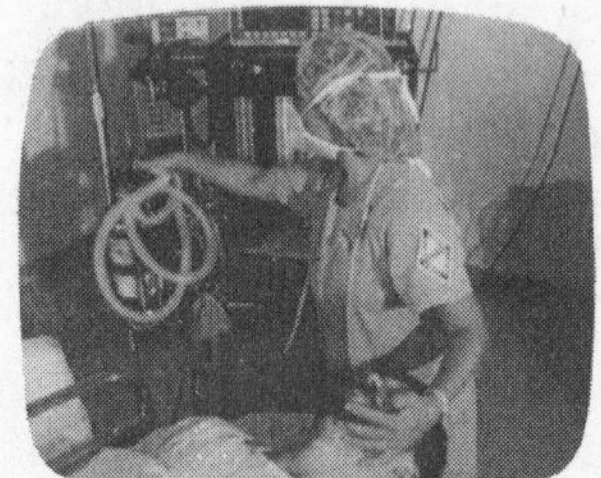

Notify ICU we're on the way.

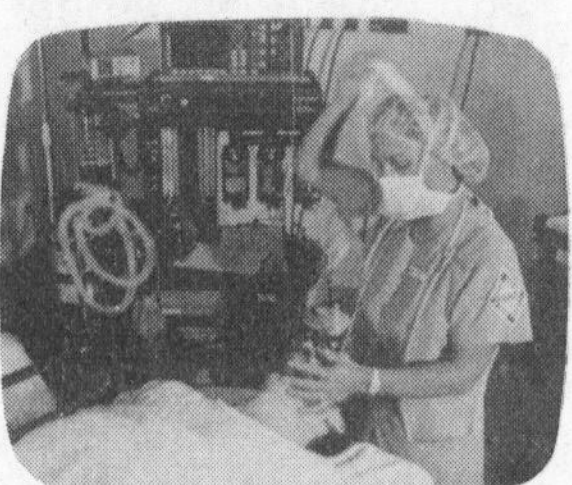

This is one of the few places where drugs belong on the job. In anesthesia they serve a useful purpose.

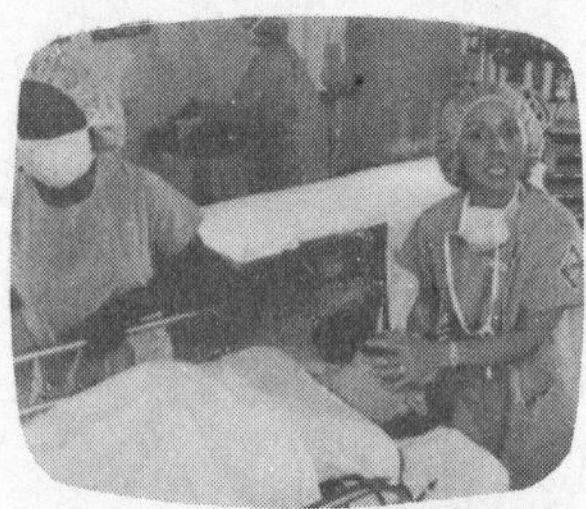

Each year too many people end up here because of drug-related accidents in the workplace. And using cocaine or popping pills creates a dangerous combination with anesthesia.

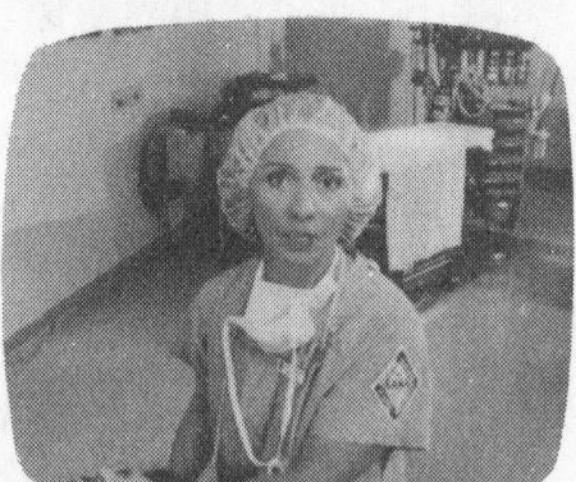

I know, I'm a nurse anesthetist. Anesthesia doesn't work with street drugs.

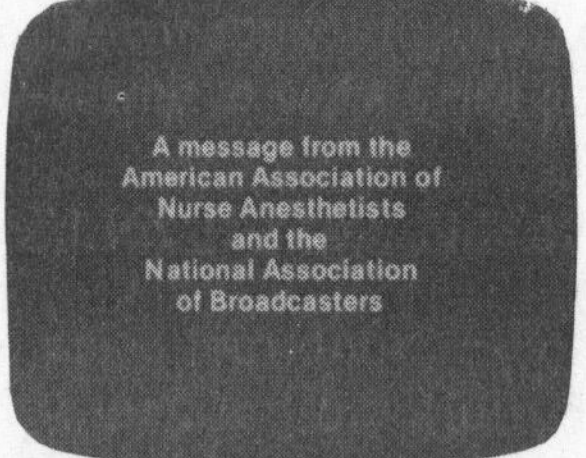

ANNOUNCER'S VOICE: Remember...drugs don't work on the job.

Storyboard for a public service spot produced by Salo Productions through Doremus Porter Novelli Advertising. The 30-second spot is one of the most effective learning tools, since every shot must count and the finished spot must still have impact as a whole. (Courtesy Salo Productions) that they learned while under that tight and rigid discipline. Their work is frequently better as a result. Advertising is one of the best areas for professional networking. Remember it is the ad agency that sends the bids to the outside producers, and it is the agency people (producers, account execs, art directors, copywriters) who then meet these people under working conditions on location or in the studios. There is no better way for you to get to know the people who handle the jobs, allowing you to move out of the agency and into a production company. Many agency people have made such a move by becoming sales reps for production companies, then going right back to the agencies for which they worked and bidding on storyboards.

PUBLIC RELATIONS

> "In the nearly ten years that I've been working here, I've noticed a tremendous movement toward videotape and away from other forms of communication. Ten years ago, they were saying, 'Should we put it on videotape?' They're now saying, 'We've gotta put it on videotape!' There's absolutely no way the audience will sit through anything else. It's the most effective medium with which to communicate. These days, everyone is video literate."
>
> Mark Bain
> Vice President,
> Burson-Marsteller Inc.

The field of public relations has one essential objective: to communicate to the public a message that will move them, convince them, or change their minds. The profession is well named, for public relations means, literally, relations with the public.

Most major corporations have a public relations department, sometimes consisting of just a few key executives, and other times boasting a full staff who perform the various public relations functions—from writing press releases to answering letters to irate customers to producing full PR programs for distribution on videotape or through satellite transmission.

As its public relations needs grow more complex, a company often hires outside PR firms to handle its communications with the public, becoming "the client" and merely supervising and approving the campaigns or the specific messages to be produced. It is these public relations firms that I will discuss in this chapter, since in-house PR is very much a part of the corporate world. (See chapter 4 for a discussion of the corporate side.)

Some public relations firms have become giants, with offices all over the globe. The two largest, Burson-Marsteller and Hill & Knowlton, can be found not only in New York but as far away as Hong Kong. Others are more modest, and some specialize in specific areas such as travel or direct mail marketing. Whichever part of public relations eventually ends up as your "home," you'll find that there is a need today to know video and to use it effectively. Some of the larger agencies have their own in-house facilities and staff producers. Burson-Marsteller, for example, recently opened a $5 million "Telemedia Center" that provides a complete range of public relations services for its clients. Other agencies, such as Daniel Edelman Associates and Porter Novelli, have broadcast service departments that supervise their clients' video projects, but use outside facilities and production technicians to finish the job.

The types of video activities that public relations departments and firms produce run the gamut from the simple to the complex, from the low-budget project to the million-dollar campaign. They include:

In-house presentations
Video news releases
Public service announcements
Exhibitions and special events
Point-of-purchase displays
Media training
Video monitoring of broadcast and TV stations
Press conferences
Satellite media tours
Teleconferencing

A good example of the effective use of video in public relations is a Burson-Marsteller project designed to help the United States win an international competition to host the 1994 World Soccer Tournament. The selection committee in Zurich had narrowed the field to three countries: Brazil, Morocco, and the United States. Mark Bain, a vice president at Burson, wrote a presentation that included a two-minute video speech by Ronald Reagan. As part of the thirty-minute presentation to the International Soccer Association, the two-minute tape proved to be a very effective tool: The United States was chosen to host the tournament.

Another example of the effective use of video in public relations is media training, teaching people to speak in front of a television camera. As Mark Bain put it so well: "Ronald Reagan didn't become the Great Communicator without practicing." People from all backgrounds—executives, doctors, economists, authors, members of Congress—are asked to appear on television. Most people need coaching, whether just to learn the proper technique in front of the camera or to overcome "incurable" cases of stage fright. Public relations firms that offer this service have proliferated and flourished. Consultants such as Dorothy Sarnoff, chairperson of Speech Dynamics Inc., a subsidiary of Ogilvy & Mather International, have become world famous.

Videotapes are replacing printed press kits at trade shows, publishing conferences, and television casting offices for such shows as "Today" and "Good Morning America." When I first began to tour the country as an author (a horrifying experience of seventeen cities in sixteen days), the publishers and their public relations people "sold" me with still photos, words of exaltation, and a copy of the book. Today, videotapes of previous appearances are sent out so that the casting directors can take an advance look at the person who is going to bore their audience for the two quick minutes that TV allows.

For these tours, the public relations companies are now investing in sample videotapes, as well as in the training necessary to project the author as a dynamic, well-versed, articulate personality—someone you'd really like to meet—instead of a reclusive, mumbling, antisocial animal (which he or she really is). The marvelous thing about all this is that it works! I have seen it work. People who would normally faint when they entered a television studio now look right into the heart of the camera in order to project their authority.

Another critical area that involves public relations companies as well as in-house departments is crisis management. The following case studies show how.

Public relations people were on the case within hours of the Bhopal, India, disaster, when the local Union Carbide plant leaked a lethal gas that caused the death of 2,000 people. The company's chairman, Warren Anderson, went to India to be seen on the spot, a move that was covered by network television and every major newspaper in the country. In addition, he made four videotapes that offered explanations of the disaster to the public as well as to the employees and stockholders of the company.

Videotape is the perfect medium in which to move quickly and effectively. The director of Union Carbide's corporate communications, Robert Berzok, was later quoted as saying, "The Bhopal incident forced us to become much more adept at using video. We had to learn to move quickly."

On the afternoon of the October 1987 stock market crash, the Merrill Lynch satellite video network produced a live program that was viewed by every employee. The message was simple: Explain the crash, project its possible effect, and, above all, ease fears. The program was aired within minutes of the close of the stock market. Judy Noble, Merrill's marketing manager, called it "a lesson in crisis management."

Consumer Reports magazine created a crisis for the American Suzuki Motor Corporation when it reported that the Samurai car had badly flunked its testing procedures and that it had a tendency to overturn when it was maneuvered too quickly and too hard. Suzuki mailed videotapes to its dealers to show that the car was safe, and at a news conference in Los Angeles that was linked by satellite to New York, other videotapes of Samurai's handling capabilities were shown to reporters from coast to coast.

If you read the papers carefully, and if you scan the trade magazines, you will begin to see that crisis management has been growing and becoming more and more popular as a form of communication. Because videotape and satellite transmission can be married so quickly, the major corporations and their public relations arms keep the technology of videotape as an effective emergency tool. Ashland Oil, Inc. responded to its million-gallon oil spill in the Monongahela River by making a videotape that showed the cleanup of that spill. The chairman of Phillips Petroleum faced his employees via videotape to explain the restructuring of the company and the reasons for early retirement and employee layoffs.

So, the next time you see the term "crisis management," remember that somewhere there was a videotape production unit and a whole staff of people trained to act quickly and effectively.

More and more frequently, that function is being taken over by public relations agencies. Thus, in addition to the usual jobs that exist within PR production units—producers, editors, writers, equipment operators, dubbing technicians—new titles and job opportunities are being created, many of which didn't exist fifteen years ago:

- *Media trainers and interviewers*, who work with their subjects in developing video personalities that will come across effectively on the screen.
- *Video monitoring services*, such as Luce, Burrelle and Video Monitoring Service, which monitor network shows, news shows, and interview programs, sending back videotapes of appearances of their clients so that they can be viewed and analyzed.

As you pursue a career in video, you will no doubt work on many productions that involve the people in public relations—both within the corporation and in the outside agencies that service those companies. During the years that I have been producing, it has been the public relations people who have most often been my clients, whether for travel documentaries or crisis management projects, for visitor center presentations or stockholder reports.

To get the "inside" scoop on public relations, I spoke with two top executives of the video production group at Burson-Marsteller: Ralph Katz, Executive Vice President, Communications Services, and Executive Vice President of Burson-Sant'Andrea Productions, Burson-Marsteller's in-house production unit; and Jim Sant'Andrea, President and Chief Creative Director of the in-house group that bears his name.

A TALK WITH RALPH KATZ

How are you using video at Burson-Marsteller?

"In a lot of unusual ways. Video walls are one use. Jim Sant'Andrea, who is one of the gurus of the multiimage, used a video wall for the Xerox presentation in Dallas. When you come through the hall, there is a video wall that is basically the sign for the Xerox exhibit. If you really want to see it well, you have to step over the threshold from the hallway into the area of the exhibit. So a video wall is used as an attention-getter and a kind of overview of some of the things that you're going to see inside."

Ralph Katz in Burson-Marsteller's state-of-the-art editing facility, the Gramercy Broadcast Center. It is used to edit a variety of videotapes such as corporate videos, music videos, infomercials, and news releases. (Courtesy Burson-Marsteller)

How else might you use video?

"We use video delivery systems as part of the architecture. We did one large presentation for a client—I'm almost sure it's one of the largest single vendor trade shows ever done. Last year it was 120,000 square feet at the Boston World Trade Center. This year it went to 150,000 square feet. And it was designed to fit together so that it just wasn't a bunch of unrelated exhibitry. The whole floor was designed so that we had video signage and video segments that were used as headers for each of the marketing areas. The foyer was a central sculpture—what we called the Theme Foyer and the Theme Rotunda—and they had built-in video constantly going on. Video walls. Video strips."

I understand that you also had an unusual exhibit at Calgary during the 1988 Winter Olympics.

"Yes, and we won the gold medal in the multimedia competition for that show. We actually produced a show every night of the Olympics in downtown Calgary where the medals were given out. It was a pyro-laser video wall show and we used eighty-one monitor screens on a video wall in Olympic Plaza. This tied in to lasers that were being projected onto fourteen-story screens on three skyscrapers. And all of that was coordinated with music that was piped into the plaza and also on FM radio. We coordinated with laser graphics and projection of eight by ten slides that projected from building to building. And that whole fantastic thing tied together, with the basic story of past and present Olympics on the eighty-one monitor screens. It was a celebration of medal winners. And the only reason the show could change every night was because of the video. By the end of the show, it was the story of the Calgary Olympics. You couldn't do it any other way but [with] video."

You also do some other, less spectacular services for your clients?

"Training is a great one, and it shouldn't be ignored. What better way than video to learn how to present. We're in a world of communications where [knowing how to] present skills is absolutely essential. You are always a salesperson. If you're in business, one way or another you're a salesperson in a service business. And we, rather than telling people, 'Here's what you're doing wrong or here's what you're doing right,' we let them sit there, watch themselves, and they know right away."

The Theme Rotunda at DECWorld in Cannes, created by Burson-Sant'Andrea Productions. The exhibition was totally integrated as an architectural sculpture, incorporating a three-dimensional environment of cosmic rings, multimonitor video walls, supergraphic murals, special lighting effects, and electronic images. (Courtesy Burson-Sant'Andrea Productions)

The focal point: The Celebration of Medal Winners Wall, highlighting each day's medal winners. The project could not have been accomplished on a daily basis without the use of videotape. (Courtesy Burson-Sant'Andrea Productions)

Downtown Calgary, scene of the nightly extravaganza.

I know what you mean. I saw one videotape of a TV interview that I did and I kept wondering why I scratched my nose so often!

"I had one four-hour session where I sat down and saw myself. Ever since, I've enjoyed presenting instead of dreading it, because I saw that you couldn't see my knees knocking! I saw that I actually moved my hands. I also saw some of the things that I did wrong, including voice mannerisms, like 'uh'—you need to point that out to people. It's much better if they watch it on video. You can stop saying 'uh' if you see that you're actually doing it."

Have many of the people we see on talk shows been trained by companies like Burson?

"Sure. Not only have we trained corporate executives, but we've trained physicians, we've trained most of the postal service sales force. Imagine that instead of having to go on a live talk show, you've been trained and briefed on a simulated talk show. If you go on live, the first time you see yourself is in a talk show situation. It's the real thing. No more. We train you and brief you with video. We set you up on the talk show set and put you through the paces. And we can play the nice presenter or we can play the bastard who sucks you in and then hits you with the zinger. We can play it any way you want—and we can play it four ways to see how you react. Using video and putting someone through a training program can really make a whole difference in the corporation and in the way everyone presents themselves."

What type of background do you look for in corporate PR video staff?

"When people call me, I always try to open them up to the corporate world. Many more corporations have the producer jobs—more than we have in public relations. I have a marketing background, combined with communications. I have a TV-Radio degree from Newhouse [Syracuse University], a master's, with a very deep marketing background, and the combination is fantastic. Corporations today are just not spending the way they used to. It's better to have a message and a purpose. So to me, marketing and communications are a perfect combination. If you can't talk to your customers, you're at a big disadvantage. You have to talk their language."

But you also had some years in advertising, didn't you?

"Yes. Five years at Ted Bates. So, when I go to my Young & Rubicam clients, I know exactly what they're talking about. They're producing the

commercials, but at public relations, we're taking those commercials and often putting them into the context of the new sales presentation. 'Hey, salespeople. Here's what's coming. Here are the new commercials. Let's give you the whole product introductory meeting.' Jim [Sant'Andrea] did a meeting for one client that showed their new campaign on a three-screen multimedia projection—with video monitors all over the hall that came alive at different points. Video fireworks!''

I assume that everyone is now beginning to use video in PR.

''I would say that we are progressive and that not everyone is using it the way we are. We're using it as part of design—for large spaces—because it says 'today' and it says 'technology.' Everybody's used to video. It's a great way of getting information across quickly. You can be totally creative with video. You can put it in almost any space. It could be a monitor. It can be projected. It's just a fantastic medium. And just look at the effects you can do with video. It's hard to make a film look 'today.' If we finish on video it can be fast-paced, it can have the most modern music; and in terms of titles, in terms of transitions between scenes, in terms of just general effects, you can't make film look 'today' because 'today' is video!''

Jim Sant'Andrea comes from the same generation of filmmakers as I. Raised and weaned on film and the hard knocks of multimedia, Jim was well known to me by reputation for many years. He is someone who has not only grown along with the new technologies, but has been instrumental in creating and patenting some of the most creative, high-tech spectacles in the world of corporate communications. Here's a part of the discussion with the ''guru of multimedia,'' as Ralph Katz so rightly dubbed him.

A TALK WITH JIM SANT'ANDREA

You didn't just start out as a guru, did you?

''My background, believe it or not, was as an art director, a graphics person. I wound up in films. In commercials. But I was always in communications. I went to the old School of Industrial Art, now called the School of Art and Design in New York. We covered photography, cinematography, sculpture, industrial design, architecture, illustration, and advertising. After Pratt and the Cooper Union, I wound up with a well-rounded background that was always communications-focused.''

Jim Sant'Andrea with a model for the interior of the U.S. Pavilion at EXPO in Tsukuba, Japan. Sponsored by Texas Instruments, the exhibit explored the history of man's inventions with video wall sculptures, digitized laser projections, and special lighting effects. (Courtesy Burson-Sant'Andrea Productions)

I've always told my students that the path into our business can start at any place.

"People come into this business from the theater route. They come in now from the technology route because of all the demand for high technology to make these things happen. Unfortunately, a lot of people who came into our business have long since perished. They came in with what we call 'the Winky-Blinky Slide Shows,' where something just moved and crackled and kicked and it was fun for a few minutes, but it didn't say a damned thing!"

Who are the ones who survived?

"Survived. And flourished. The people who understood people, who knew how to communicate, stayed with the business. To this minute, I'm still learning, and I've been doing this for over thirty years. It's a very intense, communications-focused industry, and if we ever lose sight of that, we'll probably wind up dropping out of it."

What do you look for when young people come in to see you about a job?

"What I look for—not only in a student, but in ongoing staff people—and the thing that separates the adults from the kids, is someone who

can take ideas or problems and come up with solutions that did not exist before, and that doesn't mean inventing the whole wheel. You know, the wheel started out as a slice off a tree. Now we've got these steel-belted tires. It's still a wheel. A paper clip is just a wire. It just happened to be bent right. I've never really invented anything. I've always taken what existed and made it do something that no one else made it do."

What about some of the new things that you're doing?

"The idea of the video wall has now proliferated. At Infomart in Dallas, the Xerox wall is the crown jewel of the whole exhibit. We're doing the same thing for Bell South's telephone network in a new building in Atlanta, over 30,000 square feet, with video and media being used in a very exciting and new way. The thing that's really interesting now in group dynamics is three-dimensional communications. We've designed a special theater that rotates, but the audience doesn't know it. And the proscenium just keeps opening up on new three-dimensional visuals including real people doing demonstrations. All of it is done with video. There are computers in it, live people, video phones all over the room, in the proscenium, all the electrics, the wall switches, the chairs rotate . . . so you enter the theater in one environment and when the door opens, you've no idea we've done this to you. You are exited in a whole other place in the exhibit, which ties in with our story about transporting information around the world. And as magical as that seems to be, Bell South does it as a matter of fact."

As a matter of fact?

"Sure. We're just rebending the wire again into a new paper clip."

"Xerox at Infomart," a 35,000-square-foot permanent showroom exhibit that dazzles its visitors in Dallas with a combination 37-light box and a 21-video electronic wall. (Courtesy Burson-Sant'Andrea Productions)

CHAPTER SIX

GOVERNMENT VIDEO PRODUCTION

Government audiovisual programs have long had an undeserved reputation as being boring, bureaucratic, and labored. Of course, some of them are. Over the years, however, as federal, state, and local agencies have developed their own audiovisual programs and as the people who produce the videos and films have become more sophisticated, we have begun to see programs that could hold their own with any professional production.

Several things have happened to expand the potential for the person who wants to break into the field:

- The advent of video has increased production in government agencies a hundredfold.
- Agencies have begun to form their own production units, with some of them producing as many as 150 to 200 subjects each year in all media.
- The increase in video production has meant more opportunities for independent production companies and freelance producers, directors, and writers.

A look at spending by the Defense Department alone gives us a good picture of just how things have changed. The 1987 *Federal Audiovisual Activity Directory* lists audiovisual expenditure figures for the Defense Department that far outstrip the most active corporations. From a budget of about $20 million in 1985 with 7,800 in-house productions, the department reported a total budget of over $38 million in 1987 with almost $9 million contracted to outside producers. The total figure includes production, duplication, library operations, and off-the-shelf purchases. The latter represents nearly 2,500 titles produced as generic videotapes.

And that's just one federal agency. (See the full list on the following pages of federal agencies that produce videotapes. The entire catalog giving titles by subject matter is available from the National Audiovisual Center. Write for the *Media Resources Catalog*, National Archives and Records Administration, National Audiovisual Center, 8700 Edgeworth Drive, Capitol Heights, Maryland 20743-3701.

Taping a location sequence for the State of Georgia's Hospitality Training Program. Federal, state, and local governments have increased production since the advent of videotape. This project was produced by the Georgia-Pacific Corporation's in-house unit. (Courtesy Georgia-Pacific)

FEDERAL AGENCIES THAT PROVIDE VIDEOTAPES

DEAFRF Deafness Research Foundation, New York, NY

USA Department of the Army, Department of Defense

USAAHS U.S. Army Academy of Health Sciences, Dept. of the Army

USAF Department of the Air Force, Department of Defense

USAMSA U.S. Army Materials Sys. Analysis Activity, Aberdeen Proving Ground, MD

USANM Anacostia Neighborhood Museum, Smithsonian Institution

USAPA Assistance Payments Administration, Social & Rehabilitation Service, Dept. of Health and Human Services

USARS Audiovisual Resources Section, Reference Services Division, National Library of Medicine

USBHME Bureau of Health Manpower Education, National Institutes of Health, Public Health Service, Dept. of Health and Human Services

USBLM Bureau of Land Management, Department of the Interior

USCDC Centers for Disease Control, Public Health Service, Dept. of Health and Human Services

USCDRH Center for Devices & Radiological Health, Food and Drug Administration, Public Health Service, Dept. of Health and Human Services

USCPSC Consumer Product Safety Commission

USCS Customs Service, Dept. of the Treasury

USCSTP Cadastral Survey Training Program, Dept. of the Interior

USDA Department of Agriculture

USDAVA Department of Audiovisual Arts, National Park Service, Dept. of the Interior

USDCP Office of Public Affairs, Dept. of Commerce

USDEA Drug Enforcement Administration, Dept. of Justice

USDESD Division of Educational Systems Development, Dept. of Education

USDJP Office of Public Affairs, Dept. of Justice

USDLA Defense Logistics Agency, Dept. of Defense

USDOD Department of Defense

USDOEP Office of Public Affairs, Dept. of Energy

USDPB Defense Privacy Board, Department of Defense

USDS Department of State

USDSP Bureau of Public Affairs, Dept. of State

FEDERAL AGENCIES THAT PROVIDE VIDEOTAPES

USEDA Economic Development Administration, Dept. of Commerce

USEPAP Office of Public Affairs, Environmental Protection Agency

USETA Employment and Training Administration, Dept. of Labor

USFBI Federal Bureau of Investigation, Dept. of Justice

USFDA Food and Drug Administration, Public Health Service, Dept. of Health and Human Services

USFEMA Federal Emergency Management Agency

USFHWA Federal Highway Administration, Dept. of Transportation

USFJC Federal Judicial Center, Judicial Branch, Admin. Office of the U.S. Courts

USFLET Federal Law Enforcement Training Center, Dept. of the Treasury

USFS Forest Service, Dept. of Agriculture

USFSI Foreign Service Institute, Dept. of State

USGSA General Services Administration

USHCFA Health Care Financing Administration, Dept. of Health & Human Services

USHSC Health Services Command, Dept. of the Army, Dept. of Defense

USN Department of the Navy, Department of Defense

USNARS National Archives and Records Service, General Services Admn.

USNASA National Aeronautics and Space Administration

USNBS National Bureau of Standards, Dept. of Commerce

USNHTS National Highway Traffic Safety Administration, Dept. of Transportation

USNIAA National Institute on Alcohol Abuse and Alcoholism, Public Health Service, Dept. of Health and Human Services

USNIHC Clinical Center, National Institutes of Health, Public Health Service, Dept. of Health & Human Services

USNIMH National Institute of Mental Health, Public Health Service, Dept. of Health & Human Services

USNIOSH National Institute for Occupational Safety & Health, Centers for Disease Control, Public Health Service, Dept. of Health & Human Services

USNLSB National Library Service for the Blind and Physically Handicapped, Library of Congress

USNSF National Science Foundation

FEDERAL AGENCIES THAT PROVIDE VIDEOTAPES

USNWCG	National Wildfire Coordinating Group
USOCDE	Office of Child Development, Office of Human Development, Dept. of Health & Human Services
USODEX	Office of Design and Exhibits, American Revolution Bicentennial Administration
USOE	Office of Education, Education Division, Dept. of Health & Human Services
USOPM	Office of Personnel Management
USOPOP	Office of Population, Agency for International Development, Dept. of State
USOSHA	Occupational Safety and Health Administration, Dept. of Labor
USOSWM	Office of Solid Waste Management, Environmental Protection Agency
USOTA	Office of Technology Assessment, Congress of the United States
USOTS	Office of Toxic Substances, Environmental Protection Agency
USPHS	Public Health Service, Dept. of Health & Human Services
USPTO	Patent and Trademark Office, Dept. of Commerce
USRAIR	Walter Reed Army Institute of Research, Dept. of the Army
USSBA	Small Business Administration
USSRS	Social and Rehabilitation Administration, Dept. of Health & Human Services
USVA	Veterans Administration
USVABA	Veterans Administration Medical Center, Birmingham, AL
USVADC	Veterans Administration Medical Center, Washington, DC
USVADE	Dental Education Center, Veterans Administration
USVADT	Dental Training Center, Veterans Administration
USVALC	Veterans Administration Medical Center, Lake City, FL
USVANO	Veterans Administration Medical Center, Northport, NY
USVASL	Veterans Administration Medical Center, Salt Lake City, UT
USVAST	Veterans Administration Medical Center, St. Louis, MO
USVATA	Veterans Administration Medical Center, Tuscaloosa, AL
USVIBR	Visual Information Branch, U.S. Secret Service, Dept. of the Treasury

Some of these agencies produce a great deal of their material in-house (Defense Department, U.S. Information Agency, Veterans Administration), while others use outside production companies and postproduction facilities (NASA, National Park Service, Labor Department). For outside contracting, a rather complex process is used. Called RFP (Request for Proposal), it's basically a detailed outline of the specifications on which the winner of the contract will be judged. (See page 133 for more information.)

Video is now being used by state and local agencies in a variety of ways: by fire and police departments to train new recruits; by safety and health agencies to educate the public, for teacher training, and for student safety programs. Video is also being used in courtrooms, either as a record-keeping device (in states where it is legal) or as a method of introducing evidence in a solid and believable fashion. It is gradually replacing the court stenographer.

Video's flexibility allows it to be tailored by government agencies: from top-secret information taped for the FBI to a shaky, hurried recording of a drug deal for the local police department.

I've chosen two very dissimilar groups—the U.S. Department of Labor and the Metro-Dade Police Department—to interview on the subject of video use. From them you can see that subject matter, methodology, and production techniques vary considerably. However, for both agencies video has become a vital part of their communications.

A TALK WITH STAN HANKIN
(Chief, Audiovisual and Photographic Services, U.S. Department of Labor)

Stan Hankin joined the U.S. Department of Labor right out of graduate school. With his background in marketing and advertising, his first job was to develop a training program for job seekers who needed to hone their interpersonal communications skills. Today, two decades later, he heads his department. Hankin's observations over 20 years in the field give an excellent view of just where video is going on the federal level.

I assume that your department is now sold on video.

"I think that video usage in the government is coming of age. Agencies have become a lot smarter in knowing what they need for a good video product, whether it's for communications or training or public service. Ten years ago, this was not the case. We're producing better products today, simply because there's more knowledge about what we can do with video. And I'm serious about this: I think the public's tax money is

being well spent on programs that train the government staff, and that help the public in general."

The figures show that government agencies are spending much more on video production now than they ever did.

"Yes, and I think the money's being spent better. There has been a conscious effort not to have the same agency produce six films or videotapes on the same subject. There's very definitely a public constituency out there that wants information. For example, the Consumer Information Center out in Pueblo, Colorado, had one public service announcement on the air during prime time and they got fourteen thousand responses—just from one airing."

What types of videos do you produce for the Department of Labor?

"We produce job training programs for federal employees as well as affiliated state and local government staffs. We also produce public service programming designed to recruit young people into the Job Corps, mostly disadvantaged youngsters who need a training opportunity. We also produced a minidocumentary designed to encourage industry and labor to explore new ways of developing apprenticeship programs that can meet the kinds of jobs that will be coming into the economy in the next decade—service and high tech. One of our most successful programs was 'The Business of Caring,' which focused on how companies and employees can work together to develop day care options. Another program that's a favorite of mine is one that I produced as part of a cooperative effort between the Department of Labor and the Department of the Interior with the U.S. Holocaust Memorial Council. It was called 'To Bear Witness' and it won nine major national awards, including an Emmy. It was a documentary about the liberation of the concentration camps in World War II. We used old footage mixed with a lot of contemporary interviews with people who were the liberators. Actually, we videotaped the liberators' conference here [in Washington] and then built our story around that."

Do federal agencies produce most of their own programs or use independents?

"It's mixed, certainly. The Consumer Information Center, for example, produced the spot I spoke of earlier with an outside contractor. Nonmilitary agencies use freelancers on a mixed basis—they'll have in-house people working with outside assistants such as videographers or editors. For the military, it depends upon security situations."

How is your department set up?

"Our staff consists of only two people: myself and one other federal staff person on the television side. On all programming, I serve as executive producer and when I have time—such as on the apprenticeship program—I take an active hand in writing. If possible, I remain active as director and producer. We use a great deal of outside talent to help us produce our programming—writers, directors, camera operators."

Do you have a complete facility?

"Yes. To accomplish the programming that we have to do, we basically are completely equipped with everything we need to produce a program from beginning to end, and all of it to broadcast standards—with the exception of digital effects, which we then buy at an outside facility, a postproduction house. However, if we need to have a second or third camera, for example, we use outside freelancers—or, if you want to call them 'contractors'—to assist us in production. It becomes a team effort, with government equipment, some outside equipment, federal staff, and outside staff."

How do people break in to government video?

"This continues to be a referral and word-of-mouth business, as well as people's own personal marketing effort. We do get resumes, we do get demonstration reels, and we look for certain qualities in people. We interview producers all the time. I look for the ability of people to get along with other people. It's too easy to become egotistical in this field."

What other traits do you look for?

"I look for the inquisitive mind, the person who can go one step further when faced with a roadblock. Sometimes people call me and say, 'I'm looking for certain types of footage' and 'I don't know where else to look,' and I begin to wonder to myself, how come they don't know that footage exists at the AFL/CIO or at the International Ladies' Garment Workers' Union or the American Federation of Musicians? Or at least, they might say, 'If I were looking for this, what other places might I call?' I look for those kind of people, someone with a sharp mind who can communicate clearly, at least on the phone. A lot of the other things you can be trained in."

What would you say are the big differences in producing films and tapes for the government versus, say, corporations or television?

"Every product that we produce as an in-house organization has to be a winner. Network television is the only place I know of where you can spend a ton of money to produce something and fail, and then get a ton of money to try it all over again. It's the only place I know of that affords you that marvelous luxury."

There's a big difference in budgets, too.

"I think the average now for a half-hour sitcom on television is about $400,000 or more. Now, compare that to what we must do. How many times can we fail when we show a program that we've produced? How many times can we fail in front of the Secretary of Labor or a major audience and still be in existence? What I'm telling you is that when we roll the dice on a new person, it has to be almost a sure thing. And so we look very carefully at a person's track record. We try to look carefully at what his potential is. We use him first as, say, a production assistant, to let him test himself [without] putting the program in jeopardy. It gets back to referrals, people who, for example, belong to organizations like ITVA, to which I belong, so we get to see who they are.

What about satellite technology?

"We're using it here at the Labor Department. For example, we just had a press conference not too long ago, in which OSHA [the Occupational Safety and Health Administration] leveled one of the largest fines in history against the construction company that was involved in a building collapse in Bridgeport, Connecticut. There was a technical presentation, which was quite elaborate, covering what took place with the building, and the type of construction that was used. Because it has real implications in the construction industry, we televised the presentation on a satellite hookup to Bridgeport, where a lot of local officials and construction industry people saw the actual press conference live. Then we offered it to television stations around the country at the same time. It was an ideal opportunity for the Labor Department, which certainly has a responsibility under the law to be able to let not only the interested parties know, but to let the country in general know what was happening."

THE METRO-DADE POLICE DEPARTMENT AN OVERVIEW: COMMANDER BILL JOHNSON

The video unit at the Metro-Dade Police Department was started back in 1959, one of the first established in the United States. The incredible thing is that

Police departments are using videotape in many areas, especially for training. Some videos are done in-house, others are given out for bid. Robert ''Magic'' Wands of Magic Creations in Deerfield, Illinois (left) directs a training tape for the local police department. Others are Sgt. Turnbough, K. T. Stanwick on camera, and Larry Sharfman, sound. The Uzi being held by the sergeant is a prop. (Photo: Fred Davis, Strategic Perception)

all over the country there are local government units such as this one, producing videos that are both exciting and informative, using a medium thoroughly, with most of the public (and the communications schools) still totally unaware of the production output and the scope of the subject matter produced by these groups.

Metro-Dade trains more than 2,500 police officers in its own department and, in addition, provides training to twenty-seven departments all over the country. It also produces videos for the Native American reservations as well as the sheriff's department in Key West, Florida. The total number of police officers trained both in and out of the area has now passed 7,000. The video unit averages about forty productions a year, but in 1987 it did 148 separate projects, including 100 that were part of a special series on child abuse funded by a Florida state grant. The unit's video library now has 791 titles. It is, without doubt, one of the most unusual video units in the country.

Commander Bill Johnson heads the video unit. Formerly a director of marketing for a television station and an owner of his own advertising agency, he joined the police force ''just for a while'' about twelve years ago. He's still there in a job that uses video to its fullest potential—and in some of the most unusual ways.

How would you describe your video operation?

''I guess we're sort of a combination of media relations and video production. We provide video coverage to local TV stations—certain events that they might not have footage on—soft news. They have what we might

call 'news holes' where they use footage provided by outside sources. So, we're servicing them and, at the same time, getting some good PR possibilities for us. Another thing that we're doing is going entrepreneurial and we're marketing our tapes nationwide."

To other police departments?

"Yes. But we're involved in a lot of areas. In the last ten days, we've done nine shoots on nine different projects. For our officer promotion ceremony, we did a twenty-six-minute tape that we've posted and put titles on, music under, and edited, then provided the tape to all the promotees and their families, forty of them."

How does videotape help your police work?

"This week we're doing a video lineup on a guy who made the national press. He abducted a woman, beat her nearly to death, then abducted her kid and dropped him off in Alabama, starting a nationwide manhunt. We're [sending it] all over the country to police departments, because this guy was a serial killer. Surviving victims in many states will have the opportunity to view the lineup and possibly identify this guy in other crimes. With computer technology combined with video technology and communications technology, we're making it possible to actually conduct a lot more successful investigations . . ."

The phone rings. Commander Johnson gets on another line, then comes back with yet another use for video.)

"That was a detective calling up, saying, 'I have an auto thief here who's telling us everything and he's willing to do a videotape demonstrating how he does his scams and stuff.' "

Is your department expanding?

"Yeah. There were three here, and now I've brought my secretary and a computer along, so it's already five and we're headed for more."

What's the latest on the production schedule?

"We're coproducing a show with a TV station and we'll be shooting the crime scenes. We're also producing our own show for cable television. And we're re-creating an arrest situation for a training film."

A CLOSER LOOK AT METRO-DADE: JOE KEITH

Joe Keith, supervisor of video training for the department, is not a police officer, though he did serve a stint as a reserve deputy sheriff in Houston some years back. He came to the Metro-Dade Police Department from professional television in Houston and Miami, and his background includes eleven years as a photographer-reporter-producer-assignment editor.

Bill has spoken about some of the areas in which the department is involved in video production. What are some others? Could you cover training, for example?

"Well, video can basically be used in any way that the user's imagination directs it. With video we can show that the changing of four or five words, or changing the tone of voice, might literally mean the difference between the officer's being able to legally arrest or not arrest. Video is the only way you can handle it."

Do you also do safety tapes? How to protect visiting dignitaries and things like that?

"We've done a few in the past. We were the host agency when the pope visited Miami, and we set up the security in cooperation with the Secret Service. We shot twenty-six hours of footage, both what the public saw and behind-the-lines footage, and we're currently working out the basics of dignitary protection for agencies that have to handle a papal visit or a presidential visit or that sort of thing."

You seem to have a very sophisticated operation.

"We think we're fairly sophisticated for a police department. We don't come up to Northrop Corporation or Allstate Insurance or somebody like that, but we're one of the luckier police departments in that we've been able to get support from the local government in terms of experimentation—as well as funding, so that we don't have to struggle and get on our knees and beg. They've simply said, 'You guys are doing a good job. Keep going ahead!' "

Do you use postproduction facilities in Florida?

"We do that here. We've got a full production studio, off-line and on-line editing, and duplication capabilities."

So you do the whole thing?

"The whole thing. The only job we've ever farmed out was on the child abuse project. We went outside for duplication. But historically, we've done everything in-house, except for maintenance contracts on our equipment, obviously."

And with a staff of five?

"I do have a training specialist working here—that's a county classification that essentially means 'producer.' She's a script writer, she produces programs, she edits and runs our tape library and does duplication. Everybody who works here does everything. We've all got specialized duties, but any one of us may end up with the camera. We have one position that's being filled by a police officer, a dispatcher. He's our veteran. He's been in this unit for nineteen years. However, we'll be opening between three and seven new positions in the next three years."

What kind of positions?

"Writers, technicians—technicians in the sense of people who are production-oriented—shooters, editors—knowing the basics of field maintenance. When you're out in the middle of something going on, whether it's a civil disturbance or a training tape or a cocaine lab, you don't want the equipment going down. Someone who can figure out where the malfunction is and get the equipment back operating is almost essential."

But if you need more people for production, when you need more of a crew, like gaffers, do you go outside?

"Well, normally we don't need more. But, for the papal visit, for example, we went to our civilian volunteer program in the county—it was originally designed to bring in retired people who had a knowledge of accounting or clerical work, and they kind of helped out. I also got lucky. One of the people with 'Miami Vice', an assistant cameraman, decided that he wanted to donate his services. He's put in more than four hundred hours. He's also attracted our second really active civilian volunteer, a gentleman by the name of Edward James Olmos—you probably know him as Lieutenant Castillo on 'Miami Vice.' "

Would you say that your group is typical of government video work?

"We just happen to get a little more publicity than most, but there are a lot of other agencies out there doing good work. I think that people looking at the field are totally ignoring huge blocks of government, industry, education, where video is incredibly sophisticated. Most people don't realize, for instance, that the winner of the Madonna Music Video Award last year was a university video crew from Florida International University. They did it on their off hours with rented cameras and then put it together. They won first prize."

A final word?

"I'd rather see young people aware of the realities of this world when they come into this business, because it's a fabulous career, but it's not a magic career in terms of the billing it's gotten over the past few years. It can also be a really rough one."

A BUREAUCRATIC FOOTNOTE: REQUEST FOR PROPOSALS

The Request for Proposal (RFP) is a very special and particular government system of which you should be aware if you ever decide to compete as an independent producer for a federal, state, or local government project. Government jobs put out for RFP bids can make for marvelously interesting and rewarding video samples, especially for the producer without too much experience (since the overhead is usually low and the budgets reflect this advantage) or for the experienced producer who knows the complicated, tortuous thinking of the people who write the RFPs.

But RFPs are time consuming and take an inordinate amount of research, hard labor, and budgetary magic. The federal bureaucracy has developed many methods of torturing the bidding contractor, though all of them contain essentially the same elements.

The major reason for the RFP system in government bidding is to make the job potentially available to everyone who wants to bid, regardless of experience, company size, and Congressional contacts. On occasion, two or three finalists are asked to make personal presentations to the agency executives or the audiovisual group. In the New York Police Department RFP (reprinted at the beginning of this section), the budget figure had already been established,

REQUEST FOR PROPOSALS

The New York City Police Department will accept proposals for the development and production of a videotape presentation on drug identification to be used for training and public information purposes. A preproposer's conference will be held on 10-08-87. Proposals must be submitted no later than 10-23-87. Further information is available through the Special Projects Unit of the Narcotics Division, One Police Plaza Room 1100, New York, N.Y. (212) 374-6960.

so that cost was not a factor in the selection. However, for most RFPs, you must show every budget detail, line by line, item by item, crew member by crew member, plus all postproduction costs, overhead, and profit (if any). If you're just starting out in video, I would strongly suggest attending an RFP conference if you happen to see one listed in your local newspaper, or if you are interested in pursuing a job with one of the federal, state, or local agencies.

The RFP is a long, complex document. Requirements vary slightly from RFP to RFP, but the following example from the RFP for the New York City Police Department will give you a fairly good idea of the complexities as well as the demands that you will have to face.

The Objective: Training members of the department to identify illegal drugs, and to recognize those conditions that support a reasonable cause to believe that the substance is, in fact, an illegal drug.

The Audience: Law enforcement personnel, including other law enforcement agencies in the metropolitan area, plus members of the public, community groups, etc., to promote public awareness.

Requirements:

- To depict currently popular drugs in all categories of weights and packaging common to street sales, emphasizing size, color, texture, paraphernalia, and both street and legal terminology.
- To present reenactments of street conditions which provide a basis for drug identification.
- To also produce a modular component directed to training *plus* a second component for public presentation.
- To provide a visually interesting vehicle for dissemination of up-to-date field intelligence provided by the Narcotics Division, scientific input from the Police Laboratory and standards for court testimony provided by the Legal Bureau of the department.
- To supply a videotape original for classroom use and a 16mm copy suitable for presentation to larger groups.

And so, from very beginning, the producer has some things to consider. For instance, the department wants *two* versions, not one. It's also asking for a 16mm print plus videotape master. Should you shoot in film and transfer? Or should you shoot in tape and transfer to film (not a very cost-effective method)?

Note also that the requirements mention "reenactments." Does that mean that actors will portray the principals? Or will "real" people be used? Maybe the police can play their own roles, but what do we do about convincing a drug dealer to portray himself in a street sale? Already the budget of $110,000 seems to be shrinking.

The RFP also asks for

- Eight (8) copies of the proposal including all exhibits
- The maintenance of an accounting system for purposes of audit and examination of any books, documents, papers, and records maintained by the producer
- A proposal submitted in three parts:
    1. *Letter of Transmittal* (cover letter) containing the name and address of the contractor, as well as the name, title, and telephone number of the individual to be contacted. The names and addresses of *all* subcontractors. All subcontractors must be approved by the city. Corporate information for each subcontractor. Offer valid for 120 days. Signed by contractor
    2. *Technical Response* (4 copies) including qualifications and work plan:
        - An index
        - An Executive Summary including significant features of the proposal, the technical approach, and the experience of the proposer
        - A Work Plan. A detailed description of how the proposer would carry out the requirements of the RFP, including a schedule and target date for each task
        - The tasks to be performed by the contractor
        - The number of hours as well as elapsed time *for each step*
        - Highlights of critical decision points as well as target dates for all milestones [sic]
        - City resources needed for the project

And that ain't all!

The RFP also asks for a contractor background statement, including divisions that will perform the work, a description of any litigation in which the contractor is currently involved—PLUS a list of *all subcontractors* who will be used in the project.

Also—a qualifying statement, subject to review by the New York City Department of Investigation, identifying everyone who will be responsible for the work to be performed, with no changes or substitutions without prior written approval by the city. The RFP asks for resumes of all known personnel who will or *may be* assigned to the project, a description of the corporate experience of the producer's previous work, a statement of other contractual obligations, and a statement that the vendor has no involvement in South African businesses.

Last but not least, the RFP asks for

3. *A Financial Supplement* detailing the breakdown of costs.
4. *Interim Reports.* To be completed every month of the project:
   - Scope of work completed to date
   - Scope of work completed during the month
   - Comparison of work completed with work projected to have been completed over entire length of contract
   - Comparison of actual billing and expenditures versus projected figures
   - A statement about time and cost overruns (or underruns)
   - A summary of *daily activities*, including the names of all individuals involved

Amount of time between RFP conference and RFP due date? Two weeks. A lot of work? Yes. Worth it? That's a decision that each reader must make.

Are *all* government contracts for outside producers this complex?

Yes, a great many of them are, always with varying degrees of bureaucratic obtuseness. RFPs are a labyrinth for the experienced and for the unwary. And yet, many, many producers have made their fortunes over the years on just such projects. Occasionally—just occasionally—the government is allowed to award a job to a single supplier without going through the bid process. This happens when the agency can prove that only one person or company is equipped (through experience or personnel) to handle a specific subject. It actually happened to the author *one time*.

I was asked by the Department of Energy to research, develop, write, and produce a project about the philosophical and historical perspectives of the energy problem. It was to be the pet project of the Energy Secretary. It was a producer's dream. The subject was fascinating. The budget (for once) was sufficient. The client was perfect.

After months of research and writing, and travel to such places as Davis, California, and Washington, D.C., I submitted my fifty-five-page treatment to the accompaniment of loud huzzahs and congratulations. It was exactly what "the boss wants." I submitted the budget, then went home and waited for the phone to ring. A day later I got an answer. But it wasn't the message I had been waiting for. The secretary had quit! He had left the government completely to return to the private sector. And since the film was really *his* "baby," the department didn't see any reason to continue with the project. But, thanks a lot. Good job. Good-bye. The check for the treatment is in the mail.

CHAPTER SEVEN

INDEPENDENT PRODUCTION

Paladin Productions has been an entity for about three months now. In three months, I've done more projects than in the three years I spent working for other people. Right now I've got the freedom to do that. I've done a medical film about diabetes. I've just finished cutting a music video, which I also produced and edited. Tonight I'm working on editing two documentaries on African safaris. I've got three proposals in right now for medical programming, training tapes, patient education-type videos. I sell these all by myself . . .

Steve Goodman
President, Paladin Productions
East Windsor, New Jersey

You have to earn your reputation. It's being known. It's being trusted, that you're a proven entity. You're always proving yourself. Even when I was a gaffer, I had to prove myself. Just knock over one light and there's no second chance. It's always the Olympics. You've got to prove you can do it right now!

Sandy Spooner
President, Spooner Associates
Los Angeles and San Francisco

The competition among independent producers is fierce. Independent producers can be found *everywhere* these days, especially since the explosion in communications. But despite the competition, despite the huge pool of freelance creative and technical talent, despite the fact that every client has at least ten production companies knocking at the door, this segment of the video market continues to grow, mostly through the hard work and ingenuity of the people who really want to enter—and stay.

If the previous paragraph seems unrealistically glowing, rest assured that talented people eventually find their way into the business, and many small companies not only flourish, but continue to grow.

The size of production companies varies greatly, and it's a factor to consider when trying to crack this segment of the industry:

- There are small, independently owned production companies, sometimes with a "staff" of one, such as Steve Goodman's Paladin Productions, where the owner handles as many jobs as he or she can, hiring outside help only when needed.
- Most production companies boast from three to twelve people: directors, producers (usually the owners), editors, and bookkeepers. A salesperson may be on salary or on draw (advance toward commissions). Some personnel, for instance, freelance videographers, are hired for specific productions on a daily or a weekly basis.
- There are larger production companies, many of them involved in commercial production with "star" directors/cinematographers, with staffs that range in size from 50 to 150. Included among these are the giants such as Lorimar, who are engaged in the production of television sitcoms, made-for-television movies, and even features.
- Major corporations and public relations firms that do in-house production have begun to use their high-tech equipment and state-of-the-art studios as "profit centers." In other words, since they can produce only a certain number of their own shows or tapes each year, they are hiring out their downtime and staff personnel as production companies for outside clients. This has cut into the business of the independent production companies, who formerly did all the work for their corporate clients. J. C. Penney, Georgia Pacific, and Burson-Marsteller, to name only three, have entered the independent production contest.

No matter what the company's size, you will find that production is done by staff people and freelancers, while postproduction is usually farmed out. Equipment is often rented—from research and development through the writing of treatments and scripts, and certainly through the production phase. Thus, while the "creative" aspects of production may be done by permanent staff members, the finishing of the video product (usually including off- and on-line editing) is done at a postproduction house.

The reasons for this are simple. The purchase cost of equipment needed for postproduction—complex editing suites; special effects tools such as the ADO, Montage, and Paintbox; computer-driven animation and film-to-tape transfer setups—can be high. By specializing, the postproduction houses have removed a large part of the burden from the producer's shoulders, allowing precise selection of sophisticated and constantly changing equipment, while making investments that can run into millions of dollars. On the job end, the postproduction houses provide yet another avenue for young, talented, moderately experienced beginners. Indeed, it warrants its own chapter (see chapter 9).

If we look at the careers of independent video producers, we generally find a period in which they worked freelance or on staff for a small company before setting off on their own. Though there is no "recipe" for entry into the business, nor one for success on any level, I thought it might be enlightening to expand the interview with Steve Goodman, whose quotation is one of the two that heads this chapter.

I first met Steve when he was a technician at a postproduction facility where I used to have my NTSC tapes adapted for PAL and SECAM clients overseas (remember incompatibility?). When he moved to another small company in New York, I went along with him for my transfers and some postproduction editing. Finally, at the ripe age of twenty-eight, he decided to branch out on his own.

TAKING THE PLUNGE: A TALK WITH STEVE GOODMAN

We used to say that a producer is anybody who says he (or she) is. Is that a good description of you at this point in your career?

"Yes. I primarily consider myself, right now, an independent producer in videotape programming. Though I've worked in the video business for about seven or eight years in various incarnations, I've always wanted to produce."

Did you study video in school?

"I did major in film and video productions at Queens College, the City University of New York. I was going to get out of school and go to Hollywood. Of course, that didn't happen. I started by working as a production assistant on low-budget films. It was a great experience because I learned how to produce on a budget, all the tricks of the trade, how to get things done effectively and cheaply. I still feel that I can produce on a shoestring budget if necessary."

What brought you into video?

"Well, I really wanted to stick with production, but I found that work was not that easy to get, especially steady work. I felt that getting a bit

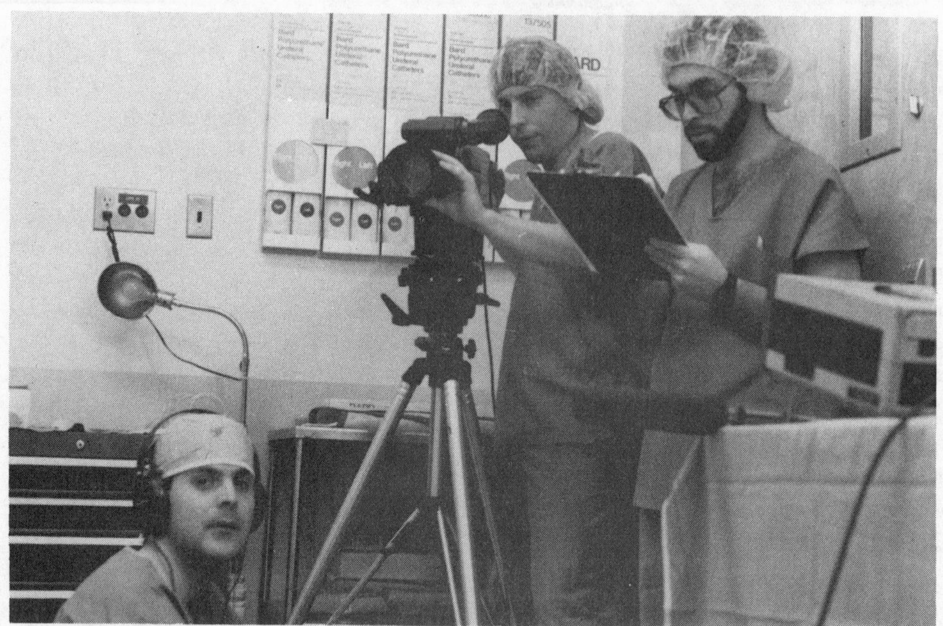

Steve Goodman (right) with Bob Koko on Betacam SP producing a patient video about a new technique for dissolving kidney stones (lithotripsy) for the New Jersey Kidney Stone Treatment Center, affiliated with the Robert Wood Johnson University Hospital.

of a business background was probably a good idea, giving me some hands-on skills. So, I wound up selling broadcast video equipment, while still doing freelance work on shoots. But selling the equipment is really what got me into the heart of the business in New York. I was selling equipment to production facilities. That's how I made my contacts.''

And the contacts brought you to the next step. That seems to be fairly typical, doesn't it?

''It's a step that a lot of beginners miss. What happened to me is that I sold every piece of equipment to a company called Video Central, which is where I met you, and it dawned on me that they're now going to need people, so I talked to the people to whom I was selling the equipment, told them that I also had a production background, and lo and behold, I became production manager!''

Steve remained a production manager for three years, designing and installing the equipment for Video Central, and eventually producing some of their industrial training films and video promotions. The department grew to the point where Steve had a staff of three working for him, but he wound up doing more and more administrative work (which is something that seems to happen to every successful executive producer). So he broke away to Picsonic, a postproduction house.

"That's where I honed my skills as an editor, learning computerized editing, which I didn't know before. Finally, after a while, it dawned on me, that whether I was selling for Video Central or Picsonic, I might as well be doing it for myself. I sell by showing a demo reel that I've put together, made up of programming that I've done over these past years—about ten projects of different types. Just looking around, I see that video is being used for more and more things. It's a medium that's permeating every aspect of our society, not only in terms of the consumer; it also seems to be a necessary business tool, not a luxury."

Should young people be learning film, too?

"Absolutely. Absolutely! I don't think there's as big a line between film and video as people have been making. They're a lot closer than people think. Learn film techniques. I see more and more of a marriage between the two. As an origination medium, I think that film will always be there. As a postproduction medium, [I think] that's where you're going to see video. As far as videotape editing goes, anyone can push a button on the equipment. It's much more important to know the aesthetics of editing, to be able to have a vision. The aesthetics are critical. You have to know what shots go together. It doesn't matter what buttons you learn to push!"

Do you also feel that video production is more than knowing the technology—at least in terms of starting a career?

"Well, learning the technical things is important, but getting only a basic knowledge of how to operate some of the equipment is all that's necessary, because by the time that a student is ready to go out and get a job after four years of college, the equipment that was used in school will be out of date. None of the equipment that I learned [in school] was what was happening in the outside world. I think you're much better off getting the basic knowledge of the aesthetics involved in editing, the aesthetics of camera work. Get a Camcorder and take it out and experiment with camera angles and composition. Most of us say that we're being raised in a video society—as 'vidiots'—but if you're going to watch that

much television, watch it with a closer eye. See how shots are done. Look for camera angles or the way things are cut together."

Anything else?

"There are more and more people coming out of schools today who have hands-on experience and skills in production. If they can combine that with any kind of business training, any kind of selling experience, it can only help. It's just another way to get in."

OK. Now you're a producer. What is the difference between the rhetoric—the fantasy—and the reality?

"I don't know what the perspective of a young person with regard to making a video is all about, but it's certainly more complicated than just taking a Camcorder and shooting. The role of the producer is still a job—*more of a business-type job. It still requires the skills that are learned through experience, that are not taught in film school. It takes the skill of being a person person, to be able to coordinate things, being able to be on the phone sometimes eight or ten hours a day and just trying to make things happen, to get people to do things for you. You have to know how to small talk and to sell and to bend over backwards to do things. So once again, I get back to that: If you can combine creativity with a business sense and with entrepreneurial thinking, then you've got what it takes to be a video producer."*

Are the hours long?

"The hours are all the time! I don't work nine to five. If you think you're going to work at a nine-to-five job, it's not for you. I'm working out of home. At eleven o'clock at night, the phone rings. I answer, 'Hello, Paladin.' I'm always working."

What is the benefit to the client of using an independent production company? Put very simply, the independent production company allows the client—whether an ad agency, corporation, television network, or government agency—the freedom of awarding an entire contract, including creative and technical elements, to one entity that will deliver a finished product ready for presentation or transmission. An agreement with an independent removes the client from the day-to-day responsibilities of the project. The contract between the parties will guarantee (hopefully) that the project will be delivered on time. And it will guarantee (even more hopefully) that the project will be delivered *exactly* to the predetermined budget figures.

Does it always work that way? Of course not! Video (as well as film) is a collaborative effort. The field of production is a *business*, not an art form. As with film, there is client involvement in the creation, development, research, supervision, and postproduction of each and every video project.

As with any business, independent production has more than its share of problems—weather disasters (rain on a day set for a golf sequence, sun on a day planned for a rain dance), budget disruptions (twenty on-line hours instead of four), and technical foul-ups (the equipment breaks down in Aruba during an airline strike). Despite the problems (or perversely because of them), many of us, including myself, have found it to be one of the most rewarding businesses in which to work. Consider these pluses:

- You are constantly learning, not only because the subjects you cover are varied, but also because no project is exactly the same as the one before. Everything—the people, the conditions, the job specifications—are different. You start all over again.
- Travel is very much a part of the job. Once we all worked in studios, never seeing the light of day. Now our productions take us all over the world. If you like to travel, production will more than satisfy your gnawing wanderlust.
- You will meet some of the most interesting people, some of the most effective and memorable executives, and some of the strangest characters, all of whom will be involved in your projects somewhere along the way.

Best of all, independent production allows you to choose your entry position from a variety of job classifications, and to make maximum use of your talents as your career progresses. It offers opportunities not only for directors and producers, but for a host of other talents: artists and set designers, actors and models, makeup artists and hairdressers, videographers and engineers, writers and researchers, technicians and prop people—not to mention financial experts and sales reps, and even the lawyers and accountants who now seem to control all of Hollywood's production.

The thing to remember as you are starting out is that there is a definite osmosis possible among all these jobs. Once you are working *in* the field, the move between categories becomes much easier. It is not at all unusual to find that people who are now firmly ensconced in their own production companies as owners, producers, directors, and videographers started out in other job categories, working either freelance or on staff, and somehow making the move successfully into the field. Still others began their careers in the film industry; as videotape became the ubiquitous medium, they either jumped over or are now straddling both film and tape.

One such producer is an old friend of mine, Sandy Spooner, with whom I first worked about twenty years ago. He was a gaffer (electrician) at that time, and we shared experiences all over the country, from power plants in Arizona and Utah to assembly lines in snowbound Massena, New York. Sandy was reliable and fun to be with, but I lost track of him for some years. That is, until I spotted an ad in *Back Stage* one day, boasting about "The Silver Spooner" and announcing his budding production company in San Francisco (now expanded to include the Los Angeles area). As Steve Goodman can articulate the process of just starting out, Sandy is able to speak to his years of paying his dues in a field that is difficult at worst, rewarding at best.

THE VIEW FROM LOS ANGELES: A TALK WITH SANDY SPOONER

Sandy Spooner started out with the idea of going into the theater, attending the National Theatre Institute, and becoming a lighting and scenic designer. "Even as a kid," he says, "I used to organize other kids in the neighborhood to do theater." But then, one day, he watched a television show being shot and noticed that "all these people were sitting around, doing nothing, mak-

On location in San Francisco, shooting a commercial for the Northern California Toyota Dealers. Sandy Spooner (with headsets) frequently shoots on film and edits on videotape, an increasingly popular technique.

ing twice the amount of money that theater people made. I said, 'This is crazy,' and that's when I went into television."

Sandy moved through jobs as production assistant and coordinator, ending up as producer of one job when both the original producer and his wife were fired. "Being at the right place at the right time," he explains. He worked as a gaffer, then began to shoot for shows such as "Real People" and "20/20." He moved to California, where he started his own independent production company about ten years ago. If we were to look more carefully at his background, we'd find that his career "ladder" was typical in that there was nothing "typical" about it! With no formal training, he says, "I've learned everything by the seat of my pants."

In your own hiring, what do you look for in people?

"I like people who have done theater, actually. They've learned to work for no money! Most students think they can start out like Coppola. But it's a lot of hard work. Too many people come in telling us what they've learned from the book, and we've been doing it for the past twenty years! I think someone has to start as the lowest production assistant—coiling cables, spray painting, working at the horrible things like picking up the trash after a shoot. You have to start out being an eager Irish Setter. Those are the people who get ahead."

Filming a hula-hoop commercial, Sandy Spooner is ably assisted by a student at the local school. The proliferation of videotape equipment has made everyone aware of production in the medium.

You're not condemning schools completely, are you?

"Of course not. But there are a lot of people who know all the stars, the movie titles, and the names of all the vice presidents at the film companies. I don't know half of that crap. For me, it's not a scientific thing. It's a profession. It's a craft, and you have to learn it. I try it, and maybe it works. It's like learning how to throw clay on a pottery wheel. I mean, you really have to throw it, hit it around—and if your hand goes in too far . . ."

You start again?

"You start all over again. People forget that this is a business. We may call it show business, but it's a business and you have to survive."

Anything else?

"Yeah. The important thing is that this is a very small business. You can't really screw anybody over because it's gonna catch up with you. You work on your reputation. People in agencies are risking six or seven months of product development on their choice of a director/cameraman. Commercials are a very tough business. There are a lot of egos in the agencies who are trying to live out being directors, but they don't understand that there's a lot of work involved, a lot of grit, dirty work. Nobody writes about that in the books."

I try! Could you describe some of the work that you're referring to?

"Well, like preproduction. It's amazing the amount of work that goes into preproduction. And budgets. Doing budgets is not an exact science, yet people always want to know exactly what the price is going to be. But it's exciting, because you're doing something different all the time. We just did a spot today about a woman being chased by turkeys!"

Turkeys?

"It's an interesting casting problem. You have to cast a turkey, and a woman who has good legs who isn't afraid of turkeys. And she has to run in high heels. It's a funny spot."

How do you build up your company?

"You go out and pitch. And sell. As you move up, maybe you can afford a rep to sell for you. I used to do that myself. I used to do little mailers. I worked out of my house—my commute used to be from my bed to my office. I called people. I did things for free. There's a lot of stuff that you

Preparing to shoot a Thanksgiving and Christmas commercial for a local supermarket, Sandy Spooner goes over some last-minute changes with the star of the spot.

do that you're not going to be paid for, that you hope at some point will come back to you. It's the favors, but you have to be careful about just who you do favors for, because there are a lot of people around who take advantage of that, too. You hear, 'Hell, stick with me, kid, and I'll pay you back,' and it doesn't always happen. There are a lot of people in this business who will rip you off—a lot of actors and actresses and crew people get ripped off, get stuck by people who come to town to do a job and then disappear.''

It's something that no one talks about much when we paint glowing pictures about the industry.

I've been burned four or five times by companies that have gone bankrupt. They do a project and then they don't have money to pay. If it's a corporation, you're screwed! You end up doing three commercials and they're out, and the only thing you've got to show for it is a whale costume.''

How do you prevent it?

''You can't really. It's a business of instinct. You try to get some money in advance, up front. You try to work with certain clients. We used to joke that this is a business of gut. If you've got a bad gut, you're in trouble—most of the people in it die at the airport waiting for a plane

that's late or canceled, because they're so worked up. It's a business of tension, of bad food, of no sleep. It's not a healthy business.''

Then what's the reward?

''I love it! It's a sickness. I mean, I just really love what I do.''

In these short years, Sandy's company has expanded to the point where he is now shooting national shows for the networks, business films for companies like Hewlett-Packard, IBM, Apple Computer, and Smithkline Beckman, as well as commercials for products such as Clorox, Ford, Emporium, and Toyota. If you ask about the number one challenge of being in business, his answer is simply, ''*staying* in business,'' remaining financially sound.

You will find, in climbing your own ladder in the business of independent production, that the rewards will eventually outweigh the problems of personality, of ego, of being only as good as your last job, of the constant balancing act that goes on between director/videographer and cast, agency executives, art directors, technicians, and everyone else who sees it one way while you see it another.

Do you find that personality is a major factor in any shoot?

''It's a challenge, and there's a tremendous amount of personality. Some of the big-name actors want a certain level of service, and sit in their limos waiting for the crew to service them. And then, there are the other ones, the real pros, like George Burns. You work with him and there he is rolling up cable. I feel that any shoot is like working with a team. I'm no god, but there has to be a leader. You can't have total chaos. Someone has to be in control. And I think you have to have a sense of humor—or 'senseless' humor.''

I suppose, like all of us, you end up with your 'war stories' and all you remember from a tough shoot is a funny story.

''Yeah. Like the documentary we were shooting in southern Mexico, and there was this guy who had hired somebody to do something cheaply. I suppose he was getting a kickback by putting us in these terrible hotels and he would pocket the rest. He put us in one hotel and we woke up and there were lizards crawling all over the walls and in the middle of the room . . .''

I remember one shoot in Ecuador where columns of ants marched up the walls and across our faces!

''The world is filled with fancy hotels like that.''

It was even called the Europa. Very posh, and at the end of a muddy dirt road.

"And a major trek through the jungle with four-wheel-drive vehicles. We were going to film those guys who jump off towers and it's going to be the greatest shot ever done for a documentary. Middle of nowhere. Machetes through the jungle, snakes. It's incredibly hot. We finally get there, dying of thirst, and they offer us something to drink out of bottles that have been reused, and you just look at them and say, 'Oh, no! Not me!' "

But the shot was worth it?

"Shot? When we got there, they had cut the tower down. There was no tower there at all! We had to go back!"

Which of your projects do you shoot on tape?

"We do our television things on tape. For commercials, sometimes it's tape, sometimes film. About 80 percent of commercials, I would say, are still done on film—with many finished on tape. I like to transfer everything to video, color correct, and then go back and select the scenes from the original negative. So, I use both."

When you deliver the finished product to the agency, is it on videotape?

"It depends. Certain projects are shot on film, delivered on film, and then the client or agency edits. If we do the project from beginning to end, we go all the way through the editing process, both off-line and on-line, and we deliver a one-inch videotape master. It gives us the advantages of both media: the look of shooting on film with the ease of editing on videotape."

A final word, Sandy?

"I'm just thankful that I've gotten as far as fast as I have, you know, in ten or fifteen years—the last ten in my own business. But, then, it never seems fast enough. It seems like it's taken forever. I still feel that I have a lot more stripes to earn. I'm open to options. I guess I never knew I'd be where I am now when I started Spooner Associates ten years ago."

What do you see in your future?

"Working. Just working—and a cappuccino!"

CHAPTER EIGHT

EXPANDING YOUR HORIZONS

Not only are production companies becoming smaller, but the good ones are also becoming national and international in scope. Jet air travel and the advent of overnight package delivery put a premium on producers who are flexible, who have good marketing skills, and who keep up with the trends *in all sections of the marketplace.*

Ray Salo
Salo Productions
Shoreview, Minnesota

Up until this point, I have been writing of the independent producer and the jobs in video with reference to the same marketplace that is serviced by the film industry—commercials, corporate communications, television—what we might call the ''standard'' needs. The only difference is that production will be on videotape rather than film. But the widespread use of video has created a whole new world of opportunity, and clever, original, inventive producers of videotape have begun to discover markets for the product *where no market had ever existed before.* All across the country, videotape producers and freelancers in the creative and technical areas have begun to specialize, targeting very specific professions or client groups, such as medicine, law, education, and the home video market.

Many of these little-explored areas present opportunities for the beginner to gain experience, acquire sample tapes, and make contacts in the field. If you look at all the ''up the ladder'' stories in this book, you'll notice again and again that the first experience of these subjects was generally outside the realm of producing or owning a company. You'll also notice that our peers generally speak of having worked for very little money on low budgets, or having been exploited when they started out. This, unfortunately, is also part of the climb.

Many of the job areas that I describe in the next few pages are low-budget operations. These smaller, leaner, low-overhead organizations offer the job seeker a much better chance of getting past the receptionist than do high-tech, state-of-the-art companies. It also follows that the staff and crew who work for these low-budget companies will receive less money for their work than their union brothers and sisters, and many times will be asked to work "for the experience." It's the reason that we find so many crew members who are hyphenates: gaffer-makeup-driver-gofer or director-videographer-sound editor. It's a great way to get experience, and many of us have begun in exactly this way.

What follows, then, is not by any means a complete listing of the markets in which you might want to work. However, I think it's a pretty good overview of just how much opportunity does exist in the areas outside the ones that normally come to mind. This is why I've called this chapter "Expanding Your Horizons." You may begin to think in other directions, begin to understand that your hobby or interest might well be the start of a video career. Most video students think only in terms of network television and directing the Olympics from Barcelona (which wouldn't be a bad assignment!). Your start may well be somewhere else. Remember, you can always direct the Olympics four years from now.

HIGHER EDUCATION

> *The blackboard is finished as an educational tool. You just can't show a professor pointing at chalk marks on a board and expect people to pay attention. Students and professionals are used to broadcast-quality graphics, and if we are going to keep their attention, we have to provide them.*
>
> Arna Vodenos
> Vodenos Productions
> Rockville, Maryland

Not too long ago, I received a videotape in the mail from a friend who lives in Atlanta. Produced by Emory University, the tape was being used to recruit students by showing facilities, faculty, and student amenities. It was being sent to high school grads across the country for viewing by them and by their parents. It was a far cry from the literature that I once received lauding the attributes of Antioch and USC. (I eventually ended up at City College of New York—it was free and a subway ride from home.)

Schools across the country have met video, and the marriage has blossomed into yet another great potential for both the communications graduate and the independent producer. Certainly, not every school system has VCRs and a large audiovisual library, but almost all of the major colleges and universities, as well as many of the secondary schools, have begun to use the medium in a vast range of communications and teaching programs, as well as in other aspects of education and public relations unheard of fifteen or twenty years ago.

One of the major reasons that schools have fallen in love with video is a very simple comparison of the costs after completion. While the actual production expense of a film is equal to that of a video, the cost of duplication is substantially higher. The average 16mm film print costs about $10 to $40 per minute, or somewhere around $300 to $1,200 for a thirty-minute film. There is no way that these higher film prices can be avoided, and the costs continue to rise.

A videotape, on the other hand, can be purchased for as little as $10 to $25 for an entire thirty-minute subject. The costs come down even further if the school is willing to make its own production and then dub locally, or if the producer will allow them to make their own dubs on the school videotape systems (a tricky business which entails copyrights, unlawful use of subject matter, etc.).

Many school districts maintain large audiovisual libraries on almost every subject from anthropology to zoology, consisting not only of their own productions, but of tapes produced by outside companies as well. Pennsylvania and Michigan, for example, both maintain excellent audiovisual services for the schools in their states.

Video has many uses in the educational field. Among them:

INSTRUCTION. The VCR has replaced the film projector in most schools across the country. The production potential of video has made teaching videos the equal of much of commercial television programming and commercials. High-quality graphics, contemporary and lively music, and up-to-date animation techniques are considered essential to keeping the interest of a high-tech generation.

Videotapes are used not only in classrooms, but also in libraries for research and independent study. ''Homework videos'' are now being produced by schools and outside organizations such as Britannica Education Corporation, the video production division of Encyclopaedia Britannica. Britannica produces about 60 tapes year on everything from astronomy to zoology. Its list currently includes 1,500 titles. Many of the tapes have been designed to work in conjunction with printed question-and-answer materials.

There is another advantage to the medium, in that guest lecturers or the best of the school staff can be recorded on videotape for posterity or for review by students who might have missed a class because of illness. Some of the seminars that I've conducted at New York University have been recorded on videotape. Video has given the NYU film school an opportunity to record one-time visits of animators, writers, directors, and cinematographers.

GUIDANCE COUNSELING AND RECRUITMENT. Video has provided the guidance counselor with a superb opportunity to show prospective college students course curriculum to help them determine if the school carries courses that meet their needs. It is also invaluable in allowing the counselor to show students just what a job in the "outside world" entails. This in turn has given video producers yet another outlet for their services. A great many corporations are anxious to show their story to new grads, especially in such fields as law and computer science, where there is a great deal of competition for top students.

RECRUITMENT. Videotape is being used extensively for recruitment for colleges and universities. Of course, nothing can replace on-campus visits by parents and students, but distances and airline fares make it well nigh impossible to inspect every college firsthand. Thus, college recruiters now carry portable VCRs in their cars, along with several copies of the recruitment tape. This allows them to make presentations to groups of parents or high school students or to leave a tape behind so that the prospects can study and decide at their leisure. Though it is doubtful that the final choice will be made because of the videotape, the tape does help to narrow the field somewhat.

ORIENTATION. The recruitment tape is often shown again to the assembled freshman class to give students a refresher on the school's facilities, programs, and teaching staff. Probably the best orientation tape that I ever saw was one that was made for Princeton University many years ago. The tape did a remarkable job of showing the scope and the physical beauty of the school, and it left the viewer with a strong feeling that Princeton was the place to be. It was actually nominated for an Academy Award.

CABLE AND LOCAL TV PROGRAMMING. Colleges and universities are busily filling public access channels on cable, providing sports, educational, and cultural programs and public affairs tapes to local stations. Campus activities are also often taped and provided to local news programs. A few years back, we were producing a film for the new visitor's center at Lake Norman in North Carolina. Part of our story was the role of Davidson College in the history and the contemporary life of the area. We decided to film part of the school's graduation ceremony. Standing next to our professional crew that day was another videotape group composed of local producers and college communications students. Their tape of the ceremony was to be used as a source of news clips for local TV, as an archival record for the school, and as a memento that could be purchased by parents and grads.

There are numerous other uses for video on the university level. For instance, videoconferencing has become an integral part of the curriculum at schools like Harvard and Columbia. Interactive video is being used extensively in classrooms and libraries. Videotapes are even taking the place of class yearbooks. (One production company now offers "video reunions"!)

In other words, every opportunity that exists in the "outside world" for video producers also exists in academia. Moreover, statistics show that though much of the school educational and recruitment programming is produced in-house by college personnel, about one-third is done by outside producers. A majority of schools also buy "off-the-shelf" modular materials for instruction purposes, which are being produced by companies across the country. Indeed, tapes are being sold the way that textbooks used to be sold. Although tapes are not replacing textbooks or films, they have carved out a very large share of the marketplace.

With over 3,000 colleges and universities in the United States, and ten times that number of secondary schools, almost all of them using videotape, you can begin to see why the field of educational video is so open for beginners and seasoned video producers. Educational video has literally burst out of the classroom and into the outside world.

So think about it. How would you produce an educational videotape entitled *Bauxite Mining in Upper Volta*?

THE VIDEO ENTREPRENEUR: A TALK WITH ARNA VODENOS

Arna Vodenos, president of Vodenos Productions of Rockville, Maryland, is probably the perfect person to discuss such topics as the roles of production and postproduction companies. Vodenos Productions was founded about eight years ago to produce medical education videos for health care professionals. The company expanded rapidly into the consumer health care field and from there has branched out into cable television, educational videos for government agencies, and international satellite videoconferencing. Only twenty-nine at the time of this interview, Arna began her career at the age of seventeen. To say the least, I found her to be an impressive young woman.

Arna Vodenos in her Rockville, Maryland, postproduction facility. As a young entrepreneur, she has been highly successful in a very competitive market.

You began your company only eight years ago in the area of corporate education videos. What other areas do you work in?

''One of the most important areas of growth is video conferencing. We're just getting started doing international conferences in Europe. Hundreds of sites. Also, medical video is a big area of ours. We've done about five hundred programs. Lately we've gotten into travel programming. I went to Florence recently and did a program in the vineyards.''

You were seventeen when you started?

''Yes. I started working as an intern in a television station, and I got a degree from Boston University in broadcast journalism and psychology. I was able to launch myself pretty quickly as a producer based on the fact that when I was still in college, I made my first documentary, which I did on my own, and then sold it to commercial television. That way I had a really nice sample when I walked out of college. That led me to a job as producer with ''PM Magazine,'' and I learned a lot of technique

there. Actually, I worked from seventeen to twenty-one in public broadcasting, getting as much experience as I possibly could. And then, at age twenty-four, I went out on my own.''

In the past, it has been very difficult for a woman who owns her own company to get through corporate doors. Have you found that problem?

''I don't find that at all. . . . Basically, I just go out and sell the clients and get the budgets and make a product and deliver the product.''

How many people do you have on staff?

''Eight people and twenty-two regular freelancers. We have two full-blown on-line edit suites and our own 3D Graphics Paintbox, as well as duplication. I have all my own equipment.''

What jobs do the staff people hold?

''I have an editor, a creative director who is an animator and a graphics person, a technical production person, a general manager, a CPA/comptroller, a receptionist, and a production assistant.''

And the freelance people?

''Writers, producers, editors. We need a lot of editors. We have one full-time editor, but I use about twelve other editors between off-line and on-line. We're running all the time.''

What do you look for when you hire people?

''The first thing is attitude and eagerness to learn. That to me is the most important thing. And I want to work with people that I can watch grow because I really get excited about watching someone grow. And we like to train people here. When I see someone learning new skills and doing them well, I feel like I've succeeded.''

What should job applicants' backgrounds be? Technical? Marketing? Communications?

''I think the background should be liberal arts. My own background is classical art and music—as a hobby of mine. It's helped me tremendously. And this may even be going against my communications background at Boston. Liberal arts with the emphasis in the art areas. And then, training in the field, actually working as a TV intern, as well as taking writing and basic journalism. These courses teach you the basic principles.''

What about the future? Do you see growth in the field?

"I think that video is the future because it's an instant tool. You can get instant playback and quick results. It's very easy to deal with computerized editing and it's becoming more and more perfected. But I'm a little bit on the other side. Because I'm a child of video, I have this tremendous urge to do film. I've learned a lot of the video tricks and what kind of equipment will do what kind of things. But I've not had much opportunity to work in film because when I came into the TV stations, they were getting rid of it. So, though I've been exposed mostly to video, I love the look of film. To me it's the comparison between oil painting and acrylics, with film being the oil painting."

I've always felt that to be successful in this field, you have to know both film and tape.

"Videotape was a great starting medium in which to work. The basic directing principles, the editing principles, in my opinion, are very similar, if not the same. And I've heard this from a lot of people. The background that I've learned in videotape is going to give me a very good background in film."

NONPROFIT ORGANIZATIONS

Before the word *nonprofit* makes you turn quickly to the next section in this chapter, hang around for a while. On the other hand, if you have ever said, "Wouldn't it be nice to do something for the world!" (and some of us really do feel that way), then this section may be just what you're looking for.

Since nonprofit organizations generally use videos to raise funds or to create public images (which will eventually be used to raise funds), their video budgets are generally lower than those in for-profit companies. Since larger production companies cannot afford to do these low-budget videos (mostly because of their high overhead), the doors to nonprofits are open to the one- or two-person teams that can produce videos at minimal cost. This can be an exciting opportunity, then, for the producer who works on low overhead or who does most of the jobs himself, and who has the urge to learn about the world and to help someone along the way. And, though the word *nonprofit* might refer to the way the agencies are structured for income tax purposes, producers generally do make a profit, however small it might be.

If you look carefully at the list that follows, you will begin to see that nonprofit can also mean a chance to travel, to cover a wide range of subjects, to gain recognition, and to acquire some incredibly moving and human samples of your work in video.

There are numerous examples of nonprofit groups:

- *Local hospitals*, as well as *local and national organizations* devoted to specialized care for the deaf, blind, and handicapped; for cancer, heart, diabetes, multiple sclerosis, and substance abuse patients.
- *Local and national fund-raising organizations* devoted to both specific and general causes, such as the March of Dimes and the United Way.

A scene from "Hands of Love," produced and directed by the author for The Little Sisters of the Poor. (Photo: Sister Mary Richard)

The crew at the Queen of Peace Residence for "Hands of Love." Left to right: Bill Shaver, sound; Mike Barry, camera; Sheryl London, art director; the author; Peter Hawkins, assistant camera. The project was shot on film and transferred to tape for distribution. (Photo: Sister Mary Richard)

- *Local and national performing groups* such as opera, ballet, and modern dance companies, orchestras and local museums and theaters. Currently, I am working on raising funds to do a videotape with a young, talented woman named Deborah Marcus, who works with the aged in movement and exercise. Eventually, the video will be used to expand the program to other areas of the city and state and to raise still more funds. There are many people just like her out there in the world and their work presents still more opportunity for those of you who are looking for a sample of your work, as well as for a feeling of just being involved.
- *Religious organizations*, which use video to record services to be broadcast over cable and local television stations. Churches and synagogues, as well as religious orders such as the Little Sisters of the Poor, have begun to use videotape as a recruitment tool for volunteers and for men and women who want to join.

An important point to remember is that the amount of work in this sector has increased since the advent of videotape. Whereas many (if not most) of the organizations in this category used film for their communications and fund-raising needs, most have now increased their production with video. And though many still produce a part of their output in-house, more than half the projects each year are given to outside producers, since many organizations do not have the facilities to produce their own work, nor do they want to make the investment in time, equipment, and money.

I have also discovered through the years that if there is one place that welcomes the low-budget producer or the one-person production company, it is the nonprofit sector. The reason is quite obvious: It is yet another area where the size of the budget has nothing to do with the quality of the product.

MEDICINE

After recovering from surgery, a patient in the past would offer to reveal the raw, sutured scar by asking, "Wanna see my operation?" Today, I suppose, the question would be different, though its purpose might be the same: "Wanna see a *videotape* of my operation?"

In the field of medicine, *everything* is now on videotape: for doctors, for students, for patients, for staff. The tapes are used for record keeping, instruction, and consultation. They may even be used as "souvenirs" of operations—patients can take them home and keep them on the shelf along with tapes of the Marx Brothers and Abbott and Costello. For the would-be producer-writer-videographer, this sector offers still another area of production opportunities.

I must say that it was not always this way. For years, doctors and hospitals kept their doors closed to the filming or videotaping of anything that went on in the corridors, the operating rooms, and the research labs. For those of us who were trying to make a living doing medical documentaries, permissions were difficult to obtain, filming situations were tightly controlled, and doctor resistance was almost as strong as what you would encounter doing a film about the CIA.

The amusing thing to me, however, was the reaction of some doctors to the filming. They would loudly proclaim, "Cameras? In *my* operating room??!! Not on your life!" After much coaxing, we were allowed in, only after we had scrubbed up, put on gowns, and dipped our cameras in Lysol. When the project was finished, though, the egos took over. Some of the most stubborn surgeons would actually ask for copies of the films in order to hold parties at their houses, where the stars of the evening would be—you guessed it—the doctors who had loudly tried to keep us from THEIR operating rooms.

Another memory of my early medical filmmaking was the initiation of new directors into the field of medical photography. One young man was sent out by me for his first taste of an operating room sequence, only to come back to the office, his face pale, his shoulders slumped, his mouth half-open in horror. His very first "patient" had died on the operating table during open heart surgery. Certainly, I did not think it amusing then, nor do I now. I just felt that it was part of being a documentary filmmaker.

Today, not only are doctors aware of the use of videotape, but they actually *demand* that it be used. Rather than banning video from their operating rooms, they have invited it inside to document those operations and procedures. Not the least of the reasons is the fact that surgeons can, for example, go back weeks or months after an operation to get a better understanding of how the treatment has progressed. The videotape provides a more accurate record of the procedure than do the written logs. Taping within the medical community has become so prevalent that we now see articles about it in magazines ranging from *Vogue* to *The New York Times Magazine* and certainly throughout the medical literature.

The field has opened up considerably in major areas of production, each of which provides lots of opportunity whether you want to specialize in medical documentary or consider it as just one of your options.

IN-HOUSE HOSPITAL VIDEO PRODUCTION. About 1,500 hospitals in the United States now produce their own videos. With over 7,000 teaching and nonteaching hospitals in the country, this part of the field still has room to grow.

I was fascinated to read in Judy Stokes's book *The Business of Nonbroadcast Television* that the first televised surgical operation took place over a closed-circuit system at Johns Hopkins University in 1937. In addition, hospitals have always staffed still photographers to record patient symptoms and post-operative responses. In fact, it was a hospital photographer, Rosemary Spitalari, who did some of the most exciting and moving pre- and postoperative filming of Parkinson's patients for my Academy Award nominee, *To Live Again*.

Audiovisual staffs that include writers, videographers, and directors have been expanding in the hospital sector, and openings do occur from time to time. Getting on a staff is an excellent way to break into the field and to acquire very effective sample tapes for your move out and up. As the technology becomes even more accepted, the opportunities grow. The Mayo Clinic, for example, now uses a satellite video system that allows a doctor in Rochester, Minnesota, to examine a patient in Jacksonville, Florida, or to demonstrate new surgical techniques to another doctor in Scottsdale, Arizona.

PHARMACEUTICAL AND HEALTH CARE PRODUCTS COMPANIES. Drug and health care products manufacturers produce a wide variety of videos, including tapes on new prescription drugs, patient information, and doctor-nurse education. Companies such as Johnson & Johnson, Pfizer, Smithkline Beckman, Baxter International, and Eli Lilly have long found it profitable to keep a constant flow of information out in the medical marketplace. As a result, some of these companies have opened up in-house video production departments. Companies also use independent producers experienced in medical videography. They have been known to spend expansively in order to promote products and educate both doctors and the public.

OFF-THE-SHELF PURCHASES. Many health care institutions buy packages, or generic information videotapes, produced by other hospitals, by independent producers, or by pharmaceutical companies. There are some generic (or modular) video subjects that lend themselves well to this type of entrepreneurial production and distribution. Tapes showing standard surgical techniques, for instance, need not be produced over and over again in order to inform the profession about advances in techniques or technology. When medical advances are made, the tapes are revised and sold as "updated."

VIDEOCONFERENCING. This technology allows hospitals and medical schools to tie into satellite networks to discuss problems and medical advances with experts anywhere in the world. It's used to demonstrate new surgical techniques and to provide access to participation in medical conferences around the country (or around the world). From a very pragmatic dollars-and-cents point of view, videoconferencing eliminates travel costs and reduces the time needed to participate in a seminar or convention. Most doctors seem to prefer videoconferencing to traveling, unless, of course, the convention is held in Paris or Rome or Las Vegas—in which case, everyone seems to go!

EDUCATION. Videotapes are used at medical and dental schools, as well as at facilities that train nurses, medical assistants, even volunteer staff. Video also provides continuing education and updating for doctors, residents, interns, nurses, and professional hospital staff such as X-ray technicians and lab workers. Every discipline is covered: psychiatry, internal medicine, medical specialties, surgery, rehabilitation. Programs are also available on such topics as doctor/patient relationships, improving hospital administration, hospice care, and disaster planning.

PATIENT EDUCATION AND INFORMATION. Videos produced by drug companies, medical schools, hospitals, and professional health associations are used to inform patients about illnesses, treatments, and surgical procedures. Some patients find that their anxiety is reduced when they fully understand the procedure being planned by the doctor. Patients are even being shown videos of their operations to help them understand the procedure. Other patients, of course, don't want to know. One patient, who was shown a video of the operation on his brain, commented that his brain was a "luscious white, like cottage cheese."

Hundreds of videos are produced each year on nutrition and exercise, cancer prevention and care, mental health, obesity, and a wide variety of general health issues.

Getting this information on videotape instead of hearing it directly from the doctor or nurse has certain advantages, especially for the older patient, the hard-of-hearing patient, and the non-English speaker. Videotapes can help communicate the message.

DOCUMENTATION. Besides documenting operations, video is used in research to record experiments and studies at various stages of progress. It is the ultimate visual record.

MALPRACTICE. The unfortunate reality is that we have become a more and more litigious society, so doctors are taking every means possible to protect themselves from malpractice suits. Videotape records of an operation or a rehabilitation program can frequently mean the difference between winning and losing a case.

COMMUNITY RELATIONS AND FUND-RAISING. Every hospital has a constant money problem. From time to time, a presentation is made to the community leaders or to the general public and a film or video with full details about the importance of the hospital to the community is often part of that presentation. Of course, somewhere along the line, a contribution will be asked for. (Not on the tape—it is an unwritten law that you *never* ask for money within the body of a fund-raising documentary!)

A video is able to present a hospital's story in dramatic terms, not just to the groups mentioned above, but also to the foundations that contribute money to a variety of causes and nonprofit organizations, many of them outside the realm of medicine. In this area, everybody is out for the same dollar, and a strong video can do much to sway the members of the board who make the financial decisions.

LAW

Recently, a headline in the *New York Observer* caught my eye: "SOON PLAYING ON YOUR VCR, RETURN OF THE DEAD TO LIVING." A New York lawyer named George Akst, along with a producer-director named Richard Pepperman, had begun a new venture called Video Legacy, Ltd. To augment the drawing up of a will, the company videotapes the "not-yet-departed" along with two witnesses, allowing a personal message to be delivered to the eventual beneficiaries. The subject can reminisce, or even rebuke a relative who has been left out of the will. Such tapes last no more than half an hour, and are time-coded to prevent tampering at a later date.

Video Legacy is still in the early stages of its growth, but Akst hopes to franchise the idea. As he comments: "With this [we've] completed the circle. [We've] brought the video camera into the delivery room, now [we] bring it to the gravesite, so to speak. It's the yin and the yang. . . ."

Before you smirk, be aware that there have, indeed, been people who have videotaped their wills by reading them directly into a camera. and that the process has already been used in court to successfully demonstrate the competence of the deceased.

Fifteen years ago George Akst's idea would have been unheard of. But fifteen years ago lawyers were not allowed to advertise. Today their videotaped commercials get plenty of play on local television stations. Fifteen years ago cameras were not seen in the courtroom. Today live cameras and videotaping are permitted.

The use of videotape in law has grown. The Nassau County [New York] Bar Association, for example, opened the Law Store, a video library of taped seminars from around the country. For a daily rental fee of $5, Nassau County lawyers can choose a selection from over forty subjects ranging from "The Art of Cross Examination" to "How to Try for Damages." One of the most popular videos has been "Representing Clients at Contract and Closing on a Single-Family House."

Independent video producers have become specialists in very narrow fields—medicine, education, law. The following interview gives you an idea of what it's like to be a video "legal eagle."

A TALK WITH BILL BUCKLEY

Bill and I go back to the mid-fifties and a company in Princeton, New Jersey, where he was an editor and I was a neophyte film producer. Bill is a prime example of someone who has become a video specialist. Although he does training films for Champion International and videos for Planned Parenthood and the American Friends Service Committee, he has gained his reputation in the legal field.

Bill Buckley, who has made a strong reputation as a documentary videotape producer in the legal field.

How is videotape used in the legal world?

"On the simplest level, depositions . . . the video version of the court stenographer. Typically, [my work is] with a doctor or a gun expert or a tire expert. Usually the plaintiff's attorney hires you, and then you have the defense attorney, who is also there to cross-examine. [Videotaping is] used for witnesses who are difficult to get to court. It varies from state to state as to whether this type of [deposition] is admissible."

Your work must take you all over the country.

"It can. It took me to Paris a few years back. It's taken me to California. And you have to know the rules of [each jurisdiction]. For example, in federal cases, you've got to have a time-code generator so [officials] can tell that you didn't tamper with [the tape]. In some states, you can only keep the camera on the witness. In others, you have the discretion of showing the attorneys in a long shot, with the witness in the middle, and then going into a two shot, and then a close or medium shot. There are a lot of things you have to know about a deposition besides setting up a camera."

What about dealing with injured parties?

"Actually, [in this area of law] you are making minidocumentaries, and it's a tough place for a person to enter video unless he or she has a documentary film background. You're into time compression. You have to take two or three hours of material and compress it into a twenty-minute tape. Essentially, you have to know how to edit effectively. And, if the defense attorney can prove that it's prejudicial, it'll be thrown out. It's a very tough documentary."

I know there are video wills. How else is video being used in the legal field?

"Reenactments of accidents. Say, a machine without a safety guard on it is sold to a company. The company had elected not to spend the extra $750 for the safety guard. A guy gets his arm or leg caught in it and is seriously injured. What you do is go down and show the machine, show someone demonstrating how the accident happened—sometimes even showing the guy who lost his arm or leg in the machine. Showing the videotape is certainly more [effective] than trying to describe the accident in detail."

What kinds of cases have you videotaped?

"I've [videotaped] tire experts on cases where a tire exploded and killed

someone. I've [taped] gun experts on cases where the safety device of a weapon didn't operate. I've had a lot of asbestos cases . . . people who had worked for Johns-Manville. It's fascinating. I've had as many as twenty-three lawyers on the defense side examining the poor dying witness, with one lawyer in the middle for the plaintiff, the guy who hired me to come in and do the deposition. And the problems of lighting all these guys, miking all these guys . . . it's a hell of a job.''

I suppose that it's not only people, but things that can't appear in court.

''Some doctors just refuse to appear. They'd charge so much that it would be frivolous of the court to insist that they appear. And as far as things—[a good example is] the bridge at Greenwich [Connecticut] that [collapsed]. They made models of how it happened, and we videotaped the models and brought the tape into the courtroom to show to the jury. Another example: You may have a case where someone has dived into three feet of water in a swimming pool. You can actually show an exact model of the pool, where the diving board is, where the ladders are, break away the pool and show a cross section, the shallow end versus the deep. Suddenly it becomes so clear, and once you show how it happened, you say, 'My God . . .' ''

SPECIAL EVENTS: VIDEOTAPING THE MILESTONES

Not too long ago, my cousin Leah was married. The wedding in its entirety was videotaped. It was a professional setup. Lights were placed at critical points in the chapel, on the dance floor, and behind the band. I was even interviewed by one of the producers about my feelings for the bride and groom. Three weeks later we were invited to the couple's new home to watch the video.

Weddings are but a drop in the proverbial bucket. There are lots of special events that lend themselves to videotaping, providing both income and experience for the novice videographer:

- Friends of mine who were building a new home on the coast of Maine were kept informed weekly of the progress of the builder through videotapes provided by an independent producer.
- People are now doing video inventories of their homes and possessions for insurance purposes.

- Artists and sculptors now have their work videotaped and provide tapes to prospective buyers.
- Applicants for job openings send not only video applications but video resumes.

Does it work? Is it viable? Can you, as my grandmother would have asked, make a living? I asked Jill Aspinwall, who with her husband, Kevin, own their own company, Hamilton Communications, in West Haven, Connecticut. Though they do a range of projects, their main business is derived from special events such as weddings.

WEDDINGS AND BAR MITZVAHS: A TALK WITH JILL ASPINWALL

How did you start out?

''[Kevin and I] first started off both having full-time jobs, and we were looking for something that we could do on weekends to start our own business. Weddings were weekend work, so we started by doing a freebie for a friend, because we needed a sample to show. From there, we developed into a full-time company. And the prices have gone up as well. People are now booking well into next year.''

Is there much competition?

''A lot of people are doing it, but we do it quite differently. We treat it as a documentary as opposed to your Uncle Joe going out there with his little camera. Though video is technically easy, we've both got a film background, which taught us composition and how to shoot for editing, the key to why I think we've been so successful.''

Where did you go to school?

''University of Bridgeport. Bill and I met there in a screenwriting class. We worked well together in school, and one thing led to another . . .''

What did you start off with? Was it home equipment?

''We started off with industrial decks, VCRs, and consumer cameras. We needed something that had low light capacity, and the industrial cameras really require a lot of light because they're usually used in a controlled situation. But with weddings, you can't really blast people with lights. We went out and bought all the equipment. We secured a loan before we even had a new car and a new house. We really chose good stuff and it's still working for us. I should knock on wood. We haven't had any problems.''

Do you carry hand-held lights?

"For the ceremony we don't use lights. We may use a hundred-watt bulb for the bridegroom's face, usually behind a podium where it's not visible, and we stay put during the ceremony, unlike a photographer. We're really unobtrusive. People get used to where we are, and then, too, they're watching the bride and groom instead of us. For the reception, we just try to bounce off lights in various areas and sometimes we'll use a camera light if the room is really dark. We're sensitive to people's needs. It's amazing, but people will tell us afterwards that they didn't even know we were there!"

What about editing?

"We've got our own equipment and I spend about forty hours editing each job. I really treat each project like an individual documentary, not like a crank-'em-out wedding video. We edit in half inch and we generally get down to a two-hour tape."

Two hours?

"Yeah. Sometimes clients even call and say, 'Did you put everything in?' If I find that I'm at the end of a two-hour tape and I still have more footage, I go into a second tape. I don't hold back because it's their one-time deal, so we really try to give them everything."

Are weddings and other events difficult to shoot?

"I think weddings are one of the hardest things to try to shoot. You get only one chance and it's very stressful. People want video but they don't want lights. And it's a long day—a very long day, and you're constantly getting blocked by people and you're trying to get great shots—and being a documentary situation, you've just got to get the best you can at the moment it happens and that's it. It's unlike a corporate video where you have a script and weeks to shoot and you can try things over and over again to get the exact shot you want. It's stressful, very stressful!"

Do you find that more and more people are videotaping important events in their lives?

"Yes. Everybody now wants their things on tape. Even my own family. I can't go to a party without bringing my camera; it's terrible. 'It's Grandma's sixtieth anniversary, you coming? Bring your camera!' It's really fun and a great way to look back and see everybody, to capture things. Photographs are great in themselves, but video—you hear people tell you

that it brings back all the happy memories in their lives. The weddings, you just live through the whole day again. At least that's the way we shoot them.''

MUSIC VIDEO

Music video represents the cutting edge of editing technology. This is true largely because the people who make [the videos] are young, brash, and not afraid to take chances. These are also the people who will let an editor make a contribution.

Glenn Lazzaro
National Video Studios
Interview in *Back Stage*

If ever there was an area of the industry that had a euphoric and meteoric rise, only to see its aura fade, then rise again like a phoenix, it is music video. And if ever there was an example of crossover, with directors and production personnel starting here, then moving on to features, commercials, and documentaries, while others were doing just the opposite, it is music video.

In the early eighties, millions of fans began to watch music video almost to the exclusion of every other type of television programming. It became so popular that *Time* magazine featured it as a cover story in 1983. It was a time when the first music video was made for over a million dollars, though most of the production stayed in the range of about $30,000. There were video singles, Top Ten Awards, and Video Grammys, and some of the best-known commercials directors, like Bob Giraldi, began to work in the field.

Then suddenly, music video was ''video wallpaper.'' The headlines began to change; the ratings at MTV began to slump and the record companies began to cut back their production by as much as 25 percent. In 1984, the *New York Times* commented that ''danger signals are beginning to appear on the horizon'' due to overexposure.

Today, music video is enjoying a boom once again. MTV has kept its ratings steadily climbing and is moving into both the European and Australian markets. Once we were saying prayers for the departed, now the patient has recovered and begun to find even greater viewer acceptance and increased total production dollars. There are now over a hundred music video programs on the air across the country, covering everything from network shows to twenty-four-hour cable systems. Celia Hirschman, president of Vis-Ability, a video marketing firm in Los Angeles, points out that music video is not only for heavy metal anymore. It has expanded to provide specialized programming in adult-oriented rock, country music, and rap. Probably the most important change is in the costs involved. Budgets now range from $50,000 to $100,000, and the ''star'' music videos can exceed that substantially.

Music video is hardly a new phenomenon. Just look at old films. *Zeigfeld Follies* (1946) consists of short vignettes, with Lena Horne, Gene Kelly, Kathryn Grayson, and Fred Astaire doing what would now be called ''music videos.'' Walt Disney's *Fantasia* (1940) did the same with animation and classical music. If we go back to the first talking films, Warner Brothers was producing short, one-reel musical films that featured singers like Al Jolson and Eddie Cantor as early as 1927.

Today, music video represents a wonderful stepping-stone in a career, no matter which direction you choose to step—from music video into commercials or features or from commercials and features into music video. Advertising agencies are beginning to develop more and more commercials based on quick-cut music, and people who have made their mark in music video are becoming very much in demand. Director Tony Mitchell, who first worked in music video, as well as Jeff Lovinger and Joe Hanwright, who launched their careers doing music videos for people like Billy Idol, Tina Turner, Carly

Music videos are being used increasingly in the corporate and commercial world. Director/cameraman Sandy Spooner sets up a music video commercial for Mervyn's Department Store, shot on film, edited on videotape.

Simon, and Duran Duran, are now working in advertising and doing commercials. And their music video background is making itself felt. As Mitchell puts it, "There are outrageous things being done in commercials now."

The crossover is working the other way as well. People like Tobe Hooper (*Texas Chainsaw Massacre*), Bob Rafelson (*Five Easy Pieces*), and top commercial director Bob Giraldi have all joined in the movement to direct music video. As a result, the headlines once again loudly proclaim "MUSIC VIDEO MANIA" and "MUSIC VIDEO STILL A HOT NUMBER" (*Back Stage*).

Even the corporate world has caught on to music video. Since many of today's young executives have been brought up on a diet of television that includes MTV, it is only natural that delivering messages to music would appeal to them. For trade show crowds, bleary-eyed and jaded, music video has been a welcome relief from the talking-head videotape or the flip chart lecture. The look of corporate videos has changed to reflect the influence of music video: quick cuts, computer animation, fog, star filters, pulsating rock and roll lights, dancers, even rock musicians dressed in vivid contrast to the customary corporate attire; more Fillmore East than *Fortune* 500.

The changes wrought by music video have only begun. Most of us see an entirely new market developing both for the freelancers and for the independent producers who have been working in this part of the field.

MUSIC VIDEO: A TALK WITH JOHN PAYSON, MTV

John Payson is a producer in the on-air promotions department at MTV in New York. In this interview, he presents an insider's view of the world of music video.

What does the on-air promotions department do?

"We're responsible for the overall look and attitude of the channel. We design graphics, show openings, the animation that goes in between the videos, the top-of-the-hour station identifications, that sort of thing."

But you don't produce videos?

"MTV doesn't produce videos itself. What we produce is all the stuff that goes on the system that is not music video: the VJ [video jockey] segments, the specials, the concerts, the news reports. The videos themselves are produced by the record companies."

How do people start out at a place like MTV?

"People usually start working at MTV as interns. When they finish their internships, if they want to come back, they're hired usually as freelance

PAs [production assistants]. Then they're put on staff as PAs and eventually they're promoted to associate producers and then on to producers. The MTV staff is virtually homegrown.''

What about freelancers?

''Well, one way that we get our staff is that people are brought in on a freelance basis—like some of our producers. They do a particular project and if MTV likes them or they like us, they do another one and then another, and possibly they move to staff. But some prefer to remain freelance.''

But you do think that internships are the best opportunity for someone trying to break in?

''Yes, but internships are pretty much what you make them. They can be very dull and unrewarding. For the most part, the people who have shown the most initiative have definitely gotten the most out of them. And they are the people who are still around.''

Do people ever go on to other things from MTV?

''Oh, sure. People go from here into the record industry. They go into radio and into television. I've seen people go all different ways and they've all started out right here.''

RENTAL HOUSES AND MOBILE PRODUCTION UNITS

If you look at the backgrounds of production people, such as videographers and technicians, you'll notice that many started out in two lesser-known areas: equipment rental houses and mobile production units.

It is probably not necessary to point out again that most videotape producers rent the equipment they use out in the field. Rental facilities offer everything from cameras to full lighting packages, and they are too often overlooked by the job hunter as a potential place in which to learn, to grow, and to move on.

Because much video rental is large packages from cameras to recorders to lights, the rental people generally go along to operate the equipment. Recordists, lighting technicians, even videographers for second units frequently accompany the equipment into the field. Thus, rental house personnel become part of the crew, whether to help set the lights or to operate the recording equipment.

We have all seen mobile production units parked outside hotels, courtrooms, and studios, transmitting special events back to television studios. (This is a far cry from the days when events were recorded and film was delivered by motorcycle messenger in time for the six o'clock news.) Mobile units are complete production facilities—a studio plus postproduction on wheels. They are equipped with mobile one-inch videotape switchers, recorders, Ultimattes, Chyrons, cameras, sound, and lighting in one compact, brilliantly designed vehicle.

Some units are a part of a rental package, such as that offered by All Mobile Video in New York, which provides everything a producer might wish for all on location. Other mobile units are a part of the local television station's hardware; they are generally crewed by the same people who might work back in the studio.

Today, anything that we can do in a studio, we can duplicate out of a truck. With the advent of digital audio and video and with the growing sophistication of the industry, not only is production a possibility, but postproduc-

A completely equipped mobile unit is tied to a car for a dolly shot in the CBS Movie of the Week, The Littlest Victims, *produced by 1125 Productions in HDTV. The unit is a control room on wheels: tape decks, Ultimatte, switcher, and camera control unit. (Courtesy 1125 Productions)*

tion—done right on the spot—is also part of the package. Graphics, character generation, digital effects, slow motion, all the swirls and wipes and zooms and patterns are there, with the most sophisticated intercom systems hooked up for communication with the crew working outside as well as with the base back home. The latest developments are being planned to include fiber optics as a transmission path rather than coaxial cable or hard wire. As Curtis Chan, the vice president of marketing and product development for Centro Corporation, which designs and constructs mobile units, says, "If you have an unlimited budget, then heaven is the ballpark!"

CHAPTER NINE

POSTPRODUCTION

The postproduction area is no longer just "post." You can build a commercial from the ground up now, production and postproduction work hand in hand. . . . With time, patience and talent, you can build anything. The editing suite has become a gourmet store; there's so much to choose from.

Peter Karp
Director/Editor,
Editel, New York
Interview in *Back Stage*

We used to say in film that "you can always save it in the editing room." No matter what the problem, no matter how much incompetence on the part of the director or the cinematographer or the laboratory, our intrepid editor, working alone in a darkened room, with rancid coffee cups littering the table, would manage somehow to find a way to "save" the project. Actually, a great many Hollywood films have, indeed, been saved by clever editing, but realistically, we sometimes expect too much from the editor. If the material ain't there, nothing is going to save it. However, the fantasy has now moved over into the videotape field, and we hear just as often, "Don't worry; we can always save it in post."

I will admit, though, that the technological breakthroughs in videotape, the "bells and whistles" as we call them, have certainly allowed the editor to play a much more important role in the look of the finished product. Directors who wail, "I should have used a longer lens" or "I should have done another take," now find that the postproduction phase of the medium is a godsend. Essentially, up until this time, postproduction was everything that took place *after* the videotape was shot: color correction, the adding of titles and effects, and some computer animation, all of it edited into a timed, complete form ready for airing or distribution. All that has changed.

Today postproduction really combines both the production and the finishing of the videotape. It is now a part of the original development and planning of the project, especially in the production of television commercials and music videos, where quick-cut editing makes all the difference. It is probably safe to say that nowhere in the field has technical development had more of an impact than in postproduction. It is also safe to say that no other area is as dependent on state-of-the-art technology and the continuing development of advanced equipment.

With the growth and changes in postproduction have come greater opportunities for talented artists, technicians, engineers, computer operators, designers, on- and off-line editors, as well as videotape production executives, sales reps, supervisors, and all the financial and management administrators who go along with any burgeoning industry. Indeed, the area of postproduction has grown so quickly that it now has its own magazine called, naturally, *Post: The Magazine for Animation, Audio, Film & Video Professionals* (25 Willowdale Avenue, Port Washington, NY 11050).

Since the marriage of film and videotape has taken place, projects are often shot on film and transferred to videotape for editing. The tape is then transferred back to film for screening.

The "marriage" has had many advantages. Color correction can be accomplished more easily on videotape than on film. Film allows for higher lighting and imagery, but the convenience and the postproduction technology of videotape can add production value to any project, as any television viewer can attest. Film can still be used for large-screen presentations in theaters, while videotape fits nicely into the VCR setup in living rooms or conference situations. Economy, however, is not a factor, since the cost of special effects in videotape can mount. Agencies and producers have begun to write articles about "keeping the costs down" in videotape. Remember, the development of any technology can be expensive, and someone has to pay for it. In postproduction, you pay for it by the hour! Someone once described video postproduction in the same terms as getting into a taxicab. Once you're in the dark, screen-lit editing suite, the meter goes on, and you pay whatever the trip costs, based upon time and the addition of equipment rental costs to achieve your "bells and whistles."

A whole new generation of professionals has now entered the field, and job opportunities have grown in direct proportion to the number of technological advances. The most interesting thing to an observer of postproduction houses is that most of the colorists, graphic artists, and editors are very young, all of them brought up on computer technology and the video screen. Videotape editors were once mere "button pushers," but this is decidely no longer the case. Given half a chance, and knowing how to utilize the available technology, the videotape editor can not only "save it in post" but can add dynamic, innovative elements to the production.

One other factor makes this a most promising area for careers in video.

Since the cost of "bells and whistles" hardware can be astronomical (sometimes well into the millions of dollars), postproduction is generally accomplished outside the production company or the client organization—and it is done *everywhere*. There are postproduction facilities in every part of the country, a far cry from the days when film laboratories were located only in major cities and after a shoot the exposed material had to be shipped by air or hand carried to the lab.

Advertising agencies, corporations, independent producers, video artists, government agencies, schools, *all* use the facilities offered by competing postproduction houses. At times, the off-line editing may be done right at the producing entity (after a post house has put the time code on the dub), but the on-line editing and additional special effects are given to an outside facility. Remember, if you were going to use a special effect once or twice or even ten times a year, the investment in high-tech computerized equipment would certainly not be economical, to say the least, especially since the equipment would probably be replaced by even more sophisticated technology within a few years.

And so, the person who is considering making postproduction part of a career path *must* know how to speak the language of videotape, while the person with a pure film background must cast aside the simplicity of editing and finishing in order to learn the "techno-jargon" of the new technology. Anthony Vagnoni, the former publisher of *Back Stage*, once wrote that if you visited a film editor's place, "the most high-tech piece of equipment you'll find may be the phone," while a trip through a video post house would feel like a "walk through a high-tech jungle, with an emphasis on smoke and mirrors." While a film producer might easily take over the editor's chair in an emergency, the video editor–postproduction artist is really irreplaceable.

What has begun to happen is that the videotape editor has become more and more like a producer, since much of the planning for post takes place before the project begins. He or she now must offer a combination of creativity and technical know-how in order to succeed in an ever more complex field. Frank Markward, a senior editor at New York's International Production Center, said in an interview that "people edit with their brains, not with machines. Things haven't changed in that respect." I heartily agree!

Notice how many of the people who have been interviewed for this book have had a background in art or graphics or even marketing. Many employers in the postproduction field comment that they have hired people to operate complex computer-generated machines like the Paintbox who have had no experience in videotape postproduction at all. It was their "portfolio" that worked for them, or their attitude, or their experience in other art-related pursuits that convinced the producers to hire them.

The technology, of course, *is* very much a part of the field, and it can be learned. Here's a quick listing of some of the more popular systems now being used in postproduction. This listing is offered to you as a courtesy by Editel, New York*—and they call it—are you ready:

BELLS AND WHISTLES

PAINTBOX. An electronic system capable of producing graphics, animation, and motion graphics, as well as typography effects, all with very high resolution. It can also be used to create complex backgrounds for use with the Ultimatte. The Paintbox was introduced into the videotape medium back

*Editel also has facilities in Chicago, Los Angeles, and Boston.

Art director Dick Cronin of Henninger Video renders his images on the Quantel Paintbox and prints out hard copy with the Mitsubishi Video Printer. (Photo: Katie Henninger)

in 1982 by Quantel and a great part of the videotape postproduction revolution is due, to a great extent, to this flexible tool, as well as to its cousins that came afterward. It can also be interfaced with the Harry and the Abekas.

HARRY. (I love that name!) Quantel describes it as a "digital video production and editing system," but others in the field would probably call it "the perfect animation tool for Paintbox." It can combine multilayered first-generation quality graphics through frame-by-frame video, and it can also compress time without quality loss. It does the job of switching by performing dissolves, wipes, and other effects, and it also serves as a videodisc recorder. Incidentally, there are various stories as to how Harry got its name, but it caught on rapidly and postproduction people used to introduce their clients to Harry as if it were a real person, which some editors think it is.

MIRAGE. A digital video effects system that allows the images to be transformed into 3-D shapes and moved with a 3-D space. It can create over eighty different effects/shapes including spheres, cylinders, page turns, explosions, and many other transitional devices that are used in videotape production (sometimes overused) from sitcoms to commercials. The television series "Star Trek: The Next Generation" uses the Mirage to create planets and stars, including a collapsing star and turbulence surrounding it. By transferring artwork to videotape, the Mirage creates the effect in about fifteen seconds by "folding over" the artwork and digitally wrapping it around a ball. The effect is the sphere in space, with a turbulent, colorful surface. By way of contrast, the wonderfully imaginative film *2001* has as its climax an exquisite and exciting trip to the planet Jupiter. Using the techniques of motion picture optical benches, the single sequence took several months of detailed and incredibly complicated planning.

ABEKAS. One of the problems of videotape is that the more generations that you move away from the original material, the more the picture quality disintegrates, the grainier the image becomes. The Abekas allows postproduction houses to maintain first-generation picture quality through hundreds of composite layers of special effects.

ULTIMATTE. A video matting system quite similar to the "blue matte" used in film, which allows the editor to superimpose an image onto any background that has been produced through another technique: painted set, distant location, etc., either through real photography or by use of a Paintbox. As the technology has improved, this matting has evolved into an almost seamless blend of elements. In HDTV it is almost impossible to tell that matting has taken place. The Ultimatte can mat foreground and background el-

The Abekas 62, bells and whistles in a box. Since it uses disk drive instead of tape, finding an edit point is almost instantaneous. (Courtesy Abekas Video Systems, Inc.)

ements in film-to-tape and still maintain first-generation quality. It can also blow up and reposition images and create ghost effects. Many of the special effects now being seen on high-budget commercials have been achieved by the use of Ultimatte.

SUNBURST. Along with the Da Vinci (wouldn't you know that someone would eventually use that name?) the Sunburst is a color correction system, the latest one designed by a color wizard named Armand Sarabia. Sunburst can enhance an entire shot or it can color correct a small portion of a frame; it can enhance the richness of a frame or a sequence, or correct for lighting problems. It can even strip color from a scene. One of Editel's colorists tells the story of a client who wanted to strip every color from a New York street scene except for the yellow in the taxis. The job was done in one pass—and in real time. Remember: You can always save it in post!

Of course there are more special effects computers, hundreds more. Encore. Palette. The System X-L (which won Sarabia an Academy Award in 1985 for outstanding engineering). Rank Cintel. The Sony DVTR. And by the time that this book comes out, there will be at least a hundred more to add to the list. The most important thing for the beginner is to remember the advice of the professionals and the people who hire other people: The technical side is important, certainly, but editors must have a creative opinion about the work they do, and they should do more than push buttons.

THE JOB MARKET

The field of video postproduction has opened up a range of jobs that did not exist fifteen years ago. With the technology advancing as rapidly as it does, new categories continue to appear. Thus, the prerequisites for the technicians and the creative people change right along with the technology.

Computer animation is a good example. At the beginning, people just

A good off-line edit can save hours in a final on-line editing session. David Kolm, a freelance producer, is working at Henninger Video for Ike Pappas Productions on "Western Change," a project for the Western Development Corporation. (Photo: Katie Henninger)

"wandered" into the art, and their training took place right on the job. This still happens in some cases, but more and more producers in the medium are now demanding a more concrete background. Many of the people whom I know in the field have indicated that there are at least five prerequisites to even being interviewed for a job:

- a computer background (gained either through a degree program or through on-the-job experience)
- knowledge of several computer languages
- knowledge of the internal structures and the capabilities of computers
- training or experience in art, graphics, and design
- sample tape

As one of the pioneers in computer animation, Judson Rosebush, once said to me, "It's not just wiggling a joystick à la Pac-Man. You have to be able to separate the toys from the tools."

And so, computer graphics artists and producers have developed specialties—no one person does it all: animators, software specialists, and operators (low person on the computer animation totem pole.)

In other areas of the postproduction business, we also find more and more people beginning to specialize: Paintbox artists and Harry operators, off-line and on-line editors and playback people, colorists, designers, film-to-tape (and vice versa) technicians, engineers, dubbers.

A TALK WITH DEAN WINKLER

Dean Winkler is vice president and creative director of Post Perfect, a state-of-the-art company that does everything from special effects to computer graphics. Winkler has earned a reputation as being a receptive and sympathetic executive in guiding young people into the field. He is also a major supporter of ACM/SIGGRAPH (Association for Computing Machinery/Special Interest Group on Computer Graphics), which conducts seminars and holds conferences where artists and members can share their work and experiences.

What background do you look for in job applicants?

"Frankly, what I look for are people with engineering degrees who are also artistically sensitive, and that's not an easy thing to find. But we pay our people very well and we're quite a state-of-the-art facility, so we can afford to be a little bit selective."

Do you mean a college background?

"I find that there's no substitute for higher education. I'm a firm believer

in it. If someone wants to catch my eye in a resume or an introductory letter, what I want to see is both *an engineering* and *an art background.''*

Well, how do people get to you? Letters? Walk-ins?

''I get about, I'd say, three resumes a week, just blind. We get a lot of press in industry magazines, so people see our name in print and then write a letter. And, by and large, I'll tell you something that doesn't impress me, the last thing I want to see on an introductory letter: someone who drops a name. They know someone at Saatchi and Saatchi—it doesn't impress me. We certainly don't have any lack of applicants. A year ago there were three of us working here. Now there are forty-seven people working at Post Perfect. So, I've got a stack of resumes sitting right in front of me about four or five inches high!''

Does an applicant need a portfolio or demo tape to show you?

''Not in an introductory position, no. Although, when someone shows me a video art tape that they've done, I'm generally more receptive. One young man named Alec Seiden approached me blind at a conference at which I was speaking. He was an MIT undergrad, so there are points right there. He asked if I'd mind if he showed me a couple of his art tapes. Now, you've got a computer engineer from MIT who's into computer graphics programming and art tapes. We gave him a job and he's worked out really well!''

And for the higher-level positions?

''Well, as an editor or colorist or Paintbox art director, yes, you'd have to have a reel. But on the introductory level, like a tape playback person, you don't need one. If you want to get in, show up at a post facility with an engineering degree and say you want to do electronic maintenance for a year. You'll get hired at any of the houses right away. That's the way I started. I was an undergraduate in engineering at Rensselaer Polytech and I worked summers at Editel. They started me fixing things and I went on to design for them.''

What about editors?

''It's difficult. The problem with a job like editor or colorist is that those people are supposed to bring a client base along with them. That's why they get paid six-figure salaries, based on the theory that someone should be paid 10 percent of the gross business that they bring in.''

Then how do they get their start?

"You have to build up your client base. You have to start at a facility, say, as a playback person. For example, we have four staff editors and we're about to hire a fifth. Then we have five playback people, and when we feel that someone is getting further along, we'll start assigning him to supervised editing work, and then we watch how he does."

What would impress you about someone on the lower levels?

"One thing that impresses me is people who have the will to come in on their own time and just use all the 'toys' to make art projects or just throw things together to make their own tapes."

They do this when the machines are down?

"Yes. And it's a good trait. I look for a lot, and those people will be promoted upward. If we feel they have the right personality and an appropriate client comes along, we'll start feeding them a little bit of editing work and we'll very carefully monitor the feedback from our clients. And that's how they build up a following."

Does the same thing hold true for Paintbox and Harry people?

"No. They come from a different side of things. We generally take people who have art backgrounds for that, usually a fine art background."

And who've had experience on the equipment?

"Not necessarily. Some of my best Paintbox people have come here right out of art school, who I've trained myself. One came from Satellite News Channel—a woman named Maureen Knapp. She had worked on a similar painting system and before that she did club video—shooting one single camera. So I guess what I'm saying is that I want to see a more eclectic background."

One more question. Do some people start out of town and then move to the larger markets?

"Again, it depends on the level. It's difficult at the editor level because you have to get your client base to move with you if you're going to command a large salary. It's more possible at the middle level, like junior editor or junior colorist. [Those people] may come here from other markets because they feel that we present a better opportunity for them."

POSTPOSTPRODUCTION

There is an area that everyone seems to forget when it comes to describing the business: *distribution*. It may not be the glamour area that you have targeted for your videotape career, but it often provides an opportunity for the beginner to learn just what is being produced in the marketplace, and just *who* is producing that product. Someone has to distribute the finished tapes, whether for broadcast or nonbroadcast use, and organizations employing many people have developed over the years to service that marketplace.

BROADCAST DISTRIBUTION. This area features such large syndication companies as Viacom, Worldvision Enterprises, King Features Entertainment, and King World. Departments include:

- *Sales*. Composed of sales representatives, many of whom travel almost constantly, selling to stations around the country.
- *Booking*. Made up of the bookers who develop programming schedules after the programs are sold by the sales reps.
- *Promotion*. Writers and copy editors develop scripts, story lines, on-air promos, and other support materials.
- *Program Development*. Responsible for the screening of independently produced programming for acquisition and the development of new ideas.
- *Shipping*. Some distributors have in-house facilities and some use outside services.
- *Administration*. Includes management and finance.

Working for distribution companies can give you an excellent overview of the field and plenty of opportunity to meet people along the way. Sales representatives, for example, generally travel in a particular geographic area or territory, selling the syndicated shows to local television stations, network affiliates, and cable systems. After a while, relationships develop, people get to know one another (especially the golfers). Salespeople have been known to move into other areas such as management or to develop their own stable of syndicated shows.

NONBROADCAST DISTRIBUTION. Companies such as Modern Talking Pictures and West Glen Communications have been distributing sponsored films and tapes for major corporations for a great many years. West Glen, for example, has distribution offices in New York, Chicago, Dallas, San Francisco, Seattle, Toronto, Montreal, and London. Though many of the videotape subjects do reach television in noncommercial time, their major audiences might include

- Civic and social organizations
- Professional health groups
- Travel-oriented groups, travel agents
- Churches
- Ski lodges, country clubs, tennis clubs, hotels, resorts
- Schools

Nonbroadcast distribution companies handle corporate films and tapes as well as public service announcements for nonprofit organizations. Companies such as West Glen also develop and produce collateral materials that accompany the films and tapes.

Jobs in nonbroadcast distribution companies include

- *Booking.* Unlike syndication companies where bookers develop schedules, bookers in nonbroadcast take the calls that come in from schools, clubs, and organizations requesting programs in the inventory. Bookers handle their own accounts, including screening requests, computer paperwork, shipping documents, confirmation notices, and follow-up.
- *Television booking.* This part of the staff handles the distribution of video news releases, public service announcements, and library programs. Each person is usually responsible for his or her own library of programs, placement on TV stations, follow-up to see that tapes are returned, tracking, and reporting. It is an excellent way in which to learn just where television stations are located, and the names of some of the people who manage them.
- *Shipping and library management.* Most distribution companies maintain their own in-house video inspection department. Special machines are set to stop automatically when there is even a slight defect in the tape. No videocassette is ever shipped out of West Glen, for example, without an inspection seal.

Now you know how *Bauxite Mining in Upper Volta* found its way to your school!

CHAPTER TEN

HOME VIDEO

So much has been written about the growth of the VCR hardware industry that we sometimes lose sight of the fact that software has grown to equal it. Each year, over 75 million commercially prerecorded videocassettes are sold. In fact, these days, no one even contemplates producing a feature film without considering subsidiary rights potential for television and cable as well as the home videocassette market. Films that have gone into and out of theaters like Christmas crowds through a revolving door (did you ever see *Raggedy Man*; *Fedora*; *King, Queen and Knave*; or *The Haunting of Julia*?) enjoy a second life on cassette, and other box office disasters (*Heaven's Gate* is the classic, I suppose) have become cult favorites overseas. Much of the loss of production dollars is made up with the home audience.

At the same time, this vast new home market has opened up nonentertainment and educational videos, most of them produced especially for the home viewer. *Billboard*'s November 1987 list of the top special interest videocassettes heavily featured sports—football, golf, skiing, hunting, even t'ai chi ch'uan. In the hobbies and crafts categories, Chef Paul Prudhomme's *Louisiana Kitchen, Volume 1* was the leader, followed by videocassettes on microwave cooking, cake decorating, travel, wine appreciation, and Chef Prudhomme's second volume!

The market also includes music videos, children's shows and games, comedy specials, instructional tapes on health and exercise, and home and car repair. These videotapes are available not only in stores that specialize in home VCR distribution, but also in supermarkets, theater lobbies, hotels, and in almost every catalog that appears like magic on your doorstep along with the junk mail. I suppose that my favorite video is still the Video Baby, for those who want the joys of having a baby without the trauma and demands of being a parent. *People* magazine called it ''a womb with a view.''

The speed with which videos can be produced, edited, and dubbed has given rise to a category called ''instant video,'' where producers are turning out subject matter almost overnight in the hope that the timeliness of the subject will create a market. After the Iran-contra hearings, for example, two companies hastily produced videotapes that contained excerpts of Oliver North's testimony. Sales of the videos produced by Ted Turner's Home Entertainment and by MPI Home Video were disappointing; under 40,000 sales each. On the other hand, MPI's instant tape of the Chicago Bears, released immediately before their Super Bowl triumph in January 1986, sold more than 220,000 copies. According to producers who have put their toes into the icy waters of instant video, there are two factors that must be considered before attempting any project: budget control and getting the video into a distribution network already overloaded with feature films and other home video subjects.

While cost control is always important, regardless of the size of your budget, for the independent it is critical, since production and postproduction expenses are only a part of the profit-and-loss equation. Once the job is done, the dubs must be made, the tapes must be distributed, and the promotion and marketing phases must begin. And, since you will be receiving only a percentage of the gross return, all these factors must be counted before the great idea goes before the camera.

Professional distributors are flooded by sample tapes, and since every one of us is totally convinced that *our* brilliant concept is the best thing since *Making Michael Jackson's 'Thriller,'* it may come as a disappointment when our product finds no market through normal channels. Nonetheless, as with everything else, the system sometimes does work. Michael Wiese provides a list of professional distributors in the back of his book *Home Video: Producing for the Home Market* (Focal Press), along with some instructions on how to proceed and on the chances of breaking into the marketplace.

SELF-DISTRIBUTION

Some producers of home videos prefer to distribute their material themselves rather than put their product into the hands of a professional distributor. In his book, Michael Wiese explains the disadvantages as well as the advantages of taking this treacherous route. Although you will receive a larger royalty than in signing with a professional distributor, you will also have to carry the expense of advertising, marketing, printing, duplicating, packaging, and shipping. You'll also have accounting fees, legal costs, and overhead. Most producers choose the professional route, obviously for good reasons.

There are success stories (and failures) using both methods of distribution. There have been ski tapes and tapes about fly fishing that have hit a particular audience strongly and have done well through advertising in catalogs and specialty magazines or through strategic placement in outlets (such as sporting goods stores). More often than not, the route of self-distribution has been a failure and Wiese strongly recommends (as do I) that you find a professional distributor for your videotape, if at all possible.

Before you take the plunge, ask yourself the questions that will help you to decide whether your idea is marketable. Some people in the field call it an "inquisition" and it can be self-imposed:

- How many people are involved or interested in the subject: how many golfers, bridge players, magicians, bakers?
- What are the demographics? All over the country? All over the world? I stopped myself from making the ultimate tape on bluefishing because blues exist only along the East Coast of the United States.
- What is the potential sales total through normal distribution channels and through specialty catalogs (such as Sharper Image, Taylor Gifts, and Eddie Bauer)?
- Why is your tape unique? Are there others like it? How many others compete with yours? Why is yours better than those already being distributed about that subject?
- Do you have a very special way in which you can promote the tape? Mail order? Appearances on television? Advertising in specialty magazines? Feature stories in newspapers?

As a result of the booming home market, a number of smaller videocassette distributors have sprung up to service the independent producer and the narrower, more specialized markets. Magazines such as *The Independent* continue to report on these small companies or chains of video stores that are developing distribution outlets for specialized subjects.

For example, in Chicago, the Video Data Bank of the School of the Art Institute of Chicago was originally the successful producer, collector, and distributor of a series of interviews entitled "Of Art and Artists." Their archives contain over 2,000 videotape programs on the central theme of contemporary art. In the past few years, the Video Data Bank expanded its involvement in experimental video, added video classics to its collection, and entered the home video market. A few years ago, Video Data Bank received funding from the National Endowment for the Arts to develop cassette packages for the home market, and eventually to enter the field of video publishing.

There is also the expanding international marketplace. Not only have Hollywood feature films found audiences in Europe, Asia, and Australia through videocassette distribution, but also other, nonentertainment subjects have begun to be marketed overseas, many of them dubbed. The number of VCRs worldwide continues to grow. The number of VCRs in the Soviet Union alone is expected to increase by about 10,000 sets each year. At the time of this writing there are two video stores in Moscow (current price for rental about 2½ rubles or $4 a day); the best news is that they're stocking not only feature films, but also documentaries, short subjects, music videos, and concert tapes.

THE HOME MARKET GOES OUTSIDE THE HOME

Since the software market seems to grow in direct proportion to the demand for hardware, it is important to note that new developments in the field help create this increased demand for product. The Sony Corporation, which pioneered the Walkman and then developed the miniature Watchman television set, has now developed the Video Walkman, a VCR that's about the size of a pocket calendar or notepad and weighs only 2½ pounds. The tapes are 8mm, about the size of a standard audiocassette, and can program up to four hours of material. Whether this will work out for Sony, who lost the VCR race to the VHS system, remains to be seen. But already the geniuses are at work developing software especially designed to go with the Video Walkman. Soon there will be video magazines that you can take along with you on the bus or train, watching them on the three-inch screen. And though the costs are now rather high for subscriptions to the few that exist in Japan, remember that the price of VCRs dropped precipitously within a few years after their introduction.

Home video has entered yet another area: the airlines. The days of in-flight movies as we know them might well be on their way out of the cabin and into history. A new system called Airvision (a joint venture of Warner Brothers and Philips) is now being installed on some major airlines, and its advent heralds yet another growth in the demand for software. Instead of the single-screen in-flight movie, British Airways and Singapore Airlines, as well as some American carriers, have installed individual video terminals and headsets in front of every seat on the aircraft, allowing each passenger to choose his or her channel of entertainment.

With this development, it seems the airlines have come full circle. When they first introduced in-flight entertainment, it was through the use of individual black-and-white TV sets that were placed in front of each passenger. At that time, one of the exciting promises that the airlines made was that you could now watch the takeoffs and landings through the placement of a TV camera on the nose of the plane. I remember eighty to a hundred passengers

Each new development in technology provides fresh opportunity for videotape producers. The new Warner/Philips AIRVISION has recently been installed in the passenger cabins of several major airlines. This is the economy section of British Airways, with each passenger controlling an individual monitor. (Courtesy Airvision)

on a DC-7 eagerly leaning forward as the plane took off, watching the runway being eaten up. Interestingly enough, everyone seemed to ignore the scene in glorious living color out the windows. In any case, the experiment was short-lived. It seemed that the passengers were terrified by the image of the takeoff and, especially, the landing as the ground came up to meet the TV camera. Then came the single screen for all passengers and the lowering of shades so you couldn't see out the windows at all, and now we are back to the television screen in front of the passenger again!

As always when a new technology is developed, there are people who move in to fill the need that the technology creates, and this newest innovation is no exception. Software for Airvision is being provided by companies such as SPAN (Spafax Airline Network, Ltd.), founded by two young entrepreneurs, Michael Perkins and Duncan Hilleary, with offices in London and New York. The potential in this market is tremendous. As Hilleary says,

"With 60 million people airborne each month, advertisers are faced with the prospect of reaching *a whole country* in the sky. This new video technology provides an increasingly attractive medium, and advertisers will be ignoring it at their peril."

Advertisers! And suddenly we begin to see yet another potential market for soft-sell commercials and programming: children's shows, information for the business traveler, fashion, sports, music video, news, comedy, feature films, documentaries, short subjects, as well as travel tips, places to visit, and some gentle commercial plugs for hotels or restaurants. As Michael Perkins comments:

> *"In the United States, it's the top 25 percent of the population who are travelers. About a third of our audience comes from $75,000-plus households, about 5 percent of the American population. To be successful, we're going to have to upgrade the quality of programming . . . to get people to watch, we're going to have to find programming that's different and stimulating and appealing. It will probably be some time before we see [Airvision] on every long-haul aircraft, but it will come."*

CAPTAIN KIDD AND THE VIDEO BUCCANEERS

I suppose that the subject of illegal and unauthorized copying of videocassettes would not normally be a part of a book on finding your way to a career in videotape. But an incident in one of my classes at New York University gave me a new insight to the problem. It deals more with the *attitude* than with the financial loss that occurs when someone dubs a tape illegally, though both are essentially tied together.

We are discussing the very serious problem of an industry that conservatively estimates a loss of around $1.5 *billion* each year as a result of unauthorized copying. Since 40 percent of all VCRs are purchased by consumers who already own at least one, it is obvious that the problem is epidemic. During our discussion, one student raised the point that there were now methods by which a tape could be encoded, thus preventing duplication by another machine. In the front row of the class, one of my undergrads snorted loudly. "Bah," he retorted. "Just give me two VCRs and two TV sets and I can bypass any system!"

My question had nothing to do with his technical wizardry, when I asked if he didn't know that it was illegal. His answer was buried in the shout of one of the women, who said, "Oh, we all do it all the time!" The thing that made me listen with disbelief is that here was a class of students, all of whom would be entering a field where *they* would be involved in the production and distribution of videotapes, and that *someone else* would be pirating *their* materials, thus creating a loss of royalties to them! I still cannot explain my students' attitude. For any one of us who has or will have a copyrighted program, pirating robs us of our rightful income.

There have been several instances where I have been asked to show a training program designed by my company for a corporate client, and at the end of a presentation at another corporation, have been requested to leave the tapes so that they might be shown and dubbed off for their own sales force. In fact, in one instance, the executive followed up with a phone call after my refusal and saw nothing wrong in asking again! Interestingly enough, this problem has come about with the advent of easy-to-use, easy-to-dub videotapes. I would assume that the over *350 million* blank videocassettes sold each year are *not* being used solely to record the television programs you might be missing when you go out to dinner.

A light may be in the distance for those of us who are quite appalled at what we consider plain outright stealing from the producers and distributors of our programs. There are now anticopying systems that work effectively, mostly against the professional pirate, rather than the amateur Long John Silver. Macrovision is one, and it does rather well. The system encodes the original, legitimate videotape, so that illegal duplication will put varying degrees of video "noise" on the copy, from a constant wavy line to garbled nonsense.

It's a start and many of the larger producers and distributors of features such as MCA, CBS/Fox, Warner Brothers, Disney, HBO, and MGM/UA are using it, as are most of the major corporations that produce training and employee information tapes: General Motors, Ford, Eastman Kodak, Burger King, 3M, and McGraw-Hill, to name a few. The system is also available in producing PAL and SECAM dubs for foreign distribution.

HOME VIDEO AND OTHER HELPFUL HINTS: A TALK WITH MICHAEL WIESE

Michael Wiese is an independent producer, and formerly the vice president of program development for Vestron Video. He is the author of four books on video, among them *Home Video: Producing for the Home Market* (Focal Press).

Wiese has also been the director of on-air promotions and production for Showtime and the Movie Channel, and was head of production for DHS Films in New York. He is a national seminar leader for the American Film Institute.

Do you see home video as an area of opportunity for people starting out?

''If you're thinking of home video alone, it's tough because the budgets are, say, between fifty and one hundred fifty thousand. It's hard to be in business and pay your overhead and earn a living if you're just a home video producer. You spend most of your money on the production, and what you get out of it is very little. It's also unlikely that you're going to see any royalties from sales unless you have a mega-hit. So I think that's a tough one.''

What about entry level?

''At the entry level there are lots of home videos being produced, and people can work as production assistants or as associate producers and learn that way. If I were starting out, I'd go to each area. I'd go to features, cable, pay TV, home video, corporate, and then I'd break down the different kinds of product that these folks made. And then I'd break that down even further into all the different jobs within that area, all entry level—in other words, the ones that pay under twenty-five or thirty thousand dollars. Then I'd go out and get interviews with those people that had those jobs, and ask how you get the jobs.''

Who are some of the big companies in the home video market today?

''There are lots. Vestron, CBS, Paramount, Lorimar, MCA, Prism, Media, RCA, IVE, Disney, Knapp Communications . . .''

When you were at Vestron, did you use a lot of outside people?

''Well, yes and no. I was looking for projects that made sense, I mean that would translate into money-making videos for the rental stores. So I looked for projects that had the producers attached. Once in a while, I would come up with an idea that I wanted produced, and then I would go out and find the producers. I would executive produce it and I'd say, 'Here's the concept, here's what we want to do. Here's the budget. Go develop the treatment or script.' And we would finance it and they would go out and make it.''

Did people ever come to you with ''Let's do one on golf'' or whatever?

''Yeah, mostly that. There were three ways that projects got made: One would be a producer who walked in with something that was already done and we would just buy it. Two, they'd come in with sort of a half-baked idea or some footage that had something to it but needed a lot of work. So we'd twist and turn the idea or material and figure out a way

to package it. And then the third way was either they would think up ideas or we would think up ideas and then we would get them written up, decide that we wanted to make them, and then go out and produce them.''

And Vestron would finance them?

''Yes. I did about two hundred acquisitions and productions in about three and a half years there. A lot of people stayed busy.''

How do people start out? Can people still go out with their home video cameras and shoot something that they can sell?

''You know, some people do go out with their home video equipment and do video press kits or interviews. One of our local people, Chris Marsala, is an interesting example. He's host of ''Variety Tonight,'' and he's producer of the local cable show, public access. Nobody gets paid. They've done a hundred shows; production assistants, cameramen, switchers, all those people work for free. Now he's gone out with a camera for the Vestrons and the others and does interviews with stars and puts together little video press kits, so you can make those leaps. I mean, nothing is lower than cable access, except shooting your wedding, but you can find those little freelance jobs on the periphery of the industry. At the Movie Channel (Showtime), I oversaw everything that went between the movies: promos, network IDs, celebrity interviews, coming attractions. And we'd often hire freelancers—they could field produce, they could write, they could off-line edit, they could on-line edit, or supervise editing, or any combination of those. And that's at entry level. You're being asked to make five-minute, three-minute, ten-minute pieces and they only take a week or two to do.''

Would someone come to you at Vestron or Showtime with a sample reel?

''A lot of people start with doing college ten-minute movies or short tapes. And while there's virtually no market for those any longer, it does give you experience whereby you can go to local television stations and show your work and produce segments for them. In other words, you might go out and interview the most quirky characters in your community, or shoot a beauty contest or sports event, or interview Sting when he's playing nearby, and then cut it into a five-minute sequence that might then appear locally or regionally or even nationally. Short pieces encompass all the skills of long-form movies or videos. You still have to write it, you still have to produce it, you still have to postproduce it. At

Showtime, people did come in with resumes and reels that showed their work. But, interestingly enough, it was not the reel that got them the job."

What did you look for?

"I always looked at producers and tried to get a sense of whether they could do the work and get the job done. How they presented themselves as people. Whether they would show up on time. Whether they were appropriately dressed. You figure that if they're conscientious enough to try to land the job with you, then they're going to use some of these same techniques and skills when they're out producing your show. So, you want someone who's aggressive, but not too aggressive."

Aggressive?

"Yeah. When I hired people to produce, let's call it 'field produce' political campaign spots, they had to be tough, aggressive, yet very flexible, because the schedules were always changing. We never had enough money, so they had to know how to make deals, they had to have some experience with knowing the best lab facilities, the best equipment houses. I looked for people who could write and produce and I wanted them to see the program all the way through if they were going to do a promo. I'd say, 'Okay, we've got Sophie's Choice this month and I need a ten-minute piece on Meryl Streep. Here's where you can shoot her; go research her background.' So they'd have to write the questions, have the interviewer do the interview, supervise the shoot, do the edit, find the music for transitions, title it, and deliver it. And by the way, 'Here's ten thousand dollars to do it!' "

Where do you see the fastest growing area at the present time?

"Desktop publishing—and soon, probably, desktop video publishing. Just as there was an explosion with desktop Yamaha synthesizers for composers, where musicians could buy the sound of a hundred-piece orchestra for five thousand dollars, video artist/producers can find computers and VCRs and cameras and create desktop videos for very low budgets. It's being used first in corporate in-house productions, where the budgets are low and they need mostly instructional stuff, but I think the same thing will happen in video publishing as the synthesizer did for music. People will be doing cinematic novels on videotape. They'll be able to sit in their attics with their Macs and their tape recorders and put it all together from start to finish."

A final question on a personal note. You're now an independent producer again. What made you go back to that?

"I just graduated from the school of hard knocks commercial pay television, and most recently, home video. I did film and video production, distribution and marketing. My efforts made my employers lots of money. Now, after twenty years, it's my turn. I also want to be able to more carefully pick and choose the projects in this next decade.

"My new video company is involved in marketing as well as production. You have to address both to be successful. I also work with other producers, marketers, distributors, and publishers. Sometimes as a consultant or executive producer. Sometimes we do everything, sometimes just a part. We produce, market, and publish videos, films, television, and books. I feel it's going to be a very busy year."

CHAPTER ELEVEN

VIDEOTAPE AND THE INDEPENDENT ARTIST

Video [Art] distribution is not a way to make a living.
David Weissman
The Independent Magazine

This is a most difficult subject to address, since video art, very much like avant-garde film work, is important; creates a multitude of opportunities for experimentation and innovation; and has its own press, its own vast following, its own exhibition galleries and museum shows. It is also the hardest area in which to make a living!

A parallel can easily be drawn to art film, in that the older medium also had its growing pains in the areas of experimentation and abstraction. From time to time, we saw something strikingly different and new, even as far back as *The Cabinet of Dr. Caligari* in the twenties. But, for the most part, art film went unnoticed and artists were undiscovered, unappreciated, and unpaid, quite the opposite from their commercial brothers and sisters who were grinding out Westerns and chaste love stories. Back in the forties, under the guidance of the venerable Amos Vogel, a group called Cinema 16 was formed and a small audience began to discover the works of Len Lye and Norman McLaren, a budding Stan Brakhage (who is still working in the field), the animator Carmen D'Avino, and a hundred others, good and bad, whose names are listed with the pioneers of the art film and who have had a substantial influence on even today's video artists.

Today a glorious film such as Norman McLaren's *Pas de Deux*, which used overprinting frame by frame and brought the image of a ballerina to life as never before, might well be done on videotape with computers in about one-fiftieth of the time it took the artist to complete his masterwork. However, even as a whole new world of technology has opened up, it remains a fact that video art is as difficult to make a living in as film art was back in the forties and fifties. With few exceptions, artists must struggle to raise funds, support themselves, and at the same time, have enough time to devote to their work. Distribution is a problem, too, though things have somewhat improved along these lines for the video artist.

While this picture may seem unnecessarily bleak, I think it is important to present a balanced view. The importance of art video cannot be underestimated, but we must also be pragmatic about the problems. Video artists and independent producers, for example, complain that it takes three times as long to raise money as to produce their tapes.

On the bright side, the proliferation of computers and home video equipment, the increased interest in video by artists both known and unknown, the development of videodiscs and interactive video have created an explosion of activity, with exhibition and distribution potential for the artist in art galleries, theaters, museums, schools, and organizations formed for the express purpose of seeing to it that the works get shown. We continue to read about video art exhibits at the Whitney Museum in New York and at the Pompidou Center in Paris, where the curator, Christine Van Assche, is expanding the museum's commitment to the medium.

Video is so potentially innovative that it has seduced some established artists like Philip Pearlstein and veteran filmmakers Grahame Weinbren and Roberta Friedman, who are now working with interactive laser disc technology. The constant struggle, the financial disappointment, the small audiences, and the battle for recognition have never stopped any artist, whether Van Gogh or Vanderbeek, from pursuing his or her artistic vision, and so it is today.

Here, then, are some things you should know about before you turn on the computers:

- Which magazines, organizations, and festivals are supportive in the field of independent production and video art.
- How to fund your project—foundations, grants—and how to proceed with your request.

- Who exhibits video art, and which places promote the medium as a part of their commitment to the artists and the independents.
- What are the financial considerations of distribution, the percentages returned to the artist, and the requirements for which the artist is responsible before someone will handle the distribution.

GETTING INFORMATION

There are two major organizations that offer the beginner a wealth of information and advice on subjects from raising funds to distributing completed videos.

ASSOCIATION OF INDEPENDENT VIDEO AND FILMMAKERS (AIVF) (625 Broadway, New York, NY 10012. (212) 473–3400). AIVF publishes *The Independent*, and a subscription goes along with membership in the organization. I have found the magazine to be the best guide to the field of art video and independent production. It covers a wide range of issues:

- Fund-raising and distribution
- Festivals, both foreign and domestic
- Listings of job opportunities, grant deadlines, equipment, and facility rentals
- News of the field: the names and the works in progress of some of the most important people in art video.

In addition, AIVF fights to protect and promote access to public television airtime and funding for independent producers, holds public seminars and screenings, and arranges member discounts with labs, rental houses, and postproduction facilities.

BAY AREA VIDEO COALITION (BAVC) (1111 17th Street, San Francisco, CA 94107. (415) 861–3282). BAVC has been in existence for well over ten years, and is unusual in that it provides both equipment and facilities for independents. It also publishes a most informative magazine, *Video Networks*, eight times a year. It is nonprofit and is funded in part by the National Endowment for the Arts and the California Arts Council.

BAVC offers complete editing suites—1-inch, ¾-inch, and ½-inch—and field production packages that include cameras, audio mixers, and lighting. The prices are reasonable, especially compared to those at professional rental houses. The organization also offers subsidized discounts to members.

Video Networks offers a broad range of articles on video art and independent production, including information about seminars and workshops on production, lighting, computer editing, time-code editing, and special effects equipment like the Chyron. It often devotes special issues to one subject. Recently, the magazine investigated grants and funding in depth: foundation information, showreels for presentation, tips on getting grants, and specifications and requirements for those grants.

For those on the West Coast, BAVC offers a resource library of media books and magazines to its members. I think that the magazine itself is a worthwhile investment for independents in any part of the country.

In chapter 13, you'll find a listing of other publications that may be of help to you, but those deal mostly with the areas of nonbroadcast television, corporate video, and postproduction. *The Independent* and *Video Networks* address the specific concerns of the independent video artist.

FUNDING YOUR PROJECT

Video artists and independents face the same realities as the people who inhabit the world of dance, theater, opera, music, painting, and sculpture. For the most part, funding for the arts comes from personal contributions, the largesse of family and friends, and the constant hunt for foundation and grant monies, none of which are ever sufficient in themselves to complete a project in any reasonable amount of time. Many of the foundations and government agencies work on the basis of matching grants—in other words, "You raise the dough, and we'll match it dollar for dollar." If we were to structure the fund-raising hierarchy, the list might look like this:

- Government agencies. Although funding for the arts has been cut severely during these past years, there is still some money available through the National Endowment for the Humanities, the National Endowment for the Arts, and the individual state commissions for the arts and humanities.
- Regional arts agencies, museums, and locally supported programs.
- Cable television. With the introduction of cable access, some help can be gotten in the area of production, equipment, and videotape recording.
- Foundations.
- Corporations. Some large organizations award grant monies or provide cash awards at festivals and student exhibitions.
- Trade and service organizations.
- The American Film Institute Independent Filmmaker Program (funded by the National Endowment for the Arts).
- Deferred payment agreements with production and postproduction facil-

ities. In New York, for example, DuArt Laboratories has been one of the foremost supporters of the independents, and many a low-budget feature film and documentary carries a word of thanks to its president, Irwin Young. Keep in mind, however, that "deferred" means just that—you'll have to pay it off eventually.

Leonard Maltin's excellent book *The Whole Film Sourcebook* (Universe Books/New American Library) has a most helpful section devoted to this very subject. It may help you to figure out the actual production costs of your tape. Michael Wiese's *Film and Video Budgets* is also a good source of information.

To obtain grant money, especially from foundations, you may have to look beyond the videotape category. Many times, the grants for production of a film or tape are buried in other categories. Just recently, I was working with a group that deals with dance, movement, exercise, and recreation for the aged. We found that it was quite typical for a foundation to reject the idea of a videotape. However, if we approached the foundation with the idea of expanding the service to other facilities, and the videotape was buried in the proposal as one method of doing it, the reaction was much more amenable.

Despite the '87 stock market crash, the mean-spirited cutting of government funds for the arts over the last eight or ten years, and the tremendous competition for production funding, there are still funds available from nearly 35,000 foundations. Most of the grants are quite small, and certainly not all of them are targeted at video.

To find out more about available grants, first check with local libraries. They're good resources of books, magazines, and other publications that provide foundation information. Be sure to check the following:

- *Annual Register of Grant Support*
- *Foundation News*
- *The Taft Corporation Directory*
- *Foundation Commentary*
- *NEA Guide to Programs*
- *NEH Program Announcement*
- *NEH Humanities*

These publications will give you addresses, phone numbers, names of people to contact, types and sizes of grants, entry deadlines, and specifications and prerequisites for applying. This last point is important in that some grants carry with them specific criteria for the applicant, for example:

- You must prove that you have additional sources of production income.

- Funding is limited to U.S. citizens.
- You must include supporting material to show that you are a capable video producer. I can't emphasize enough the importance of making a good sample video somewhere along the way, either in college or as an independent. It is critical both in getting a grant and in getting a job.
- You must include a complete synopsis of your project.
- You must include a budget breakdown: projected costs for production, equipment, lighting, travel, off-line and on-line editing, special effects, rights and releases, and contingencies.

Specific grants may have even further restrictions, so make certain that you check the rules before contacting the foundation or corporation. Just to give you an idea:

- You may have to be a member of the organization or foundation to which you are applying. For example, the Long Beach Museum of Art requires that you be a Video Council member.
- You may have to be affiliated with a nonprofit tax-exempt organization in order to be eligible. The Foundation for Independent Video and Film, for instance, excludes any applications for institutional projects, promotional uses, or public television station productions. It also excludes student productions.
- The National Endowment for the Arts requires ¾-inch or 1-inch videotape samples. It will not accept VHS.
- Some foundations require that you live in the area in which you are applying. For example, the Film Arts Foundation in San Francisco limits its small grants to residents of the nine Bay Area counties.
- Some organizations specify subject matter: nuclear power, peace, art, women. They may also specify the type of video—animation, documentary, etc.

Here are some other publications that might help you sort everything out:

THE FOUNDATIONS DIRECTORY. Called "The Bible" by those who search constantly for funding, the directory is published by The Foundation Center and is distributed by Columbia University Press. The Foundation Center (79 Fifth Avenue, New York, NY 10011. (212) 620–4230) is open to the public free of charge. I have found it to be a great place to do my research for foundation grants. The directory doesn't provide much guidance on how to get video grants per se, but it does offer a great deal of information in the subject areas and you may find hidden video grant potential in its over 3,000 entries (such as "anthropology" and "geology").

THE FOUNDATION GRANTS INDEX. Issued annually, the index lists over 20,000 grants made by foundations in the previous year, with the amounts generally over $5,000 per grant. If you study the grant descriptions, you'll get a good idea of just where the money has been going for the past twelve months.

THE GRANTS REGISTER (St. James Press). Updated every few years, the register covers about 1,300 organizations in the United States and the United Kingdom. Video and film grants are not listed separately, though there are a few listings of specific scholarships and grants offered by major universities. The rules of the funding game change from year to year. At this writing, the Corporation for Public Broadcasting has cut its funding for independent production by well over 50 percent over the past seven years. At the same time, the American Film Institute has added video to its Independent Filmmaker Program. The John D. and Catherine T. MacArthur Foundation has expanded its grant program into the areas of health, aging, international peace and security, and world environment. Its media grants are small, but the foundation seems receptive to new ideas. One of its large yearly grants, as you may know, was awarded to filmmaker John Sayles (*Matewan*, *Lianna*, *Baby It's You*), though he was given his grant as part of the foundation's "genius" program. I, for one, think he deserved it.

Failing all else, many filmmakers and video artists have funded their projects with credit cards (which, like deferred payments, must be accounted for at some time!); loans from parents, relatives, and friends; investors; and odd jobs from waiter to sales rep to computer software programmer. And, wherever the money comes from, and however you manage to get the job done, you now have to find a way to show it to an adoring public. Things are just a tiny bit brighter in this area.

DISTRIBUTION

Although video art and the work of the independents has actually been under way for twenty years or more, the breakthrough for recognition and distribution really did not take place until the early eighties. Certainly, there were some signs that people were beginning to take notice. In the late 1960s, public television station KQED in San Francisco set up a Center for Experiments in Television, and galleries on the West Coast and in Soho in New York began to offer everything from video art to lasers to holograms. But the established institutions, the places that really count—the museums, the large

One of the most prolific of the independent producers is Skip Blumberg, shown here in Thailand for the Elephant Olympics. His completed documentary, "Elephant Games," was shown on PBS. (Courtesy Skip Blumberg)

corporate spaces devoted to art—had paid scant attention to the video innovators. Possibly the first large, important video exhibition took place in 1982 when the Whitney Museum in New York sponsored a retrospective by Nam June Paik.* *Time* magazine took note with a favorable review, and Paik was featured in the *New York Times Magazine* and on the cover of *Art News*. They all seemed to sit up and take notice at once.

From that point on, the distribution outlets for video artists and independents began to grow. Unfortunately, what has been happening at the same time is that the number of video artists has also begun to grow, and at a much faster pace than that of the distribution outlets! Artist Juan Downey has commented rightly that "video arts has matured, but distributors have not." But,

*Who, incidentally, has been working in video art since the late 1950s.

for those of us who do try to find the silver lining, this essentially is the same thing.

There are essentially four major avenues to distribute and exhibit your videotape, though some may overlap, with a video distributor finding a way to show a video production on television or in a museum gallery:

- Video distributors, who provide the outlet for the artist and share the rental or purchase fees
- Museums, galleries, corporate lobbies, even theaters, schools, and—believe it or not—nightclubs. San Francisco has several clubs where video art is part of the atmosphere
- Public access cable TV
- Self-distribution

VIDEO DISTRIBUTORS

Video distributors range in size from art and avant-garde bookstores to organizations devoted to the development and encouragement of the arts. There are many; the list I've given below represents only a small segment of the growing network.

A typical and encouraging example is The Kitchen (519 West 19th Street, New York, NY 10011. (212) 255–5793). Founded in 1971, the organization has been a boon to video artists and the independents, as well as to people in the performing arts. Each year it showcases exhibitions and nearly 2,000 hours of video screenings. In addition, it provides small grants to artists, composers, choreographers, and performance artists. The Kitchen promotes programs all over the world and boasts a video archive that represents nearly 100 artists and over 1,000 titles.

Here are some others:

American Federation of Arts
41 East 65th Street
New York, NY 10021
(212) 988–7700

Black Filmmakers Foundation
80 Eighth Avenue #1704
New York, NY 10011
(212) 924–1198

The foundation publishes the magazine *Black Film Review* four times a year, which covers, among other things, black images in film and video. The magazine's address is 110 S Street, N.W., Washington, DC 20001.

Electronic Arts Intermix (EAI)
10 Waverly Place
New York, NY 10003
(212) 473-6822

One of the oldest video distributors, founded in 1973, EAI carries nearly 1,000 titles. It also has an excellent reputation for quality broadcast dubs.

Facets Video
1517 W. Fullerton Avenue
Chicago, IL 60614
(800) 281–9075

Intermedia Arts of Minnesota
425 Ontario Street, S.E.
Minneapolis, MN 55414
(612) 376–3333

The Media Project
Box 4093
Portland, OR 97208
(503) 225–5335

Pacific Arts Corporation
50 North La Cienega Boulevard, Suite 210
Beverly Hills, CA 90211
(213) 657–2233
Pacific Arts publishes the magazine *Overview*.

Third World Newsreel
335 West 38th Street
New York, NY 10018
(212) 947–9277

Video Data Bank
School of the Art Institute of Chicago
Columbus Drive at Jackson Boulevard
Chicago, IL 60603
(312) 443–3793

With archives and a library containing over 2,000 videotape programs central to contemporary art, Video Data Bank is one of the leading video distributors. Its promotion catalogs are also among the finest.

Women Make Movies
225 Lafayette Street #212
New York, NY 10012
(212) 925–0606

Founded in 1972, Women Make Movies is one of the oldest video distributors. Needless to say, they specialize in the distribution of video and film subjects about women.

In addition, the Association of Independent Video and Filmmakers (AIVF) publishes a reasonably priced photocopied guide covering a hundred distribution companies. The listing is based on their previous articles in the magazine *The Independent*, and it's indexed for genre/subjects, market (domestic and foreign), and target audiences. It also provides a listing of the companies that can provide funding for the production and completion of your project.

DARA BIRNBAUM

Program 1
Damnation of Faust: Will-O'-The-Wisp (A Deceitful Goal)
Producer: The C.A.T. Fund
7 MIN COLOR 1985

Program 2
Damnation of Faust: Evocation
10 MIN COLOR 1983

Program 3
Remy/Grand Central Trains and Boats and Planes
4 MIN COLOR 1980
New Music Shorts
6 MIN COLOR 1981
PM Magazine/Acid Rock
3 MIN COLOR 1982

Program 4*
Technology/Transformation: Wonder Woman
7 MIN COLOR 1978
Kiss the Girls: Make Them Cry
7 MIN COLOR 1979
Pop-Pop Video: A. General Hospital/Olympic Women Speed Skating
6 MIN COLOR 1980
Pop-Pop Video: B. Kojak/Wang
4 MIN COLOR 1980

SEE LONG BEACH MUSEUM ENTRY FOR BIRNBAUM PORTRAIT.
SEE STEDELIJK MUSEUM ENTRY FOR BIRNBAUM INSTALLATION.

Damnation of Faust: Evocation

Well known for her head-on investigation of television language, Dara Birnbaum appropriates immediately familiar TV stereotypes and generic fragments (from game shows, soap operas, sports spectacles, police shoot-outs, etc.) and then reconstructs them to exaggerate their repetitive, seductive forms and reveal their subtexts. These fast-paced, high energy manipulations of TV "ready-mades," coupled with rock and disco music, criticize TV's myths while maintaining the element of entertainment. "I am trying to take advantage of the vehicle while at the same time analyzing it." For her more recent work, **Damnation of Faust: Evocation**, Birnbaum abandoned TV's imaginary world to gather live footage from a Manhattan playground. Nineteenth century Japanese Ukiyo-e "pictures of the floating world" provided the formal devices to represent the fleeting nature of pleasure and daily experience. Visual motifs of pillars and fans, achieved through video wipes, plunge the viewer into the image as well as sometimes barring entrance.

LYN BLUMENTHAL

Program 1
Social Studies, Part I: Horizontes
20 MIN COLOR DUAL LANGUAGE 1983

Program 2
Social Studies, Part II: The Academy
18 MIN COLOR 1983-84

Program 3
Arcade
Lyn Blumenthal
Carole Ann Klonarides
Producer: Video Data Bank
Music: A. Leroy
Paintbox: Ed Paschke
Editor: Richard Feist
11 MIN COLOR 1984

SEE HORSFIELD/BLUMENTHAL ENTRY FOR INTERVIEWS.

Social Studies, Part I: Horizontes

Lyn Blumenthal's videotapes resist any particular pigeonhole. They play with different forms — soap opera, appropriation, spectacle, music video, high tech and low tech too. Blumenthal's trajectories spring as much from feminist practice as from media criticism. What leaps out from her "social studies" is a gift for observing the character of an event, whether a rock around the historical clock (Cuba circa 1960 via 1982 Cuban soap opera in **Social Studies, Part I**), a news event (**Arcade's** digestion of the Reagan assassination attempt), or an exposé of the "ideology of entertainment" as Catherine Lord has suggested. Noting the "minimal elegance" of **Social Studies, Part II**, Lord states that, "A freeze frame of the unpeopled Academy Award stage comprises the entire tape, neatly eliminating visual pleasure from the entertainment battlefield. As our attention is forced to the unedited soundtrack of the best picture selection (movie clips, applause, commercial plugs, even the legendary envelope being ripped open) vignettes from *E.T., The Verdict, Missing, Tootsie,* and *Gandhi* become idiotic simplifications of matters like aggression, sexism and bigotry."

10

A page from the Video Tape Review of the Video Data Bank. The Chicago Group is the largest distributor of tapes by and about contemporary artists. The late Lyn Blumenthal was the founder of the bank, along with Dara Birnbaum. (Courtesy Video Data Bank)

MUSEUMS, GALLERIES AND OTHER EXHIBITION SPACES

Some of the distributors listed above have been successful in placing video exhibitions in museums. The Whitney in New York, for example, has been one of the most active in this area, exhibiting the work of video artists not only in their main building, but also in their gallery in the Equitable Center in Manhattan, where programs are presented that are funded by the corporation itself. A recent show included interactive video art by Buky Schwartz and Curt Royston, and a video sculpture by Nam June Paik. Museums, unfortunately, generally support the more famous artists in any genre, but some of them are opening up more and more to the unknowns of the medium. For example, the San Francisco Museum of Modern Art has had several exhibitions devoted to the lesser-known lights, as has the Pompidou in Paris.

For the beginner, a more practical outlet might be a local art gallery. Both San Francisco and New York's SoHo have been leaders in this area. It pays to watch the newspapers and to read the video art magazines to keep up with just who is exhibiting video art, and then contact them directly. I have also seen displays in the windows of retail shops devoted to fashion and video hardware. After all, if it moves, someone is going to watch it!

PUBLIC ACCESS

Public access also provides a means for the budding video artist to showcase his or her work. Certainly, you may not get a huge audience, but knowing when your program will be shown allows you to notify people who should see it in advance—by postcard or letter or brochure. I don't know what it is about something appearing on television, but the moment something goes on TV, it seems to acquire some importance. "I saw your film on TV," my students say to me, in awe. Never mind that it was at 2 A.M.! Having your video played on public access gives you yet another credit to add to your resume, and the more than 1,000 public access channels that are now open have increased the chances of an audience actually watching your tape.

SELF-DISTRIBUTION

If the distribution system for videotape were better, there would be no need for any comment on self-distribution. But, as my grandmother warned, nothing in this world is ideal. The primary method used by most distributors mentioned in this chapter is catalogs, or smaller mailings that list the stock of tapes currently available. To say the least, however, publishing *any* catalog and keeping it up to date can be a constant headache. Very few distributors can even begin to offer the quality of Video Data Bank's *Video Tape Review*, and EAI has been working on a complete listing of its titles for several years.

EAI, founded by gallery owner Howard Wise, one of the leaders in the distribution of the work by pioneers like George Stoney, Skip Blumberg, Joan Jonas, and Nam June Paik, has found it a job that is incredibly complicated.

There are simply more videos being produced than the current distributors can handle. And so, many video artists and independents have taken the self-distribution route, with varying degrees of success. If this is the choice that you eventually make, I would strongly suggest that you first try the distribution cooperatives that operate as member-controlled groups and that will at least give you some idea of the problems of promotion, costs, and audience targeting. Here are two of the best:

NEW DAY FILMS (22 Riverview Drive, Wayne, NJ 07470). New Day Films was first formed to distribute films made by its own members, all of them women. Today it has expanded to include both men and women in its membership. It offers both film and tapes about social issues, labor history, mental health, sex education, women's rights, and urban problems.

THE EMPOWERMENT PROJECT (13107 Venice Boulevard, Los Angeles, CA 90066). This came out of a successful project by Barbara Trent and David Kasper when they produced their own documentary *Destination Nicaragua* and then became their own agents, negotiating nonexclusive distribution contracts with ten distributors. It worked out beautifully, with 800 videotapes sold in the first eighteen months. The documentary aired on 180 college and university stations and twenty public television stations. The Empowerment Project was then formed with about thirty video and filmmakers participating. The group acts as an agent for the producer, usually collecting a 20 percent fee.

If you are going to self-distribute without the help of an organization or a cooperative, keep in mind that the work will be even more labor-intensive than producing the video in the first place. Here are some things that must be considered:

- You will have to find the places that specialize in mailing lists targeted to your audience. Some lists are very specific, others more general: colleges, universities, professional groups, political organizations.
- You will have to make your own dubs, jacket covers, and labels.
- You will need promotional materials and flyers. Distributors generally provide the catalogs, press releases, postcards, bios, synopses, production stills, festival entries, and advertising. You will have to produce all this by yourself—and bear the costs.

Skip Blumberg promotes his own videos as well as using the standard distribution organizations. This one is for ''Women of the Calabash.'' Left to right: Madeleine Yayodele Nelson, Ahmondylla Best, Pam Patrick, and Ti'ye Giraud. (Courtesy Skip Blumberg)

A promotional piece for What Does She Want, *a home video series produced by the Video Data Bank. (Courtesy Video Data Bank)*

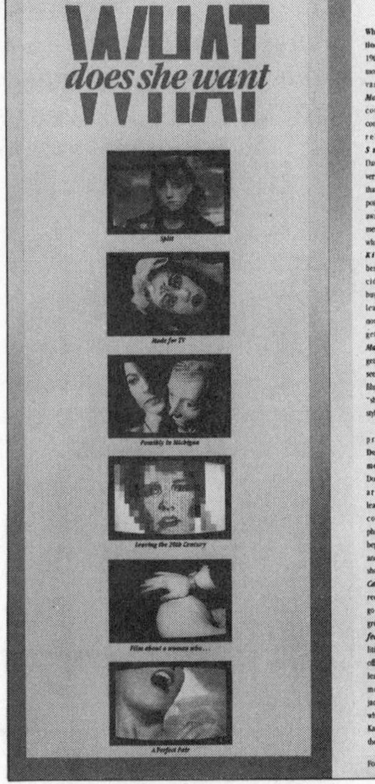

We are not sugar and spice and everything nice

program one, 80 minutes

What Does *She* Want reveals many different views of relatedness and relationships. *We are not sugar and spice and everything nice* neatly counters the 19th century family album. But instead of still and silent images pieces of dialog and movement disrupt the picture. The "album's" meaning is no longer secure but relevant. In **Ilene Segalove's *The Mom Tapes*** the messy room becomes a visual metaphor for the complications of a mother-daughter relationship. **Mindy Faber's *Suburban Queen*** contrasts David Byrne's or Jonathan Demme's versions of suburban life. Rather than poking sarcastic fun at the woman locked in a split-level, *Suburban Queen* poignantly evokes a daughter's longings. **Ardele Lister's *Split*** is a portrait of a runaway. She's angry, ironic, and cool; a girl who handles the pain of rejection as if it were merely a nuisance. **Branda Miller's** mock-rock video ***That's It Forget It*** suggests what is possible when a girl decides to invent herself. **Fronza Woods'** slapstick ***Killing Time*** asks, "What will the best-dressed teen wear to her suicide?" Next, an American family buys a **Chevy**. The generation that learned to read with Dick and Jane now discovers the joys of busing together. In **Max Almy's *Modern Marriage*** a head basking in the sun gets shot through with works. "He's perfect," a female voice proclaims, and he now seems to bask in her words. In ***This Charming Couple***, directed by blacklisted filmmaker **Willard van Dyke**, "the couple" have delusions about who "he" and "she" really are and can be, which eventually lands them in divorce-land American-style.

This Charming Couple

Modern Marriage

Bad Attitude

program two, 90 minutes

Does questioning anything mean you've a bad attitude? Does the death instinct underly the arms buildup? When a political leader is born, is this birth as constructed as "woman," to paraphrase Simone De Beauvoir? What's inevitable and what's preventable? ***Bad Attitude*** begins with a **JFK Campaign Ad**, reminding us of the father figure the camera loved, and the assassination that rocked America. ***Suzanne Suzanne*** by **Camille Billops** shows the dark underside of a seemingly happy Black middle class family. Next a ***Campaign Ad* for Ronald Reagan**: He ran on a platform that credited him with reducing California's debt, but will go down in history as creating the greatest U.S deficit. **Max Almy's *Perfect Leader*** casts a critical eye at political imagemaking. A soothing offscreen voice directs the would be leader, who with each command metamorphoses from suit to leather jacket, from coy to bold. The 1972 **Nixon Campaign**: another irony from the man who brought us Watergate. **Mary McFerran's *Homage to May 19*** dramatizes the Kathy Boudin story: a Weatherman who went underground in the 70's and surfaced in the Brinks robbery. A dangerous woman or committed idealist? **LBJ's** campaign for

JFK's Political Campaign Ad

Perfect Leader

For ordering information — Call toll free 1-800-634-8544

- Don't forget postage. Rising rates mean that large mailings can add to your costs.

Nevertheless, artists willing to put in the time and effort have found ways to distribute and promote independently. Ayoka Chenzira, who produced *Secret Sounds Screaming*, did all her own promotion, designing her brochures on a Macintosh computer, reproducing them on a laser printer, making direct contacts with potential buyers, and even setting up tables at community events to sell her videotapes. She commented in an interview with *The Independent*:

> *They're small nook and cranny places, but when you put them all together they mean a lot. Most distributors aren't good at narrowing down the markets. They might go into the women's market, which is broad, but they don't break down to psychology departments, sociology or music, looking at all the possibilities. I have the time to do that.*

Steve Roszell (*Writing on Water* and *Other Prisoners*) has produced tapes that are being used by the corrections departments in various states across the country. *Other Prisoners* was distributed using such mailing lists as the newsletter readership of the Academy of Criminal Justice Universities. Roszell duplicates his promo pieces at the local copy store. Since VHS dubs cost very little these days, he finds that he makes about 100 percent profit on his sales.

THE FINANCIAL REALITIES

With the number of videos now being produced, and with the limited markets for those tapes, the income levels of video artists seem microscopic when we compare them with the salaries offered to new lawyers just out of school or the income reported by Wall Street brokers. The total billing for one year for the top two distributors, Video Data Bank and EAI, was somewhere around $150,000 each. The top artists are lucky if their annual income tops $7,500. Juan Downey reported to *The Independent* that he had made about $5,000 the previous year through EAI rentals and closed-circuit sales, and another $5,000 for broadcast sales. Bill Viola and Robert Ashley, distributing through The Kitchen, generally report between $6,000 and $8,000 per year.

Royalties vary, and even then, the distributor often requires you to pay expenses that cut into even the modest amounts that are due you through sales and rentals. For example, you may be required to provide all or some of the dubs, or contribute to publicity expenses. Some distributors do only general mailings, listing all the tapes that are available, leaving the target mailings to the artist. It is a constant complaint in the industry. So a 65 percent or 70 percent royalty, which looks good at first glance, might well come down to half that when the expenses are met.

When it comes down to splitting fees, again, the figures vary, but they're generally in the following ranges:

- On nonbroadcast rentals, the split is usually 50/50, but it can go to as much as 70/30, with the distributor taking the larger amount.
- On nonbroadcast sales, the split can run from 50/50 through 60/40 up to 70/30.
- For broadcast income, the artist may benefit, with royalties going from 20/80 (rarely) to 50/50.

Whichever direction you decide to take with the distribution of your work, you must remember one important thing: You ain't gonna get rich!

INTERACTIVE VIDEO AND THE ARTIST

Most of us having been talking back to the television screen since the first black-and-white sets forced their way into our living rooms and our lives. Who has not "talked back" to a commercial, either vocally or by switching it off or changing channels? Gradually, we became part of the picture on the screen.

The simplest example of interactive video is the television camera in the appliance store window that catches us as we walk by and then shows us on a screen. In the world of video art, an early gallery installation by Frank Gillette and Ira Schneider called *Wipe Cycle* (1969) used closed circuit cameras and television monitors to involve visitors as both audience and participants in the work.

Early experiments with QUBE in teaching and shopping have developed into interactive video systems in department stores, in commercials and training, in government programs, and in schools. In addition, the development of laser videodisc technology and scanning infrared mechanisms like the Carroll Touch Panel, which allows a viewer to touch the monitor and change the input of the laser disc stacks, has opened up whole new avenues of expression for the video artist. And, though newspapers continue to call them "adult video games," interactive video art displays are far from games and are probably the most exciting developments in the field. The boundary between the viewer and the television screen is no more. Exhibitions have now taken on dimension, and if space allows, the installation can be complex and occasionally very large.

In an exhibition at the Equitable Gallery of the Whitney Museum in New York, Buky Schwartz's *Video See Saw* was actually a sculpture that included steel beams, two mirrors, a video camera, and two video monitors. The viewers were invited to move the armature, thus moving into the picture shown on the two arms of the armature. As each person walked into camera range, the ''sculpture'' changed. It is no different, in effect, than the store window camera that catches passersby by surprise.

In another unusual piece at the same exhibition, Curt Royston used an acrylic and oil painting of a room, a ceiling fan, and a video camera and monitor. The painting and the fan were projected onto a screen placed across the room. On the screen was the painted image of the room, the actual circulating fan—and the visitor. The screen became the reality, not the actual painting/sculpture, and the viewer became part of it.

Both these examples represent the simplest form of interactive art video. However, new technologies, especially laser discs, have expanded horizons of filmmakers and video artists alike. A recent exhibition at The Kitchen, a performance gallery in New York City's Chelsea district, reflects the current state of the art. Called *The Erl King* (''Erlkoenig''), it was developed by Grahame Weinbren and Roberta Friedman and is a collection of interlocking stories, images, texts, musical pieces, and thematic fragments centered around Goethe's narrative poem that was set to music by Schubert. Prior to the exhibition at The Kitchen, the work had been featured at the Museum of Contemporary Art in Los Angeles, the Whitney Museum Biennial in New York, and the Jewish Museum.

The installation was described, correctly, as a piece of gymnasium equipment. In the darkened room, the viewer is able to control and change and see the story in an unlimited series of sequences and track changes, depending upon where the screen is touched and at what point in the story. As Weinbren explains:

> *Working in the medium is like editing in three dimensions with the results made to look like a linear film. The track is continuous, but the length of the subject can be made to last four minutes, the actual length of the song, or up to twenty minutes by slow motion and the interactive total control of the viewer.*

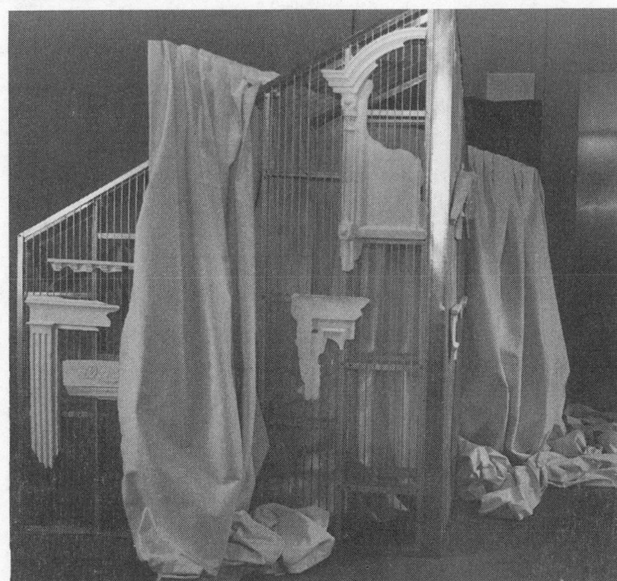

The interactive "Erl King" installation at the Jewish Museum in New York (Courtesy Grahame Weinbren)

A scene from "The Erl King," in which the viewer controls the images, the sound, and the speed of the story through laser disc technology. (Courtesy Grahame Weinbren)

Slow motion and still frames, all contribute to the time it takes to see the work. You're not bound by a specific length of time from beginning to end. As a viewer, you can escape structured time, for you are also a participant. Weinbren explains:

> *It's like driving your car through the city. The streets are laid out in a particular pattern, but you, the driver, determine just where you want to make your turn.*

When you begin to combine laser videodisc systems, videodisc players controlled by microcomputers, infrared touch screens, and the imagination and dedication of people like Weinbren and Freidman, suddenly the experience changes for those of us who sit down to watch and to participate.

- Touch the lower right corner and the German song is translated into English.
- Touch the rest of the screen and the song is illustrated.
- Touch the backup levels and you are taken to yet another branch, leaving the song behind.
- Don't touch the screen and you will be returned to watch the performer.

Roberta Friedman, commenting on the fact that you never get the same thing twice, says:

Director Grahame Weinbren with cinematographer Anthony Forma during the filming of "The Erl King." (Courtesy Grahame Weinbren)

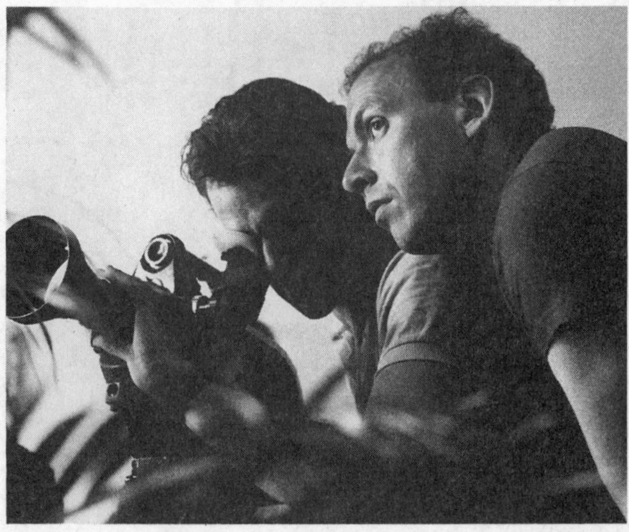

Producer Roberta Friedman on the set. (Courtesy Grahame Weinbren)

> *It's like the Changeable Charlie children's game, where you change the nose and the eyes and you get a different face each time. It's still a face you're creating, but with lots of variation and a theme.*

The Erl King, which took five years to produce, has created a new path for art video. It bridges the fine line between experimental film and video. Though it was shot on film and transferred to disc, a whole new computer language known as Limousine had to be invented in order to design the work. The raising of funds took a long, long time. (Friedman says, ''After all, we don't have the money. We're not AT&T!'') Eventually, the funding was provided by the National Council for the Endowment of the Arts, the New York State Council on the Arts, and Valley Filmworks/The Buckeye Trust. Funds for the installation at The Kitchen, where I saw it, were contributed by the New York City Department of Cultural Affairs. Avant-garde artist Robert Longo, for example, has begun directing commercials. He has long been known for his work on music videos for bands like New Order, Megadeth, and Golden Palominos. With the technology becoming so sophisticated and exciting, there will be people who will go the other way—from commercials into art video—or who will straddle the fields.

CHAPTER TWELVE

FESTIVALS AND AWARDS

ALL RULES appear in boldface. RULES must be followed or entry will be disqualified. *STANDARDS, in regular typeface, should be adhered to and any deviation may adversely affect an entry's score.*

Call for Entries
Cable Excellence Awards

However modest most filmmakers and video producers try to be, there is no doubt in my mind that we are justly proud of the festival awards that line our walls (or crowd our drawers and closets after the walls are filled). Just walk into the reception area of almost any production company. Notice the plaques and certificates—everything from an Academy Award nomination to a certificate of entry for some obscure festival, signifying nothing more than the fact that the person or group had entered the competition but had won nothing. These are marvelous for the struggling ego and have a wonderful impact on potential clients.

Apart from ego, there are good reasons to look into the festival world for your video work. Attending a festival gives you a good idea of who is doing what in your particular area, and the types of sponsors who are involved in the support and exhibition of video. Some festival sponsors are also corporate video producers (for SONY and Eastman Kodak, for example). Festivals give you a close look at the range of potential categories for your type of work (American Film & Video Festival and CINE, to name but two).

Festivals provide opportunities to network, to meet your competitors in an area of mutual interest, as well as some of the judges, many of whom may be important guests at that festival. You won't be able to ask them for a job, but you certainly can learn from their seminars, speeches, and informal chats. For example, the Sinking Creek Festival (now in its twentieth year in Nashville, Tennessee) has long featured such luminaries as Barbara Kopple, George Stoney, Faith Hubley, Les Blank, Stan Vanderbeek, Hilary Harris, and Ed Emshwiller.

If you are applying for a grant, festival awards are a plus, and there is no doubt that they are impressive to potential clients. All of us eventually become what the newspapers call "an award-winning producer," for if we enter enough festivals, there's a very good chance that we're going to win *something* at some time. It can't hurt.

A major problem, however, is knowing just which festivals to enter and which ones to pass up. The proliferation of festivals around the world has created an almost impossible choice, not to mention an almost impossible task of listing them all. At one time, there were film festivals. Eventually, their names changed and they became film and video festivals. The final evolution gave us video festivals, dedicated solely to the new technology.

There are publications that attempt to give a complete listing of all the domestic and international festivals; an awesome task to be sure. Currently, there are two good sources: *AIVF Guide to International Film and Video Festivals* (by Kathryn Bowser). Originally compiled from the columns of *The*

The only complete guide to festivals around the world.

An entry form for the CINE event held twice each year. Rules and regulations vary for each festival, as do entry fees.

97547 GOOD PRINTERS, INC., BRIDGEWATER, VA

Council on International Nontheatrical Events **CINE**

APPLICATION FORM

Closing dates: August 1 and February 1

PLEASE USE CARBONS

IMPORTANT

1. Entry information on reverse of this (white) page.
2. Complete forms and **retain white copy.**
3. **Be sure information on both sides of colored copies is filled out.**
4. Return three colored copies to: CINE, 1201 16th Street, N.W., Washington, D.C. 20036 with fee.
5. **Do not send film or tape until requested.**
6. Accuracy concerning the legal names of corporations and organizations is absolutely essential as this information will be used in printing and indexing.

Title ______

Series title (if any) ______

Original: ☐ 8mm/S 8mm/☐ 16mm/☐ 35mm ☐ Video Tape Is this your first film? ☐ Yes ☐ No

Release prints: ☐ 16mm/☐ 35mm/☐ ¾" Tape/☐ VHS/☐ Beta/☐ 8mm Tape

Running time ____ minutes Color ☐ B & W ☐ Sound:Music & Effects only ☐ With narration ☐

Year & month of Completion ______ Year of release ______ Copyright date ______

Value of print for insurance and customs purposes (See reverse side, rule 23):
(Replacement value of print or type)

Production ______
(If Amateur, Please state. See reverse side of colored forms for definition and questionnaire

Address ______

Producer ______ Director ______

Screenwriter(s) ______ Sound ______

Editor ______ Composer of original music ______

Camera ______ Other credits (specify) ______

Sponsor (if applicable) ______

Address ______

Distribution Company ______
(If not yet assigned, please state)

Address ______
(Additional distributors may be listed on a separate sheet)

Has this program previously been entered in festivals? ______ Did it receive recognition? ______

Which festivals? ______

Is this program available in foreign language versions? ______ Which languages? ______

Purpose ______

Primary (target) audience ______

Synopsis (use space below, no separate attachments) ______

All correspondence will be directed to the name and address listed below:

Signature ______ Organization ______

Name (Typed) ______ Mailing Address: ______

Position ______

Telephone No. (______) City/State/Zip: ______

IMPORTANT — OVER

Independent, it was first published in 1988. The guide contains complete profiles, contacts, fees, and other critical information.

Directory of U.S. & International Festivals of Film and Video. First published in late 1989 by CINE (Council on International Nontheathrical Events, 1001 Connecticut Avenue, N.W. Suite 1016, Washington, D.C. 20036), it is a comprehensive guide for the film and video communities.

In addition, I strongly recommend joining AIVF (see chapter 11) so that you can check updated listings in *The Independent*. Other publications, including *Back Stage* and *Billboard*, also list updates of festivals around the world. Send for the festival entry blanks and begin to learn the requirements and categories.

U.S. FESTIVALS

Although no festival is typical in terms of entry requirements, the list that follows will give you some preliminary information on just where you can place your video.

THE AMERICAN FILM AND VIDEO FESTIVAL (920 Barnsdale Road, La Grange Park, IL 60525). Now in its thirty-first year, this is one of the most influential forums for documentaries and short films. It was formerly organized by the Educational Library Association, but a few years ago, the name was changed, as was the address for entry forms. In addition to screening entries for media buyers and programmers from universities, public libraries, media centers, museums, schools, hospitals, business, and industry, the festival offers one of the broadest lists of categories for the video producer. Since each category is eligible for blue ribbon and red ribbon awards, the chances of winning are good for the beginner, even though the competition is quite keen.

When choosing a category in which to enter your work, consider carefully. For example, the category of corporate image or public relations is one into which the "big" production money usually goes. Corporations with large budgets would most likely be found there. Thus, even though your work is an "image" film, it might be better placed in a smaller, more specialized category such as agriculture or motivation, if such listings exist. It thus becomes much easier for a beginner to win an award—the competition is generally less intense.

Remember, some categories overlap, but others are particular to individual festivals. Here are some examples taken from the latest entry form of the American Film and Video Festival: SHORTS SHOWCASE (15 minutes or less)

- Original/Adapted Short Subjects or Documentaries
- Animation (Cel, Puppet, Cut-Out, Sand, Clay, Computer)
- Humor and Satire (Animation/Live Action)

ARTS AND CULTURE
- Media Arts (Cinema, Television, Photography)
- Fine Arts (Painting, Sculpture, Architecture, History)
- Performing Arts (Music/Dance/Theater)
- Arts Biographies (Portraits of Fine/Performing Artists)

THE HUMANITIES
- Literature (Portraits, Biography, Criticism)
- Literary Adaptations (Drama, Docudrama, Portraits)

- Original Drama
- History and Society—U.S. and World
- Anthropology (Primitive/Ancient—Peoples and Cultures)
- Ethnic Studies
- Philosophy and Religion

THE WORLD AROUND US

- Lifestyles: Profiles and Community Portraits
- Nature and Wildlife (Animal Studies, Zoology, Natural Phenomena)
- Science and Technology (Space Science, Computers)
- Sports and Leisure

HUMAN CONCERNS

- Family Relations (Parenting, Family, Child Abuse, Child Development)
- Human Sexuality (Sexual Abuse, Preference, Gender Roles)
- Substance Abuse (Alcohol/Drug/Tobacco Addiction, Prevention)
- Mental Health (Psychiatry, Psychology, Treatments, Therapies)
- Special Needs—Elderly, Handicapped
- Health: General (Preventive Medicine, Trends)
- Health—AIDS (Education, Profiles)*

CONCERNS AND CONTROVERSIES

- Domestic Concerns (Current Events, Social Issues)
- Environment and Ecology (Pollution, Toxic Dumping, Acid Rain)
- The Political Process (Government, Political, Legal Issues)
- International Issues
  - Global
  - Africa
  - Latin America
- Nuclear Issues (Power, Arms Race, Nuclear War)
- In the Workplace (Employment, Unions, Industrial Safety)
- Women's World (Feminist History, Abortion, Changing Roles)
- Black Studies (History, Portraits, Social Issues)

CHILDREN AND YOUNG ADULTS (Children: ages 2 to 12. Young Adults: ages 10 to 18)

- Original Works for Children (Stories/Scripts)
- Literary Adaptations for Children (Dramatizations)
- Documentaries for Young People

*An example of how categories change or are added to the list each year.

- Original Works for Young Adults and Literary Adaptations for Young Adults

INSTRUCTIONAL MEDIA (Not to exceed 40 minutes in length)
- Arts and Humanities (Art Appreciation, Art and Music Instruction)
- Language Arts (Grammar, Writing Skills, Reading Comprehension)
- Social Studies: Elementary, Junior High, High School
- Natural Science: Elementary, Junior High, High School (Biology, Earth/Space Studies)
- Categories in Physical Science, Driver Education and Safety, Guidance and Values, Continuing Education, Professional Training and Health and Sex Education

FILM/VIDEO VANGUARD
- Film as Art (Nonnarrative, Experimental, Visual Essays)
- Video Art (Nonnarrative, Experimental, Visual Essays)
- Music Video (Performance or Conceptual Music Film/Video)

FEATURE FOCUS (65 to 130 minutes in length)
- Drama (Original Story or Adaptation)
- Profiles (Individual or Community Portraits)
- Social Issues (Current Events, Domestic Issues)
- International Issues (Global Concerns, International Relations)
- History and Society (Analysis, Criticism, Recreation)
- Docudrama (Actual Incidents or Persons)
- Music and Performance (Dance/Theater/Music)
- Family Features (Live Action or Animation)

PROFESSIONAL COMPETITIONS
- Public Service Announcements (30/60/90-second spots)
- Motivation for Business (Conference "Starts," Sales Motivation)
- Training (Management Skills, Sales)
- Sales Presentation (Product, Point of Sale)
- Corporate Image (Corporate ID, Public Relations)
- Public Information—Categories in Commercial and Nonprofit
- Travel and Tourism (Travelogues, Promotion)

HEALTH CARE PROFESSIONALS
- Health and Fitness (Nutrition, Exercise, Prevention)
- Safety and First Aid (Industrial, Home, CPR)
- Medical Treatments and Procedures (Reports, New Technologies, Applications/Pharmacology, Surgical Procedures)

- Continuing Education (Patient Care, Disease Control, Medical Breakthroughs, Malpractice, Legal Issues)

HOME VIDEO COMPETITIONS
- Children's Entertainment (Live or Animation)
- Performing Arts (Music/Dance/Theater/Opera)
- Documentary/Information (History, Profiles)
- Travel (Overviews of Cities/Countries)
- How To's/Instructional (Gardening, Auto Repair, Cooking)
- Health and Fitness (Exercise, Nutrition, Preventive Medicine)

STUDENT PRODUCTIONS
- Entries must have been produced while applicant was in high school or college

SINKING CREEK FILM/VIDEO FESTIVAL (Creekside Farm, 1250 Old Shiloh Road, Greeneville, TN 37743). Not only have I always loved this festival for its name, but along the way some years back, I got to know MaryJane Coleman, who has run it for twenty years. And so, I have become a fan because of its support for student and independent filmmakers and video producers. Its entry fees are modest, and the $7,500 in cash awards that it pays each year can go a long way to encourage beginners. I am not the only professional who has tried to support the event in my writing and in my contacts with others in the field. Sinking Creek is a perfect example of the small festival that has become well known in the film/video field, and its seminars and workshops have boasted many more names than those that I wrote about at the beginning of this chapter. The cash awards may be modest, but they help to embellish a resume sent to potential employers or clients.

ITVA VIDEO FESTIVAL (6311 North O'Connor Road, LB-51, Irving, TX 75039). Categories include employee communications, interactive video, sales/marketing, information, public service, public relations, and training. The thing I like most about this festival is that all entries receive a written evaluation, whether they win or not.

The festival culminates in an awards ceremony on the final night of the annual international conference. More than 2,500 entries from around the world are submitted. The competition is open to professionals, but there are also Special Achievement and Student Achievement awards.

THE MONITOR AWARDS (The ITS, 990 Sixth Avenue Suite 21E, New York, NY 10018). The interesting thing about this festival is that it recognizes achievement not only in categories like music video, television programming for children, sports, and news documentaries, but it also honors individuals: directors, editors, lighting directors, camera operators, directors of photography, computer art designers, computer technical directors, special effects designers, and audio mixers. The most recent competition brought in almost 6,000 entries.

There are hundreds more festivals, so I would suggest that you stay on the lookout for some of the more specialized ones, as well as those that may take place in your own community. Here are some of the more interesting competitions:

- *Vision of U.S.* A video contest administered by the American Film Institute and sponsored by the Sony Corporation. Categories include fiction, nonfiction, and experimental.
- *Various student competitions*. Usually, student competitions are open only to those currently enrolled in communications, film, or video courses. Competition information is generally available through high schools and colleges in almost every part of the country. Student competitions are so numerous that I couldn't even begin to list them—check your school bulletin board to see which ones are currently being held.
- *New York Independent Film and Video Expo*. In existence for over twenty years, it is designed to recognize the wide variety of independently produced works.
- *Water Pollution Control Video Festival*. Possibly *the* classic example of specialized events devoted to video. Held as part of the California Water Pollution Control Association annual conference, it includes categories in safety, operator training, and public education.
- *Local and community festivals*. The Downtown Community TV Center in New York City recently ran its own festival of video work, with a special showing of high school student tapes. About 50 miles outside of New York, Suffolk County ran a film and video competition that garnered over 200 entries from as far away as England, the Netherlands, and California. The awards totaled $7,500 in cash, scholarships, and merchandise, and the winners were the subject of a thirteen-week series on the county PBS station, Channel 21.

Keep in mind that even the more suburban and rural areas of our country are, today, very much involved with both film and video. In Suffolk County, New York, for example, where the local festival was held, commercial film and video producers pumped over $40 million into the economy in one year, totaling 150 shooting days. Both the films *Wall Street* and *Masquerade* used Suffolk locations for sequences, so it is not too unusual to see areas outside

Hollywood and New York beginning to pay attention to their homegrown talents.

INTERNATIONAL FESTIVALS

If you think there are great and uncounted numbers of domestic festivals, wait until you begin to scan the list of those that are held overseas. The most famous names come up time and time again: Oberhausen and Annecy (not to mention the hype extravaganza of the feature world, Cannes). Film and video festivals have proliferated wildly, and more cities that sponsor festivals are added every year: Hong Kong, The Hague, Locarno, San Sebastián, Montbéliard, Haifa, Toronto.

Entries, shipping problems, deadlines, rules and regulations, all can complicate the international festival scene. Entries for international festivals can also be expensive and time consuming. There is a fairly simple way to get your feet wet in foreign competition, assuming that your video can first overcome the barrier of domestic competition. The Council on International Nontheatrical Events (CINE) runs a semi-annual competition in Washington, D.C., with many of the same categories used by the American Film and Video Festival:

Agriculture
Amateur
Animation and Children
Arts and Crafts
Business and Industry
Documentary
Education
Entertainment/Shorts
Environment/Nature
History
Medicine
Oceanography
Persons
Public Health
Safety and Training
Services
Sports
Travel

In addition, there are special categories for amateurs and students.

At the Washington competition, winners receive CINE Golden Eagle awards for their work. The festival enters its video and film winners in international competitions, where they can vie for additional prizes and awards. For some filmmakers and video producers, this has been their introduction to the international film and video community. From here they have gone on alone to garner prizes and recognition.

Some festivals are by invitation only, such as the Worldwide Video Festival in The Hague, Netherlands. This noncompetitive event is more a viewer's festival than a video contest. It is funded by the Dutch Ministry of Culture, the city of the Hague, and Sony Corporation. The program staff scours the world for entries.

RULES OF THE GAME

In choosing which festivals to enter, there are a number of considerations that must be taken into account, not the least of which is just what it's going to cost to enter your tape.

FEES. Entry fees vary considerably, but typical charges are $12 for tapes one to ten minutes in length, $20 for ten to twenty minutes, $30 for twenty to forty minutes, $40 for forty to sixty minutes, and $75 for tapes over ninety minutes in length. Major festivals (CINE, American Film and Video Festival) can charge up to $140, depending on tape length.

Generally, there are special entry fees for students, which can be less than half the normal entry fee for professionals, though they still may run as high as $50 per entry. If you should go the CINE route and win a Golden Eagle, you will be required to pay the extra entry fees for the international festivals they select and to provide ¾-inch dubs in the proper format.

Local and regional festivals, especially community-run events, are sometimes available to video producers at no charge, or at worst, for a token fee to cover the cost of mailings.

FORMAT. Most festivals now require ¾-inch format, though some do accept VHS. Up until last year, Sinking Creek was limited to 16mm film, and their move to film/tape again shows how the changing world affects every aspect of our field. For international festivals, format is particularly important, since not all are equipped to screen NTSC. Make sure you inquire thoroughly.

In an article in *The Independent*, video artist Jeffrey Kimball reported from the 1986 Venice Film Festival that he had asked in advance whether or not the organizers would provide projection according to U.S. NTSC standards. He was told that they would. Later he found that although they did have a compatible NTSC deck, they did not have an NTSC-compatible projection unit! As a result, his four screenings, already scheduled and publicized, had to be canceled. Finally, two days later, Kimball tracked down a 16mm print in Rome and finally got his screening, but with a greatly reduced audience, of course. His weary comment: "I was once again reminded of Murphy's Law."

SHIPPING. Most festivals require that you wait until you are notified before sending off your videotape. Usually, they require first-class postage or UPS shipment and they will not accept collect packages (no matter how famous you've gotten to be!). Pay attention to the requirements for marking your videocassette case and the videocassette itself. Some festivals require that there be only one entry per carton, even if you are competing in several categories. It also pays to insure your package, since most festivals disclaim any responsibility for loss.

DEADLINES. Look carefully at the dates for entry blank submission as well as for delivery of the sample videotape. Make sure your choice of shipping will meet that deadline, since entries are rejected out of hand if they arrive late.

Some other requirements to look for:

- U.S. citizenship
- Membership in the sponsor organizations (for example, the National Academy of Cable Programming)
- Nonrefundable entry fees that must accompany the application

Even though you have chosen a category in which you think you stand the best chance, most festivals reserve the right to change your designation and place your entry in a category they deem more appropriate.

There's no doubt that your first experience in the festival world will be a good one, even if you only receive a certificate that says that your entry was actually shown to an audience. For even that first certificate of participation can look good covering the crack in the bedroom wall.

No matter how many years we have spent in the field, no matter how blasé we say we have become, how jaded they accuse us of being, the notification that we have won still brings a thrill to those of us who have worked on the project as a team. The latest one for our small company, a lovely bronze plaque from the Columbus Film and Video Festival for *The Story of Juan Diego*, has taken its place on the wall. It seems that there was yet another crumbling piece of plaster that needed covering . . .

CHAPTER THIRTEEN

SCHOOLS AND TRAINING

I should give some background on what's happening in journalism education and broadcast education on college campuses. The reason we set up a course in corporate television at the University of Kansas was that we noticed that our graduates were going into corporate television instead of going to work for broadcast stations. Or, they were going to work for stations for two or three years and then going into corporate television. So, we figured this is stupid. Why don't we just offer a course in corporate television and shorten the market curve. And that's what we did.

Linda Lee Davis
University of Kansas
ITVA Conference, Las Vegas

There was a time when no one went to school to learn "communications." Instead, you learned on the job, by wrapping cable, running for coffee, and listening in awe as crew members told war stories. This may still be the best way to learn, but the rules have changed considerably.

Without a doubt, the four most important communications schools have been the University of Southern California, New York University, the University of California at Los Angeles, and Columbia University. But look at the others, and don't denigrate them: there are about 1,200 communications programs in the country today with well over a hundred thousand matriculated students. (NYU alone boasts over 1,000 undergraduate and 200 graduate students in its communications school.) Northwestern University, Boston University, Emerson College, Temple University, the University of Pennsylvania, and Syracuse University all offer fine programs. They have helped to change the rules, giving today's graduate a far better chance of getting a good reception from the industry than ever before.

With the explosion of videotape, the rules have changed once again. Along with the 1,200 university programs, hundreds, if not thousands, of other courses, degree programs, industry education seminars, lectures, and workshops have begun to compete for students. For the beginner, the choices can be overwhelming. Which school or course should you choose? Indeed, should you choose *any* school or course? Or should you get a job first and *then* choose a school or course in order to expand your horizons? Let's say you do choose to go to school. If there are thousands of courses offered, which ones will help the most?

I suppose the key question is: Will going to school help you get a job? As my grandmother used to say when she couldn't give a definite answer, "It depends." I telephoned Don Blank, who is director of television and photography operations at Georgia Pacific in Atlanta. His operation is run both as an in-house production unit and as a profit center for outside work. The staff consists of fourteen people. Blank gave some tips on starting out.

BREAKING DOWN THE DOORS: A TALK WITH DON BLANK

Well, are students breaking down the doors after they graduate?

"They're pounding down the doors! Unfortunately, they don't know anything. It's worse than that—they don't know that they don't know anything. I just don't believe they're being taught what they need to be taught in the undergraduate studies in most of your colleges. Most colleges and universities are not teaching what students need to know to actually get into the business, to actively participate in the business."

For example?

"Well, one of the students who has interned here had never heard of SMPTE time code, and this was a senior. So, I had the opportunity to meet with the professors and I made a comment about that. I told them, 'This student doesn't know what SMPTE time code is.' And one professor said, 'Well, we don't teach it.' And I said, 'Why not?' And he said, 'Because we don't have equipment that uses SMPTE time code, so we don't teach it.' I said, 'But the whole world revolves around SMPTE time code, so even if you don't have it, you could at least explain what it is.' And he said, 'We don't bother because we're teaching these students for the long run to be managers of television production, not camera operators or tape editors!' Well, you're never going to get to management until you work your way up, starting as a camera operator or as an editor!"

Where do you learn what you really should know?

"Well, we find that most of the people who work here are coming out of the West Coast colleges rather than the East Coast and tech schools. We seem to get great people out of the California school systems, out of the Oregon schools, and out of the Washington schools. We're also finding that some out of the Midwest are pretty good. But in the East, they seem to be lacking."

Where do you see the differences?

"The main difference we seem to find is that the schools that really have an active commitment to television and video as a profession have built broadcast facilities there. They have mobile units there, they're doing local sports. They're out doing something rather than just teaching it. And they're all using professionals in the industry to support their teaching staffs. They're actually working in the industry."

This conversation with Don Blank covers all the salient and critical elements about schools and training. I'd like to expand on each point in order to help you choose the school or training program that will help give you direction in your education and your entry into the industry.

COLLEGES AND UNIVERSITIES

Even if you are already out of school, have had two careers and are changing again, or plan to take some continuing education courses, I urge you to read what follows, since the parameters are just as important for the graduate as for the freshman, just as critical in the selection of one course or seminar as of a four-year program.

SCHOOL LISTINGS

The original "bible" was the *American Film Institute Guide to College Courses in Film and Television*. It is now published by Peterson's Guides (7th edition, P.O. Box 2123, Princeton, NJ 08540). Although certain listings may be out of date, you can get a pretty good idea of types of programs offered, equipment available for student work, degrees (if any), course titles, scholarships, and above all, faculty. Another critical area to look for is the school commitment in terms of philosophy versus production, studio work versus location.

Schools should offer "hands on" experience for best results. Instructor Doug Eisen in the Video Production Workshop of Film/Video Arts with some of his students. (Photo: Paule Epstein)

AREAS OF INTEREST

There is a whole range of video production jobs that are exactly paralleled in film. Directing is essentially directing. Scenic design, makeup and hair, writing, even cinematography and production management are quite similar and are typical "crossover" jobs. It takes a casting director the same time, effort, and talent to find actors and actresses for video as it does for film, and the actors and actresses themselves couldn't care less whether the job entailed motion picture film or one-inch videotape (or live television or stage). Five or ten years ago, the jobs were much more blended or hyphenated. But videotape is gradually maturing and job categories today are more rigidly structured and less flexible. Knowing this is important, of course, in both choosing your school and getting a job (see chapter 14).

I would strongly suggest finding a college or university that teaches both film and tape, since the fields intermesh and will continue to do so. Even if your primary career goal lies in video or television production, just remember my grandmother's advice: "It can't hurt!" You can certainly major in videotape production and postproduction, and then take some elective film courses to get the "feel" of the entire picture in communications today.

COMMITMENT

Ideally, the school should have a commitment to video and to the field as it exists in the "outside world." Does it spend more money for the football team than for the students in the communications field? Has it expanded its commitment as the field has grown? This is an area worth investigating if and when you get to the point that a personal visit is in order or when you speak to someone who is doing the final recruitment for the school. It also doesn't hurt to speak to some of the undergraduates or graduate students during your visit to the campus.

TECHNICAL EQUIPMENT

This is an even more critical area than it ever was in film, since video equipment and technology change almost as rapidly as dress codes on campus. If you recall, Steve Goodman mentioned in an earlier interview that by the time he had graduated from school, all the technological equipment in the videotape field had changed. Find out what equipment is available and is being taught. Is the school keeping up to date? Learning videotape editing and production on outmoded equipment is of little value when you get out and have to face an unfamiliar piece of technology.

HANDS-ON WORK

Make sure the school has enough equipment and allows enough time for you to work on your projects. There are many schools that offer editing facilities, but not enough to let each and every student spend a sufficient amount of

The on-line editing room at Film/Video Arts. Kamala Washington (seated) and Rosemary Abitabile work at the final edit stages of a video project. (Photo: Paule Epstein)

time on the equipment to become proficient. The same holds true with cameras, lighting equipment, and special effects computers, such as the Chyron or the Paintbox. Check to find out if you can work with some of the more sophisticated technology in your off time. Some of the most successful geniuses in video have made their marks with work done at 3 A.M.

INSTRUCTION

Are the teachers at the school actually working in the field? Or are they video philosophers? One of the advantages of schools located in major production centers is that they can generally recruit at least a part of their teaching staff from the industry that surrounds the area. Schools like NYU and USC, for example, boast some of the best-known teachers in the field. With videotape, with the industry spreading to every section of the country, even the smaller schools can now offer part-time professorships to local, active video producers and technicians.

You might also check to see if there are courses offered (by professionals) in adjunct subjects that may not seem very glamorous at first, but that are more important to your getting a job than your studies in editing or production: corporate and entertainment law, copyrights, finance and accounting, marketing and distribution, promotion, publicity, management, music, advertising—even studies in ethics, aesthetics, and art appreciation.

A VIDEO SAMPLE

If you have attended a school for four years, and you have been at a fairly well-equipped institution with a commitment to the industry and your future—*and* if, during that time, you did not make an effective, professional, personal, interesting sample video, then you have wasted your time! My feelings about this could not be stronger.

Student sample videos have opened doors for their producers. My own production manager, Sally Simmons, was "discovered" by me when she was a student at New York's Global Village through her sample videotape documentary.

Many schools find ways to tie in with professional outlets, allowing students to participate in what will eventually become their sample videos. In Chicago, for instance, Columbia College, Loyola, Chicago State University, Governor's State University, and Northwestern all participate in a program that appears on local cable as "Music Alive." The schools produce music documentaries in cooperation with the Chicago Office of Film and Entertainment. The student production crews benefit from the experience, have the

Music video production takes more than just handling the camera. Students at the Art Institute of Atlanta Music/Business Video School learn to handle the 48-track sound equipment. (Courtesy Design Schools)

thrill of seeing their work on television, and acquire samples that can be shown to prospective employers.

WHO ARE THE GRADUATES?

The success of the school in placing graduates should have a lot to do with your choice. Not only does it show the "track record" of the school, but it also means that out there in the "real world" are people who might well be receptive to you when *you* finally graduate, since many of them come from exactly the same school. The old school tie of Harvard or Yale or Middlebury has always worked in business and government—and it certainly also works in video and television.

OTHER PATHWAYS

CONTINUING EDUCATION

Continuing education programs are available in schools across the country. For local colleges or universities, continuing ed courses have become an important source of income, and many programs now offer courses in video, covering all aspects of production and postproduction as well as finance, management, and promotion. Courses in home video production and distribution are also available. In some schools, it is easier to find professors and lecturers who are active in the field teaching courses in continuing ed, since they do not have to be tenured and can devote as little as two hours a week to their classes.

For the student, continuing ed has several advantages. First, courses can be selected individually and not applied toward a degree. This allows you to pick and choose according to your interests. Second, continuing ed offers networking opportunities and allows you to share experiences with others who want to make a major career move. This can be very supportive and enlightening.

There are even tax advantages for those who qualify under Treasury Regulation 1.162-5, which permits income tax deductions for registration fees and for travel, meals, and lodging costs if they are undertaken to maintain or improve skills required for your employment or to meet the specific requirements of your employer. Thus, if you are an employee of a corporation and work in the audiovisual department, you may very well qualify for a tax deduction for continuing ed courses.

The range of courses offered at most schools is incredibly broad. Certainly, not every school everywhere offers *every* course, but if the college or university doesn't offer what you want, there's a good chance that you can find it at one of the other teaching institutions or groups (see page 244). Here are just a few typical offerings chosen from selected catalogs:

Videotape Production Workshop
Special Effects and Computer Graphics
Directing
The Role of the Producer
Documentaries
The Business of the Music Business
Editing (Off-Line and On-Line)
Electronic Video Editing
Writing for Nonbroadcast Television
Writing for Television
Budgeting for Film and Video
Video Electronics
Corporate Video
Broadcasting and Film Law
Postproduction Sound

Art Direction for Film and Video
Cinematography
Producing a Commercial Spot
Cable TV Production
Experimental Video
Makeup for "Beauty and the Beast"

THE PRIVATE SECTOR

The preceding list is only part of what is now available to the beginner, the continuing education student, and the professional interested in learning about new technology and in keeping up with the constantly changing field. The offerings include complete and well-planned programs that cover a range of communications subjects, as well as specific courses of instruction about a single piece of video equipment, such as cameras or editing computers. The trade journals are filled with advertising and the mailbox overflows with information about courses that are now available. Sometimes the overabundance makes the choice of subjects difficult.

The list of available schools, courses, and seminars would fill its own book. The conventions, workshops, and professional conferences held each year would easily fill volume two. Whichever path you finally choose, whichever school or course you decide to take, be sure to investigate thoroughly. Ask a lot of questions, find out just what the registration fees include, whether or not financial aid or scholarships are available (should you need them), if there is some help finding a job after the course is completed, and which graduates are currently working in the field and at what jobs.

The places outside the colleges and universities that offer video instruction can be broken down into several major categories.

PROFESSIONAL. Many of these institutions are licensed by state departments of education and accredited by various associations and trade groups. Though some of them are geared to the professional and are very short term, others offer courses that take from one to two years to complete and are quite thorough in their coverage of the field.

For example, Education Management Corporation, for which I have produced several career guidance films/tapes on the subjects of fashion, art, and paralegal studies, expanded the curriculum at its six schools to cover the music business, including music video. The Music Business Institutes (a part of EMC's design schools) are now located across the country at the various EMC Art Institutes. (Write Education Management Corporation, 300 Sixth Avenue, Pittsburgh, PA 15222 for information on the school nearest you.)

Video production is a critical part of the curriculum, but following the advice of many of the professionals in the business who recommend a well-rounded education, the schools include a range of subjects important to everyone who decides to make video a career (such as some of the examples I've listed below). If you have read the interviews in this book carefully, you find that over and over again the advice is to broaden your scope: The camera can always be learned. It is the marketing people who become successful, the people who know how to sell, and the people who know and can put to use an overview of the industry who end up in management and holding the top jobs.

Just as an example, if you were to pursue a career in music video, you would certainly need to know about video production. In addition, you should probably learn about

Audio recording and production
Concert production
Broadcast media
Marketing analysis
Music promotion
Salesmanship
Publicity and public relations
Advertising
Business management
Copyright law
Contracts and negotiations
Communications
Business math
Resume preparation

Did the producers of Michael Jackson's "Thriller" have to know all that? You can bet your bottom dollar that they did! And, if you pursue any school program, you should be asking the questions that will let you know that you'll be learning about the *business* of videotape rather than the *glamour* of it (most of which doesn't exist, anyhow).

There are small and successful schools geared, for the most part, to the professional already active in video or television. Weynand Associates (6273 Callicott Avenue, Woodland Hills, CA 91367), which has been in business for a little under ten years, specializes in on-site training, going directly to the production company or facility to give in-depth, hands-on training in the operation of computerized videotape editing, VTRs, production switchers, and digital effects units. The company offers weekend courses and seminars as well as intensive forty-hour training sessions.

Although the company's advanced classes generally are made up of professionals, Weynand's videotape operations classes, taught in New York, Chicago, and Los Angeles throughout the year, attract about 60 percent who have no experience at all or who are college grads. The remaining 40 percent are off-line editors anxious to learn about one-inch editing—plus some producers, directors, and audio engineers.

These two examples are at opposite ends of the spectrum. There are many more organizations that fall in between. The Center for Media Arts, for instance (226 West 26th Street, New York, NY 10010), includes video courses as part of a broad training curriculum devoted to television, photography, graphics, audio, advertising, and commercial art. Here, too, the courses range from intensive production through repair and maintenance and the final job search.

Way up in Rockport, Maine, is a school that is supported by a great many corporate members of the industry, including Panavision, Eastman Kodak, and DuArt Video. The International Film and Television Workshop (Rockport, ME 04856),* which operates only during the summer, offers courses for people just entering the field as well as for working professionals who want to upgrade their skills. Besides being located in one of the most glorious natural areas in the world, the workshop features a staff of well-known professionals. Every film subject from production to the use of the Steadicam camera is covered. Courses in video include

Introduction to Video Production
Advanced Field Production
Camerawork for Video
Film Lighting for Video
Video Editing (Basic and Advanced)
Location Sound Recording

Recently, the workshop joined with ITVA to expand its corporate video courses and added the same subjects plus directing, design, and interactive video on the corporate nonbroadcast level. Courses generally run one to two weeks, and accommodations and meals are provided as part of the fee.

And those, of course, are but a few examples. A more comprehensive listing of the schools that are now advertising in the trade journals appears at the end of this chapter. Get ready to be overwhelmed. There are many of them!

NONPROFIT MEDIA CENTERS. Many of these are funded by state councils on the arts, by foundations, and by the National Endowment, as well as by local community cultural affairs departments. Some of them also receive a part of their funding from the corporate sector: television networks, banks, the motion picture industry. The media centers offer courses and provide equipment and space for young video independents who need to learn and to work on their own projects.

The nonprofit group Film-Video Arts (817 Broadway, New York, NY 10003) has a program that includes media training in production and postproduction as well as courses in scriptwriting, directing, and camera maintenance. In

*Some courses are also conducted in Ojai, California. Write for information.

addition, the group periodically presents screenings of films and videos. Its production rental equipment (subsidized for nonprofit projects and students) includes editing suites, video production packages, and lighting.

Such centers may take some searching out, since they generally do not have the funds to advertise extensively. Yet they offer the most perfect and economical opportunities for both learning and production of a sample project. Generally, too, their staffs are composed of local professionals who support the groups.

CORPORATE CLASSES. From time to time you'll read about a seminar that is sponsored by a major corporation. The Chyron Corporation, for instance, recently opened a three-classroom facility in Melville, New York, with additional classes held in Walnut, California, and at the sites of customer installations. Though they are geared to the professional technician, Chyron's four maintenance courses and five operator courses for the Chyron and the Scribe are appropriate for anyone with a knowledge of digital electronics techniques and microprocessor systems. They're good ones to keep in mind as you begin to get your experience in the field.

Other companies offer professional seminars and classes, which are generally announced in the trade papers and magazines. Eastman Kodak traditionally conducted professional seminars whenever it developed a new film stock, and it continued the programs when it entered the videotape field. JVC and its Professional Video Communications Division have also sponsored hands-on training workshops in nonbroadcast video production. I suppose that one of the things that tempted people to attend the JVC seminar held about a year ago is that the location for the workshop was the ski resort of Steamboat Springs, Colorado, and the modest fee charged to learn about JVC's newest equipment included instruction, all equipment, and materials—plus continental breakfast and lunch.

POSTPRODUCTION FACILITIES. More and more postproduction houses are teaching the craft of off-line and on-line editing during their downtime hours. There is one group in New York, for example, formed by a cooperative of producers who needed economical editing costs, that uses its studio as a classroom, and its control units, character generators, special effects generators, and audio mix boards as a perfect hands-on facility. One of the best things is that all students who complete the course can then use the facility at reduced rates.

If you live in an area where only a few editing facilities exist, you might try something else. Rather than waiting for a facility to look for you, you might try asking if it would give a course to a small group of students. It may well be something that the company never thought of doing.

Professional membership organizations in the video field have begun to offer courses specifically designed to teach the latest technologies. The Association for Computing Machinery's Special Interest Group on Computer Graphics (ACM/SIGGRAPH) conducts seminars and courses, and holds an annual conference on computer graphics and interactive techniques (ACM/SIGGRAPH, P.O. Box 95316, Chicago, IL 60694). Since the organization is now national, some of its best people have begun to offer specialized courses in the field of computer graphics.

Carol Chiani, president of the New York chapter, teaches at the City of New York Research Center, retraining union cartoonists in the discipline of computer graphics, as well as at the New School and at Pratt. However, she also teaches her own workshops, from one-day seminars to thirty-hour courses (Video Computer Animation Workshop, 503 Broadway, Suite 504, New York, NY 10012). I must say that her course title, for one brought up in the simple world of 16mm or 35mm, is rather awesome, but I'm certain those who have grown up in the world of computers will understand it all: *Introduction to Painting techniques and tools on a 32 bit, 16 million displayable colors paint system. Software, Lumena/32, Tips/32, Rio, Genigraphics P/24, paint system.*

The thirty-hour course covers:

Operating system and software overview, terminology
Freehand drawing, perspective, pixilation, scaling
Storyboard and animation techniques
Spatial and color transformations
Masking, embossing, image processing, stenciling
Airbrush, custom brushes, Anti-Aliasing, text
Transparency and overlays, color camera
Video digitizing

Note that here, too, as in all the disciplines of video, it is not a matter of sitting down at the computer and just "doing" it. The prerequisites are broad, even including such things as an "old-fashioned" lesson in freehand drawing.

COMPUTER GRAPHICS: A TALK WITH CAROL CHIANI

What was your background before you became involved with computer graphics?

"I was selling video equipment. I have an art background, and I like editing a great deal. I went to a SIGGRAPH show in Boston and that was it! I was gone! I saw the work being done there and I came back and said

to my boss, 'You've got to get involved in this technology. This is the way the editing suites are going to go.' So he got a system and I had to learn it by myself—there was no place to study it, absolutely nowhere. And then, as I was learning it, I also began teaching it, giving demos. My boss said, 'Get out of here. This is really what you want to do. Take the computer.' So I started courses basically because I wanted to learn. It's the same reason that I started SIGGRAPH in New York—because I wanted to join the organization. It's simple!''

And what about your students? What are their backgrounds?

''It runs the whole gamut. That's why it's difficult to teach a rigid curriculum, because the backgrounds they bring are so diversified, from one end of the spectrum to the other. It takes time to bring them to the same point because some of them will sit there and think that the computers will solve all their problems and they leave their brains at home . . . and so I say, please, please bring everything that you know, every talent, every experience that you have, bring it to the computer. I tell my students that anyone can be trained on a computer, but you really can't train them to understand design, I mean, unless you take classes in that.''

Must you be an artist in order to do computer graphics?

''Yes, but let me explain what I mean by 'artist.' The word transcends the art community. It goes into editors, graphic artists, illustrators, fine artists, programmers—everyone has this innate sense of art, this sense of aesthetics. I believe that we're all artists in some form or another—even scientists. I mean, the work that comes out of them—from mathematical equations—absolutely magnificent. I think mathematicians are frustrated artists and vice versa—because I think artists are frustrated scientists, so this technology bridges the two. If you're not an artist in the sense that I've described, then the computer becomes a very expensive bookend, because you need that creativity.''

Does a teacher have to keep up with the changing technology, I mean in updating the equipment constantly?

''(Laughs) I'd like to say no, but yes, you have to because the tools that [the students] need, the mythology of the language, the thought processes, are all dependent upon the equipment, so you try to get the equipment and/or the software which is most closely related with what's going on in the industry. The schools just put in courses because they

wanted to get in on this technology, and they're only recently upgrading their equipment."

Where do you find most of your students going when they have gotten their training?

"Generally the 3-D people go to the places that have the hardware, like the animation houses. My 2-D classes usually work for people like AT&T doing industrials, or NYNEX, or places like Exhibit Technology. There are jobs for them. What I'm hoping that my students understand is that they should be making their own applications. For instance, people who are experienced in the fashion industry—take it back to your industry and incorporate it there."

Do they just knock on doors? Write letters?

"No, most of it is networking. I would say that 90 percent of it is networking. For example, in SIGGRAPH the people who are involved in the organization are also involved in the industry. And 90 percent of the jobs that you're going to get depend upon personality, how you're going to get along, because it's such a team effort. It's really a very communal industry, so how you work with other people is top priority."

What about computer graphics shows and industry conferences?

"Certainly. And that's what SIGGRAPH does. Every year we have a lecture series and we get some very prominent speakers to donate their time."

Are they real places for people to learn or to network?

"Both. Both."

And it's all changing rather rapidly, isn't it? I mean, still changing.

"Yes. I had one woman—it was really funny. She said she used to go into a bar and conversations were like 'Where do you live? What's your birth sign?' And she says that now, if she and her friend go into a bar and she starts talking about computer graphics, there are about twenty men around her saying, 'I hear you're involved in computer graphics.' But the truth of the matter is that there aren't as many people as we think are out there. There's still a lot of education to be done."

LECTURES, SEMINARS, EXHIBITIONS, SPECIAL PROJECTS, AND WORKSHOPS

These exist in every major city in the country, at every conference and trade exhibition. They are sponsored by every professional organization, and are generally open to students, trainees, and beginners. Look for announcements in the trade papers and magazines. You'll find a wide range of lectures, seminars, exhibitions, special projects, and workshops offered. If you attend—even as a beginner—there are two distinct advantages to be gained: the actual learning, of course, *and* the chance to hear professionals speak and to network with them and with the other attendees.

If you can't travel to one of the conferences or seminars, or if the cost is too high, chances are that you'll spot something taking place near you if you keep looking carefully. For example:

AMERICAN FILM INSTITUTE (John F. Kennedy Center, Washington, DC 20566 or P.O. Box 27999, 2021 North Western Avenue, Los Angeles, CA 90027). The institute has become well known for its seminars, which are conducted across the country and led by some of the most impressive names in the field. Some of the seminars are specifically related to film, but others are "crossover" subjects (writing is writing). A past listing might give you an idea:

Directions on Directing
Filmmaking Grants: How to Finance Your Film and Video Idea
The Music of the Movies
Acting in TV Commercials
Publicity Strategies
Anatomy of a Made-for-TV Movie
From Script to Screen
Selling Your Film or Video Project to Pay TV and Home Video
Independent Film and Video
How a TV Network Works

AFI also conducts summer workshops in video, production, writing, and television, and sponsors an Academy Internship Program funded by the Academy of Motion Picture Arts and Sciences.

DIRECTORS GUILD OF AMERICA AND OTHER PROFESSIONAL ORGANIZATIONS. From time to time, DGA offers seminars on computers, HDTV, and other hands-on subjects. The guild's special projects will be of interest to you once you begin to work your way through the communications field, and many veteran directors (the author included) take advantage of the seminars to keep up with the technological changes.

The Broadcast Designers Association has held seminars in various cities on video production techniques, including postproduction, cable in-house design, and desktop publishing.

Post Effects in Chicago holds an annual open house, along with demonstrations on the technologies of shooting video, editing, and motion control.

Apogee Productions in California has conducted one-day programs for the UCLA Extension Program covering special effects: new bluescreen photography, integration of live with animation, computer graphics, HDTV, traveling mat techniques, and getting your production dollars on the screen.

In Seattle, Digital Post & Graphics has conducted a series of seminars covering the mock production of a sixty-second TV commercial, including digital editing, graphics, compositing, animation, and effects that use the Quantel, Harry, Encore, and Paintbox. These particular seminars were limited to professionals, but they are a good example of just what is available as you become active in the field.

Almost every media membership organization conference today includes video in one form or another. Some conferences are closed to outsiders (nonmembers), but I've always found that there's a way to get a ticket if you really want to attend: a friend in the industry, a supplier, an exhibitor, or someone your family once did a favor for. It's certainly worth a try since these conferences are an excellent way to keep up with new developments. I do have one word of warning, however. If you don't want your mailbox stuffed with brochures, booklets, circulars, and letters offering video equipment bargains, *don't* put your name on even one mailing list! Since all lists are sold to other organizations, filling out even one postcard will bring an avalanche of mail for the next year at least. (The author once made that mistake—and the deluge has not diminished two years later.)

INTERNATIONAL TELEVISION ASSOCIATION (6311 North O'Connor Road, LB-51, Irving, TX 75039). ITVA sponsors both local and national conferences on the subject of corporate television. These seminars cover a large range of subjects important to the beginner. ITVA's conferences provide some of the best networking opportunities that you can find in a field where everyone admits that contacts pay dividends. Some typical topics are:

Hiring the Right People—And Keeping Them
Supervising, Motivating, and Evaluating Creative People
Career Options for Professional Video Managers
Small Business Setup and Management

Getting the Best Young Video Pros
Beginning a Career Path in the Corporate Video Business

One of the seminars held at a recent ITVA conference in Las Vegas was titled: "What Do I Do Now That I've Graduated?" Although directed to college students and grads, it was just as valuable for career changers. Conducted by Donald Bis of Allstate Insurance, Ron Osgood of Indiana University, and Lee Vogel of Kansas City Life Insurance, it covered a range of informative subject matter:

I. Preparing for the job market while still a student
   When to begin
   Getting an edge
   Resources
II. Life in the ranks of the Learned Unemployed
   On becoming a statistic
   Daily schedule
   Relationships
   Professionalism
III. The real world
   Resume distribution
   Interviews
   Career considerations

VIDEO EXPO (c/o Knowledge Industry Publications, 701 Westchester Avenue, White Plains, NY 10604). An annual event for video communicators and professionals, it's sponsored by Knowledge Industry Publications. Video Expo features exhibitions of the latest technology, and seminars and workshops open to both the beginner and the working video expert in writing, production and postproduction, management, budgeting, lighting, and interactive video. In addition to sponsoring the event, Knowledge Industries publishes video reference books and magazines, including monthly technology and management publications and books on editing, computer graphics, and lighting techniques.

ACM/SIGGRAPH (P.O. Box 95316, Chicago, IL 60694). Someone once described attending SIGGRAPH's annual conference art show as "stepping into the museum of the future," since the most dramatic work done over the past year is on display. Seminars and workshops cover computer terminology, object-oriented computer graphics, and computer animation and design.

COMPUTER GRAPHICS SHOW (c/o Computer Pictures, 2 Village Square West, Clifton, NJ 07011). Sponsored by *Computer Graphics* magazine, this is an annual major event on the East Coast, with exhibitors including almost every category of computer manufacturer and segment of the industry: TV advertising, broadcast graphics, corporate video and training, business corporate graphics, and desktop publishing.

One of the most exciting seminars at the recent show in New York was on the subject of TV advertising and broadcast graphics. It featured the luminaries of the industry, all under one roof: Bob Abel, Phil Heffernan, Bruce Lyon, Alex Weil, Robert Greenberg, and Carl Rosendahl. Topics included:

Past, Present and Real World Future of Computer Graphics
Supercomputers and the Latest 3-D Software
The Designs of Network Television
The Integration of Graphics
The State of the Art and How to Use It

VISUAL COMMUNICATIONS CONGRESS (475 Park Avenue South, New York, NY 10016). The exhibition is sponsored by a group of industry magazines, including *Media Horizons* (same address). Seminars range from the legal aspects of video production to marketing, proposals, location production, postproduction, and special effects.

INTERNATIONAL COMMUNICATIONS INDUSTRIES ASSOCIATION (3150 Sprint Street, Fairfax, VA 22031). ICIA is a trade group of the professional communications products industry, and includes manufacturers, producers, agents, distributors, and educational and trade publications. It holds an annual convention and trade show called COMMTEX (Communications Technology Exposition). Topics covered in COMMTEX seminars include video production, multi-image, computer graphics, interactive video, and audio technologies.

From time to time, you will come across smaller organizations that sponsor seminars that might be of interest to you. For example, the International Center of Photography in New York has conducted a workshop called "Women in Video" that covers the history of women's video from the early seventies to the present.

You'll notice that even conferences have changed to include video, just as festivals have done. Indeed, I soon expect to see a promotion circular arriving in my already overcrowded mailbox heralding the next group of seminars being conducted by the American Film *and Video* Institute!

"DOWNTIME" ON-THE-JOB TRAINING One of the best learning experiences you can find doesn't come from a structured "course." Your first employers will probably allow you to use the video equipment during the company's "downtime"; that is, on your own time after hours. I can't recommend taking this opportunity strongly enough. Many beginners have made their samples during the night or over the weekends, and many of them have become proficient in computers like the Paintbox and Harry while the rest of the staff was home watching the Rose Bowl Game. All other suggestions aside, this is one of the best training opportunities open to you at the entry level in video. So use it!

PUBLICATIONS

There are hundreds of books that might go into a bibliography for any career guide. Some are very helpful, others are better left unread.

Books on video are just beginning to fill the shelves of bookstores and to be reviewed in trade magazines. When you are trying to decide which one to buy, ask yourself:

- Is it written by a professional who is working in the industry? Is it up to date on the latest technology?
- Is it specifically geared to video (such as electronic editing) or is it also applicable to film? In other words, will a lighting book or a book on writing be just as valuable to you no matter which industry it covers?

Many are found in the reference sections of your local public library or college library, particularly if the school has a communications program.

BACK STAGE TV FILM AND TAPE PRODUCTION DIRECTORY (Back Stage Publications, 330 West 42nd Street, New York, NY 10036). An excellent compilation of the names, addresses, and backgrounds of professional companies around the country. It lists film and videotape producers, post-production facilities, advertising agencies, equipment suppliers, and special effects houses.

KNOWLEDGE INDUSTRY PUBLICATIONS (701 Westchester Avenue, White Plains, NY 10604). Publications include:

The Home Video and Cable User
The Video Register
Home Video and Cable Yearbook
The Teleconferencing Resources Directory

The company publishes a constant stream of video-oriented books on specific subjects (ask for *The Video Bookshelf* catalog) and offers a Professional Video Book Club with discounts for members. Every so often you will also see an item describing the publication of a local or regional guide to video production or personnel. The Boston chapter of ITVA publishes just such a guide. Listings are free for ITVA members and $20 for nonmembers. Magazines are a perfect way to keep up with industry news, technology advances, even the gossip that accompanies any profession. Here is just some of what's available covering the complete range of disciplines.

A/V Video. Montage Publications, a Knowledge Industry Publications Company. Monthly. (25550 Hawthorne Boulevard, Suite 314, Torrence, CA 90505)

Back Stage. Complete service weekly for the entire industry. Back Stage Publications. (330 West 42nd Street, New York, NY 10036)

Business TV. TeleSpan Publishing Corporation. Quarterly. Specializes in corporate satellite television networks. (50 West Palm Street, Altadena, CA 91001)

Computer Pictures. Electronic Pictures Corporation. Bimonthly. Devoted to TV graphics, electronic effects entertainment, TV and broadcast graphics. (2 Village Square West, Clifton, NJ 07011)

Corporate Television. Media Horizons Inc. Monthly. Official magazine of ITVA. (50 West 23rd Street, New York, NY 10010)

E-ITV (Educational-Industrial Television). Broadband Publications. Monthly. "The Techniques Magazine for Professional Video." (295 Madison Avenue, New York, NY 10017)

Electronic Display News. Raceatron Inc. Bimonthly. Covers everything from baseball's Diamond Vision to interactive point-of-purchase kiosks. (1705 Joppa Road, Baltimore, MD 21234)

Film/Tape World. Monthly. Official publication of the San Francisco Film and Tape Council, covering Northern California. (P.O. Box 3390, San Mateo, CA 94403)

The Independent. Monthly. Association of Independent Video and Filmmakers. Possibly the most complete magazine for the independent video artist and producer. (625 Broadway, New York, NY 10012)

In Motion. Bimonthly. A regional film and video magazine that covers the mid-Atlantic production scene. (421 Fourth Street, Annapolis, MD 21403)

Millimeter. Monthly. A Penton publication. Covers all areas of film and video production, with emphasis on the commercial field. (826 Broadway, New York, NY 10003)

Post. Testa Communications. Monthly. Devoted exclusively to the post-production aspects of video. (25 Willowdale Avenue, Port Washington, NY 11050)

TeleSpan. Monthly newsletter on corporate satellite television industry. Does extensive market research in this field. See *Business TV* for address.

TV Technology. Monthly. Engineering news magazine devoted to broadcast, with some corporate video hardware news. (5827 Columbia Park, Suite 310, Falls Church, VA 22041)

Video Computing (The Journal of Interactive Video and Optical Storage Technologies). Monthly. Slick tabloid news format with color. (P.O. Box 3415, Indialantic, FL 32903)

The Videodisc Monitor. Monthly. Newsletter on videodisc developments and technology. (P.O. Box 26, Falls Church, VA 22046)

Videography. Media Horizons Inc. Monthly. Aimed at video producers in broadcast and nonbroadcast fields. See *Corporate Television* for address.

Video Monitor. Communication Research Associates Inc. Monthly. A newsletter with broadcast and business information for people in marketing and training. (10606 Mantz, Silver Spring, MD 20903)

Video Networks. Bay Area Video Coalition. Eight issues/year. Gives regional information for the independent. (1111 17th Street, San Francisco, CA 94107)

Video Systems. Intertec Publishing Corp. Monthly. Emphasizes technical and management systems in corporate video. (P.O. Box 12901, Overland Park, KS 66212)

Video Times. MPCS Video Industries. Quarterly. Covers trends in video as well as stories about people who are active in the industry. (514 West 57th Street, New York, NY 10019)

Visual Communications. Maclean Hunter Publications. Monthly. (777 Bay Street, Toronto, Ontario M5W 1A7)

After you've taken the courses and studied the books and worked until 3 A.M. to learn the equipment and paid your dues, is it all worth it? I mean, can you really then go out and get a job?

The answer is yes. If you really want to crack the industry, you'll find a way to break in somehow. Here is part of a letter that was written to me by Kevin O'Connell, who was a student in one of my classes. His statements are fairly typical in a field where nothing really is "typical" or "standard."

> *I wanted to let you know that school has paid off and I have been working in the television field for the last four months.*
>
> *The company I work for is called Sports News Satellite, a branch of Phoenix Communications. It's an entry-level position and most of my time is spent watching and logging sports telecasts. But along the way I have learned how to edit ¾-inch tape. I'm currently working on my third musical piece on baseball highlights and I've also cut several game highlight packages. Everything we produce at SNS is sent via satellite to over 150 TV stations around the country to be used on news programs.*
>
> *It's a growing company, and I'm aiming to be a producer by this time next year. To get to that point will involve many all-night work sessions and completely forgoing a social life, but I think it will be worth it.*

CHAPTER FOURTEEN

GETTING A JOB: WELCOME TO THE REAL WORLD

Original ads for help wanted page.
Credit: The Personnel Pool, Back Stage

DIRECTOR WANTED
We are looking for an established L.A. based director to Represent, out of our Hollywood office, in conjunction with the other talents we represent from Down Under. We are an aggressive organization with offices on both coasts, as well as an affiliate in Sydney, Australia. If you have an outstanding reel, an excellent attitude, and consider yourself a director who likes to bring something to the party, please contact us.
DUCK WEST
DUCK DOWN UNDER
1821 N. Canyon Dr.
Hollywood, Ca. 90028
(213) 465-6693

Producer/Bidder Wanted
Opportunity with growing production company for individual with min 3-5 years experience as line producer/bidder with established union (prefer Nabet) production house.
Send resume and salary requirements in confidence to:
Producer
Box #IPR 030687
c/o Back Stage Publications, Inc.
330 West 42nd Street
New York, NY 10036

MUSIC REP
Established music production company known for it's young, contemporary sound seeks an ambitious sales representative to present our music for major advertising accounts and film/TV work. Persons with contacts will be strongly considered, although experience is not as important as personality and energy. Salary plus commission. 212-246-6468, Mon-Fri, 11-5.

COLORIST:
Northeast Film to Tape Transfer Facility Seeks Full Time Colorist with Rank Cintel Experience; a Solid Video & Film Background; Engineering Capabilities a Plus. Please Send Resume in Confidence: Box 187B, Back Stage Box 102, Bridgton, ME 04009.

EXPERIENCED COMMERCIAL FILM EDITOR
WANTED BY BUSY POST PRODUCTION HOUSE, NATIONAL COMMERCIALS, IN MINNEAPOLIS MN. PLEASE SEND RESUMES AND ¾" or ½" SAMPLES OF COMMERCIAL WORK TO:
EDITRONICS & ASSOCIATES
1401 THIRD AVENUE SOUTH
MINNEAPOLIS MN 55404
ATTN: ADRIENNE
(612) 871-4322

5000 EDITOR
Tired of the NYC commute?
VIDEOCENTER OF N.J. is seeking an experienced 5000 Editor with knowledge of ADO effects to join staff immediately. Good starting salary & hosp. benefits. All inquiries kept confidential.
(201) 935-0900

WANTED
COMMERCIAL DIRECTOR
Aggressive commercial production company is seeking an established commercial director to be represented in the Washington/Baltimore/Richmond area.
Please respond with a reel and/or a list of directorial credits to:
RPS
2000 P Street, NW Suite 200
Washington, D.C. 20036
(202) 775-0990

Shop Foreman; Immediate opening; Construction, management, drafting. Shop constructs scenery, decor and cabinetry. Send resume/Salary to Design Imagery, 14 Putting Green, Northfield, N.J. 08225.

SEEKING REP
Established Video Production Co. with excellent reel is looking for an established rep with commercial-industrial contacts.
Call 212-315-5095

One of my old friends in this crazy business, Emily Cohen of Studio Labs & Video in New York, told me this story. She was interviewing an applicant for an entry-level position in the company and the young woman, just out of school, had a lot of questions. Her interrogation of Emily went something like this:

- What are the benefits? Do I get health insurance? Major medical? Sick leave?
- How many vacation days do I get each year?
- How much time do I get for lunch?
- When am I eligible for a raise?

When the "interview" was over, the applicant had not asked one single question about the job! Needless to say, she wasn't hired. Actually, the questions that she asked are quite legitimate—but only at the right time. The competition out there is fierce. Like everyone, you'll be nervous before an interview (at least, you should be), especially when you're just starting out and your resume looks terribly bare of any flesh on the bones. But, if you start out with the understanding that most people are hired on "gut feeling" as well as on their ability to communicate that they can do the job and do it well, then you are already light-years ahead.

I have read about ten thousand letters of application, along with attached resumes, and I've interviewed a great number of people, both creative and technical. Thinking back to the ones whcm I've hired, I come to the conclusion that it was the overall impression they made that counted more than their resume. That, plus a good, solid film or tape sample, generally wins me over.

With over 100,000 students now enrolled in communications courses (and that includes only the *matriculated* ones), and with career changers also swelling the ranks of those who want to pursue video careers, the competition has created a buyer's market. One of the most interesting examples of the current situation is the story of Ralph's Groceries in Los Angeles, which has its own training program for employees. Looking for a video production specialist, the company ran a small ad for just one day. *Four hundred* applicants answered the ad, out of which the company screened twenty people who were actually interviewed.

The good news is that in all my years in the business, I have found that the people who pursue the job hunt intelligently and with the commitment necessary to keep at it through the disappointments generally seem to make it. I have seen beginning resumes, very sparse and with large spacing to hide the lack of experience. Then the resumes return a year or two later and the job listings and the experience are now there.

While reading this chapter, cull from it the things that seem right for *you*. There are no rules in this business, no single career path or word of advice that works for everyone. And remember, above all, that video is a business, with all its attendant financial worries and daily problems. Too many colleges and private schools are ''selling'' video as ''show business'' and ''glamour'' without regard for the realities of the job market and the complexities of the job hunt. A participant at the ITVA Conference called today's grads ''the masses of the learned unemployed.''

Indeed, if you accept the fact that the key word is ''business'' in broadcast, cable, corporate video, advertising, and production and postproduction, you can begin to understand the reasons that so many people with marketing or sales backgrounds are now in the top management positions. If you remember during your interview that everyone's interest is in the bottom line—and that *you* represent a part of that bottom line—then you have truly begun to understand the industry.

STARTING OUT

It's probably a good idea to have some idea of what it is you eventually want to do in the field. Is it editing that catches your interest? Directing (be careful, because that's where it seems *everyone* wants to go)? Graphic arts? Makeup? Management? Writing? Special effects? You don't necessarily have to keep on that career path once you're on your way, but when you're starting out you need to choose a direction. The comment that ''I will do *anything* just to get started'' is, unfortunately, a drawback, even if you will do ''anything'' just to get into the business. If your prospective employer knows what your interests are, he or she can place you more easily in the overall plan of the corporate or production structure.

Once you do get in, you'll probably find that your interests will change, with much depending on pure, unadulterated chance.

Marcy Carsey and Tom Werner, the producers of some of the top situation comedies on television (''The Cosby Show,'' ''A Different World,'' ''Roseanne'') ignored the fact that everyone had advised them that situation comedies are dead. They took their background in programming at ABC, *took second mortgages on their homes*, worked out of an office above a shoe store, and made the bet that they'd win. The rest, as they say, is history.

In an article for *EITV Magazine*, Candace Kavensky wrote of her own experience in making her way to the job which she now holds, that of production supervisor at St. John's University TV Center:

- In her college communications course, her professor stated, "There are no jobs in television." Twenty people stood up and left the lecture hall.
- Her first job was in the news department of an independent station in Washington as an intern at the assignment desk. In her words, "Interns were responsible for changing the black ribbon on the AP and UPI teletype machines." But she got experience in editing news copy.
- On a recommendation from the assignment editor, she became a secretary in the newsroom.
- Six months later she was promoted to producer, and "allowed" to work Saturdays, Sundays, and weekends, as well as most evenings.
- She then became a unit manager, and instead of going out with the crew, she hired a producer. Again in her words, "A great broadcast journalist eats, sleeps, and has nightmares about news. I only had nightmares."
- So, she moved to a university as production supervisor where she writes, produces, and directs thirty-minute programs.

Typical? No. Everyone's story is different. If I were to detail every single twist and turn in a hundred careers, there would be a hundred different stories. Your own path will be different from all the rest.

A TYPICAL/ATYPICAL CAREER PATH: A TALK WITH LAURA JANS

At the age of twenty-six, Laura is now a colorist at National Video Industries in New York. She runs the film-to-tape transfer rooms and the color correction service for this very busy postproduction company. I first met her when she was working her way up and was the operator on the Chyron at DuArt Video. She then moved to Studio Video and then on to Post-Perfect. With almost ten years of experience already behind her, she offers insight into the elements of the job hunt and the potential career paths in video.

How did you start out?

"I started out volunteering my time at a broadcast station right after high school. That was nine years ago, when I was seventeen. I volunteered in the evenings and I ended up quitting my other full-time job and working as a volunteer full time. Eventually, I got an internship from the city."

What were your duties?

"I was a broadcast engineer. I was doing programs for the air. When I first began, I wanted to be an on-line editor in CMX [an electronic on-line videotape editing system]. But everyone told me that there was no way in the world I'd ever be able to do that."

Obviously there was a way. How did you do it?

"I just told my boss that's what I wanted to do and I was volunteering my time in order to learn CMX editing. My boss liked me and recommended me to someone uptown. From there I moved to a post facility—Reeves Teletape—and I learned to play back for CMX editing."

Did you have any formal training? School?

"I took a course in CMX with a private instructor from CBS. But my original background in school was art. Then I studied fashion design, sculpting, and pottery."

And then, after Reeves?

"After Reeves, I went to Unitel, another postproduction house. I worked freelance there and they hired me on staff. I did that for three years, went to DuArt, and then to Studio, to Post-Perfect, and finally here to National Video Industries."

What advice do you have for someone just starting out?

"You have to know a little bit about the field and you have to be able to say what your goals are, what you're going to do in order to reach those goals. You have to be ambitious and, of course, you're going to have to start out at the bottom. You have to be willing to dedicate yourself to something that doesn't pay well, that demands long hours, because there's a lot of sacrifice in moving up: vacations, family life, social life, sleep, lunch, even primary necessities."

Would you say that's typical?

"It sure is. You get up very early in the morning, rush out the door to get to work, making sure that everything is ready for your clients, being booked solidly back-to-back throughout the day, lucky if you eat lunch. If you do eat lunch, it's usually while you work. Then, not getting home until nine or ten o'clock at night."

What do you see as your future?

"I want to be a producer. I want to produce feature films."

Any final words of wisdom?

"I personally think people should try to get into the field first. School is great, but to learn video I think you really need hands on. It's not hopeless to get in. It's very difficult. There are four-year communications grads looking for jobs. But it's not hopeless. It's how badly you want anything. If you want something, you'll achieve it!"

FINDING THE JOBS

The first word of advice that anyone can pass on to you is that you must be disciplined. Unless Dad is chairman of the board at a major network or advertising agency, or CEO of a *Fortune* 500 company, there is a good possibility that you'll be at the job hunt for at least a moderate amount of time. It takes as much effort to find that first job as it did to go through all the final exams at school—possibly even more. If you're knocking on doors, you have to get up, get out, and get started. Lee Vogel recommends that, if you are going to invest in anything at all, make it a good interview suit or dress. There was a time when the people in our industry prided themselves on the blue jeans look. In some places it's still the mode. But, generally, everyone is conservative these days, and well dressed.

There are several areas in which you might begin your job search:

DIRECTORIES. There are national directories put out by organizations such as ITVA, as well as books published by companies like Back Stage. Its annual *TV Film and Tape Production Directory* is a good investment for the beginner. It lists almost every category of company involved in our business—production, postproduction, ad agencies, equipment houses, special effects—and it gives the names of the people who are involved with those companies.

Trade newspapers and magazines carry articles about jobs, and frequently list the regional services available to video producers and clients. The advertising industry also publishes listings of agencies and the names of the executives and creative staffs. *Film/Tape Production Source Book*, published by Television/Radio Age (1270 Avenue of the Americas, New York, NY 10019), lists names of ad agency producers, TV film and tape commercial production firms, and producers and distributors of public relations, business, and informational films.

Government publications can give you information about job potentials and the departments that are currently working in film and video. I've mentioned the National Audiovisual Center on page 121; you might do well to request its *Directory of U.S. Government and Audiovisual Personnel*.

Every industry has some type of publication that lists its member organizations as well as key personnel. I suggest that you visit the library first if there's any area that holds your interest. Many of the publications that I've mentioned are fairly expensive.

FILM COMMISSIONS. Every state now has a film/video commission designed to help producers shoot in their areas by providing location scouting help and personnel lists in the technical and creative areas. Commissions have always encouraged both film and video producers to contact them when they need any kind of help, from scouting to production to postproduction. Though generally called "film" commissions, one of my oldest friends with the California group, Kathleen Milnes, wrote to me when I asked if "video"

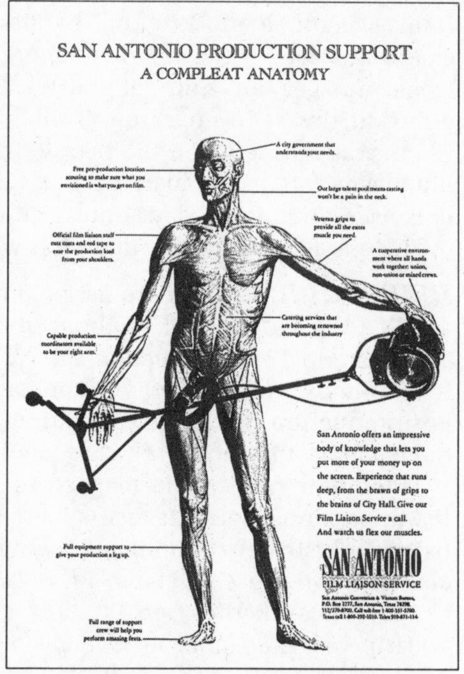

The state and local film commissions are generally quite helpful in the production of videos. They are also the best source for learning just who the production and postproduction people are locally. (Courtesy San Antonio Film Liaison Service)

Director Gary Sinise (crane) stages shot for "Miles From Home" near Worthington, Iowa. (Courtesy Iowa Film Office)

was as good as "film": "We help everybody! The medium is not the issue."

Essentially, state commissions were formed to actually help with the production of features, TV shows, commercials, business films, and videos. You can well imagine the income generated by the visit of a full feature crew (100 or more) for six to eight weeks! However, they also welcome small video crews of only two people.

There are specific areas in which they can be of help to you. Most commissions have listings of the facilities, production and postproduction houses, and equipment and studio facilities available in their areas. If your choice is to work in a particular state, that listing can be of utmost importance in starting your job hunt. Later on, of course, you can keep the commissions in mind as you produce your film or video work, since they are quite remarkable in helping to select locations, make arrangements for additional personnel, and generally pave the way for permits, accommodations, and all the little details that drive production managers crazy. I have used them extensively.

At one time, the commissions operated only on a state level, but increasingly cities are forming film commissions to encourage local production. In Stamford, Connecticut, the Mayor's Film Commission now has a directory of forty-six pages that lists everything from production companies to recording studios, costume and wardrobe suppliers, talent and casting agencies, even helicopter services. Again, all of the listings give company names and addresses, as well as the most important element of all: the *name* of the person who runs the company.

TRADE MAGAZINE AND NEWSPAPER ADS. When the field of video began to grow in importance, and especially when corporations began to expand their in-house video operations, ads like this began to appear in *Back Stage* and other trade publications. The question is, I suppose, whether or not such ads are effective means of getting your foot in the door, and there I have some severe reservations.

As I pointed out at the beginning of this chapter, even a small ad brings hundreds of people clamoring to be interviewed. At best, because of the huge response to most ads, you may be in for a frustrating experience. Your letter may not even get the courtesy of a reply. On the other hand, I am a great believer in trying *every* avenue—including the answering of an ad in the trade papers. You may well be the one they choose, possibly because some-

Original help wanted ads. Credit: The Personnel Pool, Back Stage

EDITOR

Fast growing, people oriented, Midwest facility looking for **HOT** Editor, preferably familiar with Paintbox, Mirage, Abekas A62 and, of course, CMX. Perks include: pool, company boat, catered lunches and long hours working with crazy, creative people. Salary commensurate with skills and experience. **Meek need not apply**. Contact: Terry Hamad, **Instant Replay Video Productions, Inc.**, 1349 E. McMillan St., Cinti, Ohio 45206 (513) 861-7065.

thing in your background is just what they're looking for. I always try to remember that the film director Hal Ashby got his first job when he went to the State Department of Unemployment—an even more impossible way to break in, one would think. So, ads do work at times. But, generally, I am lukewarm about them, even though I have decorated the opening of this chapter with a glorious sampling.

RECRUITERS. For the average communications graduate, the campus recruiter was once as rare as a cross-country skier in Miami. I remember doing a seminar on careers at Northwestern University in Chicago one snowy night, and the seminar leader was a wonderfully articulate IBM executive. He was quite specific on what the graduate was to tell the recruiter when he or she visited the campus. In my own miniseminar after the orientation, I warned the participants that they would atrophy before they ever saw a recruiter come through the door. It just didn't happen. Today it does—and because of video.

Corporations are now recruiting at colleges. In addition, the faculties of the communications schools are being asked to recommend top students. A part of the reason is that many top directors in Hollywood are film school grads (Spielberg, Scorsese, Seidelman, Lucas, Lee) and the other part has to do with the explosion of video in all areas of communications. Cable companies, such as Cablevision, are now holding "Career Nights" in order to attract young, fresh talent. And schools are being approached to recommend interns for television stations, postproduction houses, and advertising agencies.

INTERNSHIPS. You've noticed that many of the people interviewed for this book began their careers as interns. Indeed, an internship has become one of the most sought-after and rewarding first rungs on the ladder. Without doubt, it is one of the best ways to meet people, to get to know how a professional organization operates, and to learn the technological and creative aspects of videotape and television. For those who are unsure of their final destination or career goals, the internship programs are also a marvelous way to decide just which road you might want to follow. Some internships are a part of college curricula and course fees are charged. Others, particularly those available in the larger, more active companies in advertising and television, do pay a small stipend, sometimes enough to live on during the internship period.

I must admit at this point that I have ambivalent feelings about internships. On the one hand, I have always believed that someone should be paid for the work that he or she does, whether a volunteer or an intern. The industry has always had a reputation of being exploitative. Interns work very hard at a variety of odd jobs for little money (or none at all). I still think that internship is of tremendous value to the beginner or the college student.

Internships in some areas have been a boon to minorities, opening the doors to training and experience. For example, the 4As (American Association of Advertising Agencies) has a Minority Intern Program that has graduated almost five hundred students since its inception in 1973. (For information: 4As, 666 Third Avenue, New York, NY 10017.) Best of all, of the twenty-six agencies that participated in the program this past year, sixteen offered jobs to the interns. During the course of their programs, the interns are paid $250 a week (higher for graduate students), though this is not the norm for most internships.

Smaller internship programs are also available. The Lowe-Marschalk Summer Creative Internship Program, for example, pairs students with art director and writer teams. Participants have come from recommendations by the Urban League, the Children's Aid Society, and the New York City High School of Art and Design.

The best way to find out if an organization has an internship program is, of course, to call or write. The local television station might well offer one. Even small production companies, always pressed for funds, will occasionally take on a student for the summer or after hours. There is yet another reference work available in the career or education section of your local library. Its title is quite long, but a look through the book is worthwhile: *Directory of Internships, Work Experience Programs and On-the-job Training Opportunities* (Ready Reference Press). Although it has only a small section devoted to radio and television, you might look more carefully at all the other categories, since you may well find a program in an organization that includes communications and video. Theaters, foundations, museums, corporations, state and federal departments fall into this category. One of the book's most valuable assets is that it specifies just what is being offered to the intern, should he or she be hired:

- Stipends vary from zero to $12,500 for a one-year term.
- Sometimes housing is included or a fee is paid in lieu of facilities.
- Some require that interns pay the cost of transportation and meals. Others will repay those costs.
- There is generally no guarantee that the internship will lead to a permanent job. Some, though, mention that they do look at interns to fill the first staff opening that becomes available.

Even if you find nothing that suits you as you inspect the books, you will at least come away having learned just what questions to ask of a prospective employer who might offer you an internship. And only you can answer the questions: Am I being exploited? Or is this the greatest opportunity, the one I've been waiting for?

NETWORKING. The reality is that most job opportunities in any field come from word of mouth. Someone knows someone who knows someone who needs someone to replace someone who just went somewhere. Just yesterday the telephone rang and a voice from the Midwest told me that I had been recommended by someone in the South and would I be interested in producing their film? Whether at the beginning or at the apex of your career, networking is very much a factor in your advancement.

Certainly, those of us who have been active for many years will have more of a network out there, assuming that we are reliable, that we come in on budget, and that we make our deadlines for delivery. However, there are ways for the beginner to do the same thing, by getting involved in the groups and organizations that make up the industry. I have already recommended that you read as many of the trade magazines as possible in order to find out where things are happening, and I strongly suggest that you make an effort to actually attend some of those functions and conventions.

ITVA, for example, is invaluable for making contacts. It has a national directory of members and organizations, and its regional vice presidents are available to help members. The interaction between members and potential employers is fully realized at its annual conference.

And ITVA is not alone. There are other organizations all across the country, and most of them run conferences, conventions, and seminars. There are engineering conferences, consumer equipment conventions, computer animation and graphics meetings and conferences, multimedia exhibitions, and training conventions.

Check to see if organizations allow nonmembers to attend events. Many have special entry requirements, in which case it is always possible to contact a member who might be an acquaintance of yours or a company that is exhibiting at the convention in order to get a pass. Once there, the opportunity to ask questions, to see the latest technological advances, to meet professionals in the field, and to absorb the "feel" of the industry is invaluable to the beginner and the veteran both. I have never failed to get an entry pass to a members-only convention or conference—just by contacting an exhibitor and asking for a ticket.

Networking will continue throughout your career, whether you call it by that name or something else, and the people you will get to know are the ones who will probably be most valuable in getting you to the next rung on the ladder. I must say this, however. Along the way, you will no doubt hear the cynical comment, "Well, it's not *what* you know, it's *who* you know!" Not really. The contacts that you make are only half the story. *Who* you know can help. But, from that point on, *what* you know is more important. You had better be a consummate professional, dedicated, talented, willing to work hard, and committed to your craft *before* you ask someone for a job.

AGENTS. Getting an agent is generally an option that you have after a few years of success on your own. Some very talented people find it difficult to sell themselves. The daily, face-to-face meetings and negotiations with potential employers, especially for freelancers, can be wearying and frightening. Thus, once a reputation is made, some people, particularly directors and writers, begin to work in the "stable" of an agent, who may have as many as twenty to fifty people for whom he or she negotiates, develops marketing plans and strategies, and works out fees. Many of us find it quite difficult to "talk money." Others find that the constant quest for work takes time away from the jobs that are already under way. An agent becomes at least part of the answer.

GETTING THE INTERVIEW

It helps to be organized. You have to compile the lists and make index cards or whatever form of record keeping seems to suit your personality. You should keep track of the calls you've made, follow-up dates, what was said, next steps—or "X" the card as a dead end. Without some sort of discipline, finding a job can get to be a paper mess, a disorganized chaotic clutter.

Depending upon which book or magazine article you read, you will be given advice that contradicts every other piece of advice you've read:

- Call first, then write.
- Write first, then call.
- Don't just "drop in."
- By all means, "drop in"—what can you lose?

I know people who have gotten jobs by dropping in, though I am firm in my dictate that you *never* drop in without an appointment. Sometimes a letter is the proper advance notice of a call (although it might alert the recipient that he or she should not be available when the call does come).

What I've suggested is merely that—a suggestion. You will have to determine your own preferences, depending on your personality. I personally prefer a call first, followed by a letter. This seems to be standard procedure with most executives.

Before you even call the company, you should have the *name* of a person to call. The way to get the name is by calling the target company or by checking one of the directories that I recommended earlier. Without knowing a name, the chances are that you will never get past the receptionist. If you do not get past the telephone voice of the receptionist, write a letter to the contact person, explaining the reason you would like to speak with him or her. Then call again in a few days.

At that point, you will have to make a decision. Most people in our industry are rude and unfeeling. (Possibly that is true for other industries, but I have not had the experience of trying to get a job interview in steel or aluminum.) Sometimes it doesn't pay to stop there and on the third call, you may even get a person with whom you can speak and sell yourself. You will be rejected. Some people, forgetting that they, too, once looked for a job, will be curt, officious, and overbearing. You may even be surprised. Some will be kind, responsive, empathetic, and courteous, and you will never hear from them again. Secretaries will ask who is calling and "what company you are with" or "I'll see if he/she is in" (sitting only three feet from his/her office), or will get your phone number wrong after telling you, "I'll give him/her the message." Get used to it. It still happens to those of us who have been around for forty years or more. You are not alone. You merely hang up and try again somewhere else.

The most common answer that you'll get from your request for an interview is "Send me a letter and resume," and you'll then move to the next time-consuming, frustrating step.

WRITING THE PERFECT LETTER(!)

Whether you decide to send a letter and then follow up with a call, or to follow up your call with a letter, the same rules will apply. The letter *must* be addressed to a real person, not a title. To this day, I still receive letters addressed to "Production Manager, Symbiosis" or "To Whom It May Concern." Make sure you have the correct spelling of the person's name and the person's correct title (titles change, too), and make each letter personal. There is only one type of letter that is worse than the generic "To Whom It May Concern" type, and that's the form letter: the letter that has been photocopied or done on a computer, with a name inserted—often crookedly—at the top.

When you do write the letter, keep it brief, and try to make it original enough so that the person who spoke to you on the phone will recall the conversation. Too often, the request for "a letter and a resume" is merely a way to postpone doing anything about the telephone call. It is often the letter and not the resume that moves a prospective employer to action. In one page, then, you will have to project your personality, your experience (if any), and your desire to work for that particular company.

DEVELOPING THE RESUME

Prospective employers always ask for resumes (even from old-time professionals). However, resumes can sometimes be very important, especially if you get to the interview stage of the job hunt, where you will have a chance to emphasize your strong points or hobbies. Unfortunately, the statistics show that about 95 percent of all resumes are discarded after a glance or a superficial reading!

If the resume *is* effective, it may be so because of something that catches the eye of the scanner. You would be surprised how many times the add-ons about hobbies and adjunct experience can be more important than all the "meat" about your experience with the Sony Betacam or the Ikegami or the Paintbox. For example, second languages, sports, and crafts might be just the thing that an employer is looking for. For instance, on every overseas trip, I try to bring at least one person on the crew who speaks the language, whether it be assistant camera, production assistant, or sound. In that way, I can be fairly certain that the translations given to me while on location are accurate and have not gone through the censorship of a hostile government.

Your first resumes will give information about school projects, the space filled with fairly lightweight nonprofessional experience or internships. Don't worry. The most amazing thing to me is how fast resumes grow.

Most resumes include references, and these can also be adjusted to meet the needs of the particular company to which you are applying. The simplest way to do this is to say "References upon request." Or you might list the people who would be most supportive of you in the type of job you're after. At the beginning, references might be professors, counselors, even personal acquaintances with some impressive backgrounds or professions who will write letters of commendation. Eventually, it will all change as your experience grows, people retire or move on, or you move into another area of the field.

The resume should be changed to meet the requirements of the prospective employer: energy, training, fund-raising, etc. You will find, however, that, no matter how much experience you acquire, no matter how many projects you've worked on, a potential client looks down at the three pages covering fifteen years and says, "Yeah, it looks good. But have you ever done anything on *insurance*?" One thing that I've learned is that everyone in a position of authority is convinced that no one from the "outside" could ever learn enough about their company to do a film/tape for them. Learn to expect it. Then talk your way out of it. I do it all the time!

DO YOU STRETCH THE TRUTH?

Actually, I was going to use the word "lie." People have been known to do it. I walked into an interview many years ago where the person who preceded me had actually stolen one of my credits and put it on *his* resume. I can only say that if you do stretch the truth too much, take credit for things you have not done, or invent things you would like to do, you won't necessarily get the job, and the story may come back to haunt you at some future date. The industry is too small to take this chance. Remember that employers do talk to each other about the people they've hired or are thinking of hiring.

I was amused to read the other day that a new form of resume has entered the marketplace: the certified resume! It's a resume that certifies that every piece of information in it has been based on polygraph tests given to the job seeker. Frankly, I have no comment other than to say that I think it's a conceit. It's no substitute for checking references. I like to talk to former professors or employers and probe in depth about personality, work habits, craft. This will give you a much better sense of the person you are considering than any stamped piece of paper.

VIDEO RESUMES

Another new form of resume is the video resume. It is usually a short tape (about three to seven minutes) that allows the viewer to actually see the personality of the applicant as he or she describes talents and abilities and the type of job that he or she is looking for. However, if you consider the statistic that so many resumes are tossed into the "circular file" with only a glance, it seems unrealistic to expect a busy executive to take the time to watch a tape, then turn to see that forty more are sitting on the desk waiting to be screened. Video resumes may grow in importance, but I don't think that they'll ever replace the personal interview.

PREPARING FOR THE INTERVIEW

They've said Okay. They've set a date. They will see you. Bring a resume. Bring a sample (more on that later). You still have a lot of work to do.

Over and over again, I have been asked by job applicants at interviews, "What is it you *do*?" It is amazing to me that they had not checked my background or the background of my company to find that we do documentaries. This step is even more critical if you are interviewing for a television network or for a corporation. How could you possibly appear for an interview without first learning about the company's activities, products, size, structure, philosophy? You still have some homework to do.

Research the company to which you're applying, whether it's a small production or postproduction house or a *Fortune* 500 corporation. If the company has printed material, you might ask that it be sent to you before your interview date.

Other than the company itself, there are many other sources of information:

- Annual reports. Some are available at the library.
- *Wall Street Journal*, *Forbes*, *Fortune*, and other newspapers and magazines devoted to business. Articles, commentary, even stock listings can help you.
- Trade and professional journals. Articles about audiovisual production and postproduction companies appear in these publications.
- Advertising. Study the ad campaigns of the particular company. They will give you an excellent idea of the company's philosophy—and its product line.

As Donald Bis, AV consultant with Allstate, puts it, "The interview is a 'do-or-die' situation. It's where you make your first impression and, hopefully, it's a lasting impression."

THE BIG MOMENT

When it comes to how to behave during an interview, the best advice that I can offer is that *you* should be the one in control. If the interviewer does all the talking, then you have missed the opportunity to sell yourself. The interview is your best chance to speak of your experience, your aspirations, and your qualifications for the position.

If the job is for an AV position, you might ask to take a tour of the facility. It's also a good time to keep up a running conversation, to give information about yourself and to show that you know the field.

Project energy and enthusiasm. Be brief in your answers to questions, but don't be afraid to expand into an anecdotal account of a specific part of your experience. You may find that you and the interviewer have common interests apart from the specific job—a hobby, sport, college, something that puts you on common ground.

This is an informal industry, but I would certainly use "Mister" or "Ms."

when first meeting, until you are told or get the sense that first names are okay.

And by all means, dress appropriately for the interview. I am reminded of a story told to me by a friend, Christine Marsh.

For an interview at NBC, Christine thought carefully about how she should dress, and picked her clothing with an eye toward the first impression, the executive look. Walking up Fifth Avenue in New York on her way to Rockefeller Center, she was caught in the middle of an egg fight between two groups of touring high school students. Splattered with egg yolk, with only five minutes to the interview, she could not stop to change. So she plodded on, knowing that the executives she was meeting would understand. One block further, the skies opened up and it began to rain, destroying the look she had worked so hard to achieve and sort of scattering the egg yolks a bit more. That's how she showed up to the interview—a wet egg wreck. And—they understood and laughed with her. It turned out to be an icebreaker—she couldn't be anything else but "herself."

Ultimately, it's your attitude, personality, and personal values that factor most heavily in the decision. Your overall career goal, your values regarding your work and your personal life style, your attitudes toward loyalty, authority, and independence will all be considered.

One final rule: Above all, don't discuss salary and benefits until the job is either offered to you or the interview has reached the point where it is appropriate for the interviewer to communicate that information to you or for you to ask.

You may be called for a second or third interview. At such times, prospective employers have been known to invite job seekers to lunch. Frankly, it can be awkward; it's difficult to juggle food, look comfortable, and answer questions at the same time. This follow-up interview is frequently a "test" to see just how you would handle all those complexities, with an eye toward your demeanor with clients at future business luncheons.

The best advice that I can give you about luncheons like these is passed on to me by Christine Marsh. She strongly suggests that you order food that is easy to handle while you talk. Above all, she adds, "Don't order spaghetti!"

THE DEAD-END JOB

There is a critical question that comes up quite often and it is a very valid one: What happens if you are offered a job, but you feel that it's a dead end? Secretary, bookkeeper, receptionist—beginners, and even today especially women, are generally the ones offered the jobs that might well lead nowhere. However, I know at least six women who began as receptionists and eventually became producers, and I know of two young men who started in the record library of radio stations and eventually moved to producing their own feature films! So a ''dead end'' might not necessarily be a dead end if you choose to make it a stepping-stone.

Remember that once you're ''inside'' the organization, you have a chance to meet the producers, the executives, the people who can help you make a move. You can also spend your free time in learning the equipment, be it in off-line editing or on the Paintbox, or in watching the professionals work. Don't turn down the job too quickly, certainly without investigating the structure of the company, the chances for promotion, and the history of others who started out at the front desk, for example.

And then, if after a few months, you still think that the job is a dead end: *leave*!

THE FOLLOW-UP

Immediately after the interview, write a short note of thanks to the person who saw you. Or, follow it up with a phone call if it seems more appropriate. Then, about two weeks after that, you might write yet another note, just

There is no single path into the industry. Mauri Swantek, on camera at left, got his first job with Atlanta TV station channel 69 after graduating from the music/business video course at the Art Institute of Atlanta. (Courtesy Design Schools)

reminding the person that you are still interested and helping him or her to recall your interview. You might send of a copy of an article or a newspaper item that you had discussed during the interview. I generally send one of my books, though I'm not sure that anyone really reads it.

Be persistent but polite. You have to keep at it because timing is important. I have had many people say to me, ''I'd like to hire your company,'' and then I never hear from them again no matter how many follow-up calls or letters I send. (There is currently a man at one company that practically told me that the next project was mine and that my work was ''superb.'' That was six months ago and if he reads this, I am still waiting.) Nevertheless, I still continue to send follow-up letters—and so should you.

There is yet another area in which the follow-up is important. Nothing may have come of your interviews. The people who saw you will have forgotten you or you will have become at best a dim memory (unless you had come in with egg on your clothing, drenched by a storm), and in the meantime you have been acquiring experience and your resume has grown. At that time, you might want to renew your acquaintance with the people who were kind enough to give you the time early on. I know that I appreciate a letter from someone who was interviewed by me but who ended up taking another job. Remember, the industry is small. I actually keep a file of these letters, never knowing when I will be able to use them.

Karen Gustafson, who was interviewed by me when she was a recent graduate, just out of communications school, wrote me what is an example of the perfect interview follow-up letter. The letter commented on the ''outside chance'' that I would remember her, and that she was writing to thank me. The letter goes on:

> *Although I started out as an intern, I now have the title of assistant producer on two of our current projects. As in most small companies, that position encompasses many areas, but it has also introduced me to the numerous components that comprise a production. One of the more distinct advantages of the position is the opportunity to go on my first long-distance shoot. We will be visiting your eclectic city in November . . . and I am thoroughly enjoying my experience.*
>
> *I just wanted to let you know that I appreciated your previous time and interest. If you see our film crew in the city, stop by; it would be a pleasure to meet you, I'm sure.*

Yes, all of this takes time. But it is the people who are willing to take that time who eventually make their mark in the industry and are remembered, even if we didn't hire them in the first place.

In Celebration of

National Cable Month

CABLEVISION

Will hold an Open House for Area High School and College Students to Learn about Careers in:

- ★ ADVERTISING
- ★ CUSTOMER SERVICE
- ★ ENGINEERING TECHS
- ★ INSTALLATIONS
- ★ NEWS
- ★ PRODUCTION
- ★ SECRETARIAL
- ★ SALES

WEDNESDAY

April 27th

2:00 PM-8:00 PM

CABLEVISION

28 Cross St. Norwalk, CT

FOR INFORMATION
Please Call 846-4700

The cable industry has been a boon to beginners in the videotape field. This is a poster from Cablevision announcing a career seminar for the purpose of recruitment. (Courtesy Cablevision)

Roger Grant and Phil Dixon, working as freelance videographers for Videotakes, Inc., packing up after a day of shooting the celebration of Martin Luther King, Jr.'s birthday. (Photo: Katie Henninger)

THE FREELANCER

If you think that interviewing is traumatic, how do you think that freelance people feel—always having to interview for work, living between feast and famine, and yet mostly loving every tough minute of it? Many of the corporate AV departments have been cutting back in recent years and have been moving toward the use of freelance help to fill the gaps in production and post-production. In other areas, only freelance work is available—in makeup and hair, for example, or acting, or even in most areas of writing. It is terribly expensive to keep paying staff salaries during quiet times, and so very few organizations boast staff videographers, editors, and directors.

People who freelance out of choice love the freedom, regardless of the trials and vicissitudes of the constant job hunt. You can be certain that, as a freelancer, you will have weeks or months of downtime, when you can enjoy going to museums, ball games, and movies. But suddenly a job appears (just as you were beginning to worry that everyone had forgotten you), and the moment you take that job, the phone rings and three more are offered.

For the freelancer, there is a constant struggle to maintain strong relationships with producers and clients who may hire you. For example, you take a job that will last three days. No sooner do you agree and all the details are worked out than you get an offer that conflicts with this job, but lasts three weeks (on location in Paris). That is a conundrum, is it not?

Some producers will ask you for a "first refusal." This means that should another job be offered to you for the same time period, you must notify the first producer, who is required either to give you a firm commitment or to let you take the second offer.

Some producers would simply let you off the hook on the three-day job so that you could take the longer one, and you will not have suffered in reputation. However, some will not. You have a choice. Either you break your word, in which case you will never be asked to work for the first producer again, or you take the shorter job, because you are committed.

Now, when the shoe is on the other foot, there are some (many?) producers who commit you to the shorter job, making you leave the longer one to someone else, and then cancel their shooting, leaving you without any work at all. Technically, a producer should pay you for the time that was committed, but except in strong union shops, this is seldom done. You can always use the time to go to a museum, sporting event, or movie, if you can afford it.

Knowing the problem of cancellations, sometimes by the client or agency, occasionally by a producer who is not ready, the strongest organizations in our industry have laid down rules by which the freelancer benefits. The Directors Guild of America is one such group. Others include the stage unions that work in television and the film industry. Recently, the Association of Independent Commercial Producers (AICP) in Seattle negotiated an agreement to protect the freelancer in the Northwest Region:

- First refusals, with the production company committing to the crew member who calls reporting the offer of an alternative job.
- Working hours: eight- or ten-hour day including lunch.
- Overtime at 150 percent of hourly rate for the eleventh and twelfth hours, 200 percent thereafter. However, overtime is not paid to producers, directors, production managers, wardrobe assistants, or production assistants.
- Split days (four hours in morning, four late evening) at straight time.
- Turnaround: a minimum of ten hours between the wrap and the next

crew call. This is an important part of any work schedule, giving the crew enough off time to recover.

- Cancellation: the production company is allowed to cancel without penalty anyone who has been given first refusal, but if the member has been inked (or hired), a full rate must be paid for each canceled day.

The contract also calls for specific zones, travel time pay, payment for parking and meals, per diem rates, and contingency days (in case of rain).

All this, of course, is an ideal situation and it is included here just to make you are aware of what is possible—*if* you have the clout. These are just some of the things that have to be considered if you choose to freelance (or if you are forced to freelance):

- You will tend to be insecure: Will I ever work again? Why doesn't the phone ring?
- You will have to budget very carefully. Though freelancers generally get more money per day than staff people, the income is inconsistent and spotty. You'll feel wealthy one day, impoverished the next.
- You will work on a variety of projects, each with a different subject and with a different set of problems. As a result, you will become more experienced in meeting any kind of situation in the studio or on location.
- You will not experience the closeness and camaraderie of a team.
- You will also not experience the politics that infect almost every organization.
- More than in any other work category in the industry, you will have to face a personal or social life that is practically nonexistent. The divorce and separation rate in our industry is very high. Videographers and directors may be gone for as long as seven or eight months out of the year. I know one cameraman who was home only *three days* in an entire year.

Freedom or frustration? Feast or famine? It is yet another decision that you will have to make.

UNIONS

Probably the most frequently asked question in my classes is: Will I have to join a union? The answer to that is no, maybe, and yes. The film industry is heavily unionized in the areas of feature films and television sitcoms, network and commercial production. In most other areas, and especially in video production, the unions do not play as much of a role. Added to that, the "right to work" states, such as Florida and Texas, have expanded their production capabilities without union control.

To get to the ''no'' first, you can work in this field without joining a union. There are enough nonunion shops around to provide employment for a vast array of producers, directors, actors, and technicians. If you are starting out, you can ignore the union situation and meet it as it becomes a problem. For, as you progress, you may find that union signatories are your next step in your career. Thus, we get to the ''maybe.''

Early on, you might want to check the union of your chosen discipline (editing, directing, videography), in order to learn just what the requirements are, how you can join, and just what joining will mean in terms of wages, benefits, and, especially, job opportunities. Union listings are available in trade publications such as *Back Stage*'s production guide, and locals are in most major sections of the country. Study the applications carefully. Some unions have a Catch-22 requiring that you get a job before joining, but then you find that you can't *join* unless you have a job! Others are known as ''father and son'' locals. A listing of the membership would show people with exactly the same last name—fathers, sons, daughters, and assorted relatives. Certainly, they don't publicize that fact. Getting in may be difficult, until you've made your networking connections.

The answer is ''yes'' when you are being hired for a union job or when your goal is a union segment of the field. At that point it will become critical that you find a way in, and I guarantee that you will. Somehow, everyone I know who started out in a nonunion capacity has eventually found a way to break into the union that controls the contracts in their part of the field. Once in the union, you will probably not be allowed to work for a nonunion shop.

For the present, the best advice I can give you is not to worry about it and try for a job. When the time comes for union membership, you'll know it only too well and you'll eventually join if you must. Put it in the back of your file of ''Things to Do.''

THE SAMPLE TAPE

If you are going to move through the industry, the sample tape will be one of your most valuable tools. Especially if you freelance, you should be collecting samples of everything that you do. A good, professional sample on a subject that relates to the job you are seeking can frequently mean the difference between beating the competition and not getting the job.

If you are a gaffer or a grip, if you work in the area of tape that keeps you behind the scenes, then your jobs will depend on experience and recommendations. But if you are in any of the creative fields, then some kind of sample is almost a necessity. Writers should have sample tapes of productions done from their scripts, if possible, or typewritten samples of their scripts or treatments. Producers, directors, independents, editors, art directors, makeup and hair experts, computer animators, set designers, videographers, sound people, music editors, and composers—all should be working toward acquiring something that can be shown as samples of their craft.

Some people invest their own money to make a short sample tape, with a running time from five to fifteen minutes. Others make up a reel that consists of several segments of various types of productions on which they've worked. The ad agencies generally require this, looking for a variety of styles on one reel. For the client who is buying a documentary project or a corporate videotape, having a sample that closely approximates the problems of the new job is usually the best sales tool. This, of course, can be a problem, since not all of us have made every type of film or videotape on every conceivable subject. There is nothing as frustrating as showing your best work, your Academy Award nominee, your Golden Eagle winner, and then having someone turn to you and ask, "Yes, nice, but don't you have something that's more in line with what *I* want to do?"

More experienced employers, people familiar with the field, will look at most any subject that's professionally lighted, shot, and edited. They will want a full explanation of just what it is you did for the production or completion of that sample. Some other points:

- Never take credit for something that you did not do. Sometimes there are cooperative samples produced in college, with an entire class involved. Explain what is it that you did, and if you were responsible for only one segment, which one it was.
- Try to show a short sample. Most people do not have the patience to sit through an entire program. However, it is a great frustration to come into a screening and be told that "I don't have much time. Can you just show me a couple of minutes?" It happens, though.
- Several subjects or one subject? I prefer to show one complete videotape of one complete subject. It gives the viewer an idea of my ability to deal with continuity, pacing, and storyline. Agencies prefer several samples on one short reel, television having a short attention span. You might have to make up two different kinds of samples.
- If possible, don't screen until you've had time to explain the objectives of the videotape, the audience for whom it was intended, any special details that might be important in selling you—such as production problems that you overcame or budgetary limitations (without making excuses for lack of money). Everyone likes to hear war stories. Is there some

particular story of interest to your audience that will make them more interested in watching it?

- Label your tape and its case for return. It will help when you telephone a couple of weeks later asking what happened to your sample. You might even provide a shipping box in which it can be sent to you.

If someone should ask that the tape be sent instead of screened in person, be sure that you enclose all the information on a card or letter in the tape jacket. I usually use an index card and include such information as target audience and objectives. Whether you're present or not, the videotape sample is a selling tool—and it has to help sell *you*.

Remember this on your job hunt: There will be disappointments and rejections. And there will be some hopeful interviews and opportunities. Balance them—in the scheme of things, you don't have to win 'em all. You only need *one* job offer to get you started. Only one.

WOMEN AND MINORITIES

In 1977, when I wrote *Getting into Film*, it was necessary to devote an entire chapter to women in film. They were such a rarity in the industry that the chapter focused on how a few brave women had managed to make their way in a male-dominated industry. Unfortunately, at the time the situation was even worse for nonwhites, regardless of sex. But since then, tremendous changes have taken place in film and in video. Women and minorities have made many inroads in the field, and each day brings new changes. So now there is no need for a special *chapter* on opportunities for the disadvantaged. At the same time, it would be Pollyanna-ish to believe that video, like any industry, cannot be a tough row to hoe for women or people whose skins are not white. The following section deals specifically with this unfortunate situation.

First the film field and now the videotape industry boast women and minorities as well as men in the editing suites. Casting has also become the domain of women. Advertising agencies took the lead in the late seventies and early eighties to open up new opportunities for minorities, including internship programs. (But even here, the end of the eighties saw an article in *Back Stage* titled: "Minorities in Advertising—The Great Disappearing Act of the 80's.") For Hispanics, the opening up of the Latin American markets, particularly in Mexico, has created some new job opportunities. Puerto Rico has also become a growing market, with obvious results in the demand for Hispanic-specialist directors and technicians. There have even been new rising stars like Nick Mendoza in Hollywood, who has seen the volume of work in his production company increase both in magnitude and in budget for Spanish-language commercials.

Corporations have begun to fill many of their middle-level executive positions with women and minorities and, as a result, the production units for video projects have been chosen on a more equal basis. Companies like Anixter (see page 84) have begun to staff their AV positions with women, and small production companies have sprung up with partners representing a wide assortment of ethnic groups. Arna Vodenos (see page 154) is but one of a group of women who have successfully started their own production and postproduction houses. Another example is SVP, a Greenwich, Connecticut, firm owned by Judy Outhank and Kathy Harding, who together boast over thirty-five years in corporate work.

Judy Onthank (seated) and Kathy Arms Harding, whose Greenwich, Connecticut video production company, SVP Communications, boasts such corporate clients as Rockwell International, USAir, AMAX Corporation, and Restaurant Associates. (Photo: Gretchen Tatge)

The perception of gain might belie a very different reality, however. While television has begun to hire more minorities on camera, and more significantly, in the behind-the-scenes production areas, when we look at the statistics and the reports in trade magazines, we learn that the share of jobs held by blacks, for example, in the broadcast industry was declining by the mid-1980s. In cable television, the figures were even more distressing, with only about 3 percent of the officers and managers on the local level in the minority groups. Looking at the overall picture, there are about 10,000 licensed radio and television stations in the country, and blacks own somewhat less than 3 percent of them.

Are there bright signs ahead? There are some areas where management positions have begun to open up to minorities and women, even if they are not at the very top of the power structure. We are now beginning to see new faces that are not the typical men of twenty years ago, with the old school tie and the male bonding, and it is quite refreshing.

Jeannie Tasker, director of television services for National Advanced Systems, a computer marketing service, comments:

> *I find there are a lot of women in very key roles now. In fact, I was at a meeting on teleconferencing earlier in the week and one of our speakers mentioned that most of the major teleconferencing networks in the country are headed by women: Kodak, Hewlett-Packard, Merrill Lynch. I don't know how to explain it other than to say that my observation is that women make better managers—that women bring to the job a greater sensitivity, all of the things that supposedly kept them in the past from getting to the top. I think our greater sensitivity—and perhaps it's my bias—allows us a greater perception of what's going on. I think, too, that you're finding more women in higher places now because we're just deciding that we want to do what it takes to get there!*

The most positive thing that has begun to happen is that more and more support groups have sprung up, both for training and for networking. Some have been around a long, long time (Women in Film and Video, for instance); others have formed recently to share information, exhibit the work produced by their groups, and provide a specialized forum dedicated to the progress of their members. Fifteen years ago, for example, much was made of the fact that Brianne Murphy was the first woman to become a member of the Cameraman's (sic!) Local of IATSE (International Alliance of Theatrical Stage Employees) in Los Angeles. Today, with over 3,000 members in the IA camera guild, roughly 150 are women, 10 of whom are camera operators. With over 500 directors currently doing commercials, only 15 are black! In the non-union videotape field, the numbers are much larger, as they are in television studio and location production.

One of the major support groups for women is Behind the Lens, an organization of professional camerawomen founded by Bri Murphy (P.O. Box 1039, Santa Monica, CA 90406). The directory lists members, along with their qualifications, credits, union affiliations, and telephone numbers. It has gone out to more than 1,000 industry contacts.

Other groups that provide support are:

WOMEN IN FILM (Many chapters have now added "video" to their organization name). Started with only twelve members less than twenty years ago, this remarkable organization now has chapters across the country in almost every major city, plus seventeen chapters overseas in such countries as Australia, Japan, Denmark, and Canada. For information on the chapter nearest you, write to Women in Film, 8489 West Third Street, Los Angeles, CA 90048. The group's seminars on job opportunities in the field can be invaluable to a beginner. Recently, for example, the New England chapter conducted a public meeting/seminar on the subject of "Minority Women in Broadcasting." Other chapters do the same, and the author has been the guest (honored, I assure you) at both the Atlanta and New York chapter meetings to discuss careers.

Essentially, Women in Film (and Video) is committed to

- Increased employment opportunities for women
- Depiction of women in film and video as fair and varied as that which exists in reality
- Greater visibility of the accomplishments of women
- Networking
- Professional excellence

THE DIRECTING WORKSHOP FOR WOMEN. Established by the American Film Institute in 1974, the organization provides professional women an opportunity to direct their projects on video. It's funded by the Ford Foundation, the National Endowment for the Arts, plus other corporate and public foundations. The enrollment is severely limited, but its program has been very supportive of women directors like Lynn Littman, Karen Arthur, Lee Grant, Jenny Sullivan, Elizabeth Clark, and Lesli Linka Glatter, whose short subject was nominated for an Oscar in 1984. (American Film Institute, 2021 North Western Avenue, Los Angeles, CA 90027)

There are numerous festivals devoted to the works of women. The *AIVF Guide to International Film and Video Festivals* lists ten specifically devoted to women, plus countless others that have special categories for subjects about women. This does not include the entries of women who compete in the general categories. Though many exhibitors of independent videos admit that they have been less than enthusiastic in the past in showing the work of women, this neglect is being rectified to an extent by some distributors and exhibitors. In San Francisco, for example, Video Free America now estimates that about 50 percent of the tapes in its exhibition programs are produced by women.

There are even specific financial programs for women entrepreneurs. One of them, the American Women's Economic Development Corporation, has been a leader in lobbying Congress to provide training funds for women who want to start their own businesses. The organization sponsors seminars on starting a business, each one led by a different specialist. They have been invaluable to women. One success story is Janet Kealy, who started a production company, Knickerbocker Film/Video Associates, with Peter Meyer. The seminars, she said, "saved me a lot of difficulty." (American Women's Economic Development Corporation, Lincoln Building, 60 East 42nd Street, New York, NY 10165)

Janet Kealy, president of Knickerbocker Film Video Associates, accepts the CINE Golden Eagle Award from Robert Kelly, for her videotape "We Were There!" (American Express)

Most of this also holds true for minority groups. Magazines, trade papers, and local newspapers will occasionally print an article about a film festival devoted specifically to minority or third world subjects, or the availability of scholarships or financial help to minority groups or individuals. Ideally, of course, the mainstream will open its doors, but membership in the organizations I've mentioned can be of invaluable help in networking and in exchanging ideas, as well as in actually getting your work shown. The scholarships that are available can also help in providing you with an eventual sample video to be shown to prospective employers in the broadcast and nonbroadcast fields.

Nonprofit groups such as the Black Filmmakers Foundation and Black and Hispanic Images have begun campaigns to make New York the black and Hispanic production capital of the world. Groups offer funds for film and videomakers, sponsor seminars, and lend equipment.

Film/Video Arts (FVA) receives grant support from various corporations and foundations, and offers a Scholarship Assistance Program for blacks, Latinos, Asians, and Native Americans. (Film/Video Arts, 817 Broadway, New York, NY 10003)

Keep an eye out for seminars and special conferences on the subject of job opportunity for minority video producers and trends in television, cable, and business. From time to time the American Film Institute holds seminars especially devoted to minorities. One of them, "Contemporary Black Perspectives in American Media," was reported as "an extraordinary gathering . . . not just another how-to-get-a-break-in-the-business event preaching the old truisms of persistence and perseverance to naive industry hopefuls" (*The Independent*, in an article by Monona Wali). The most important element for the participants was the involvement of twenty-six panelists and speakers, all of them experienced, and all capable of speaking about the fantasies, the myths, and the exclusion of positive images of blacks in the media. By offering the experiences of people who have obviously overcome the odds and become influential members of the entertainment industry, seminars like these can be of more help than a hundred books on video in examining racism both on screen and in the hiring practices of our business.

AIVF lists nearly thirty "third world" festivals, including those specifically targeted to blacks, Asians, Africans, and Native Americans.

There is a new organization that now joins the others devoted to the minority artist. The International Agency for Minority Artist Affairs (Adam Clayton Powell Jr. State Office Building, 163 West 125th Street, New York, NY 10027) sponsors a Black Film Festival presented by the Museum of African American History and Arts, plus a State-of-the-Arts Conference that covers:

- How to survive and prosper as an artist
- Copyrights and contracts
- Proposal writing
- Housing, tax exemptions
- Film/cable TV production
- Networking, time sharing, and marketing

There are many more such groups. The Education Department of the Seneca Nation on the Cattaraugus Reservation in upstate New York, for example, has begun a Native American Screening and Video Production Workshop, cosponsored by the Film and Video Center of New York and New York City's Museum of the American Indian.

Well then, is all this a solution to the problem? No, certainly not. All of the information is merely a stopgap and another way to begin to break down the barriers in the field that still keep both women and minorities from the top jobs in film and video.

I am not a Pollyanna. I do not believe that persistence and perseverance are the key to breaking down the barriers. And yet, I think persistence and perseverance *are* necessary weapons in the struggle. Along with a lot of screaming about it. Along with good professional work. Along with timing. And luck.

"LET'S HAVE A SHOW, MY AUNT'S GOT A BARN": A TALK WITH PAT KOGAN

I first met Pat at a seminar at 1125 Productions, where she is an executive. The advice she gives in the following interview—on training, experience, the climb up the ladder—is a perfect summary of what it takes to succeed in this business.

Was your background in communications?

"No, my background was in art. I was a graphic artist and photographer. I started out in art school doing everything from weaving to sculpture to graphic design. In those days, the big role model was Mary Wells. It was the first time that women had come to some kind of prominence in doing something major, and I was going to take over the advertising world! But when I got out of school, I realized that I hated working under those conditions."

After two months of working in advertising, Pat moved to a TV station in Philadelphia as a news graphics person and photographer.

> *"And then somebody that I knew said, right out of the old Judy Garland movies, 'My aunt's got a barn, I've got a script,' and we put together a company to do a feature film. It was called Rosebud Films Goodtimes Incorporated and I was the only full-time employee."*

Was the film ever produced?

> *"Oh yes. It opened and won a special jury award at the Atlanta Film Festival and probably played three drive-ins in Texas. And that was the end of it. But I got to do the costumes, the makeup; I was the assistant director. I was also the still photographer on that. And we did the costumes out of Woolworth's!"*

She wound up at the Art Institute of Chicago at a time when the experimental video movement was just starting out. Nam June Paik was at Cal Arts, Phil Morton and Dan Sandin were just starting to work with the image processor at the Circle Campus, and Stan Brakhage was also teaching there.

> *"There was a big avant-garde theater community [in Chicago], and there were lots of inflatable structures and sixteen locations and seventeen dancers, the early pulse lasers and holograms had begun to come to life. Six audio synthesizers interfacing with biofeedback—and interactive video environments with people falling asleep after eighteen hours of dancing around. At the school, I developed a program for myself and it turned out to be the first master's degree in experimental media. We just learned how to do everything ourselves, how to light, how to run around the country and plan shoots, how to work with cameras, and how to tell a story in pictures."*

At some point, she says, "you outgrow the art background and a bad edit isn't art anymore." She began to make phone calls, and finally joined the Joshua Light Show, since video synthesizers and light shows all fit together.

> *"And being a woman in the field was pretty high profile; there weren't that many of us floating around. There were a lot of producers, but there weren't many people who weren't afraid of hands-on. Then one day, George Honsher, who was in charge of special projects, said to me, 'You've done whole productions from top to bottom, but you haven't the faintest idea of the right name for the right light, 'cause you never learned studio stuff. You have a wonderful sense of production, a wonderful sense of direction, but you can't direct a crew professionally because you just don't know the right name to call things!' "*

During the seventies, a lot of corporations were starting their first television facilities. AT&T was one of the most important because they also owned the phone lines. So, Pat went to AT&T and tells one of the funniest "how I got a job" stories that I've heard so far.

> *"I walked into AT&T for what I thought was going to be an interview. There was something going on and they said, 'Get in there!' They literally shoved me on camera while the program was going on the air. During the time I was on camera, the headset went dead, so I was shooting a live feed with no direction from the booth. To say the least, it was kind of interesting."*

She began to freelance for AT&T, doing production assistant work, set design, construction, lighting, camera, some editing, and then directing her own programs. At one point, she realized that it might be time to incorporate, since she was doing all the work for a corporation and might just as well be doing it for herself. She and her husband formed their own company, which started with a few corporate clients and then expanded to a wide range of *Fortune* 500 corporations. A short time ago, she joined 1125 Productions, one of the leaders in HDTV production.

What about being a woman in the video field?

> *"There's a tradition both in film and video. There's no real problem with women in producing capacities. There never really has been. We may not be up to the male count, but you're never looked at strangely. For a while, in technical positions it was tough, and in directorial positions it was difficult, and engineers start giving you a line about how you have to talk their language before they pay attention.*
>
> *"There was a time—which isn't true anymore for people starting out—that if you were building something on a set and you were a woman and the others were men, if the woman picked up something to carry, one of the men would stop what he was doing to help her, whether she asked for help or not. So, someone who was watching the situation would say that she was incompetent because she couldn't carry her own weight."*

You say it's changed?

> *"There are now a lot of mixed crews. Some of the best camera operators that I've worked with—heavy-duty hand-held stuff—are women. There's one woman I work with who does major sporting events. She travels all around, does primarily hand-held things, out of helicopters, stuff like that. It's not common, but I don't think it's a major issue. I don't think*

there are barricades. There are biases. *And I think that if a man comes in and says, 'I'm an engineer,' no one's going to question it. But if a woman comes in and says it, you're going to get, 'Oh really?' That 'Oh really?' means you've still got to prove it. There are times if I'm very direct or if there's a lot of pressure, people say, 'Oh, the bitch.' If somebody else did the same thing, it would be passed over.''*

What is your impression of the young people who come to see you?

''I guess what really shocks me is that the young people seem to want an encapsulated answer—a path to success that is going to guarantee them a job. And what I usually say to them is, first of all, 'What direction are you interested in?' And usually they can't answer that because they're fresh out of high school or college. When I say, 'What is it you like to do?' they keep trying to make a job out of that. I mean, how do you like to spend your time? Are you good with your hands? Those are the things that are really important.

What advice can you give beginners?

''Expose yourself to as much as possible. Learn how to think. *Whether you're going into a technical area, a production area, or directing, the main thing to do is to expose yourself to situations that teach you how to think, how to approach things analytically and diagnostically, things that teach you how to move fast and give you a lot of exposure in dealing with people. Those are the skills that are ultimately going to make a difference in terms of your ability to do something—not the specific training. You'll find ways to get the specifics when you're closer to the job that you are eventually going to take. You probably won't even find that out until you begin working, and you're probably going to go through a couple of jobs before you find out what you're going to eventually do within the industry. But you're not going to be worth anything unless you learn how to think.*

''It doesn't necessarily have anything to do with which school you go to, it doesn't necessarily have anything to do with which course of study you take. If you follow your instincts and follow your abilities, you're going to wind up doing the right thing. And that's a much more visceral decision than an intellectual one!''

CHAPTER FIFTEEN

THE FUTURE IS BEHIND US

In my opinion, video is a new golden age like the end of the thirties in Hollywood.

—Oliver Stone
American Film magazine

I learned many years ago never to laugh at predictions. Back in the seventies, a friend of mine predicted to me that some day the very basis of the way we think about and use information would be revolutionized by computer technology, that maybe instead of collecting slides or photographs, we would collect video clips, or that instead of going to museums, we would visit solid-state walls on which images were inherent in the walls themselves, constantly changing, controlled by computers. I wasn't so sure myself, but now, in the nineties, aren't we transferring our 35mm slides to videotape, and attending shows at museums of video technology?

When it comes to video technology, predictions actually tend to lag behind what is really happening now in editing suites and computer facilities across the country. Technologies that had only just begun to surface when I began writing this book are now being replaced by newer, more useful developments in both the consumer market and professional fields.

In this final chapter, I would like to share with you two of the technological developments taking place in video that herald the future.

Remember that it was only about ten years ago that video was considered a rather crude, unwieldy technology. However, with the advent of original negative film transfer to tape, the refinement of one-inch editing technology, special effects innovations like freeze frame and variable speeds, and picture manipulations with the Quantel and the ADO, videotape moved into every part of the communications business. Since then, we have seen a vast range of electronic systems with letters and numbers that boggle the mind and the memory.

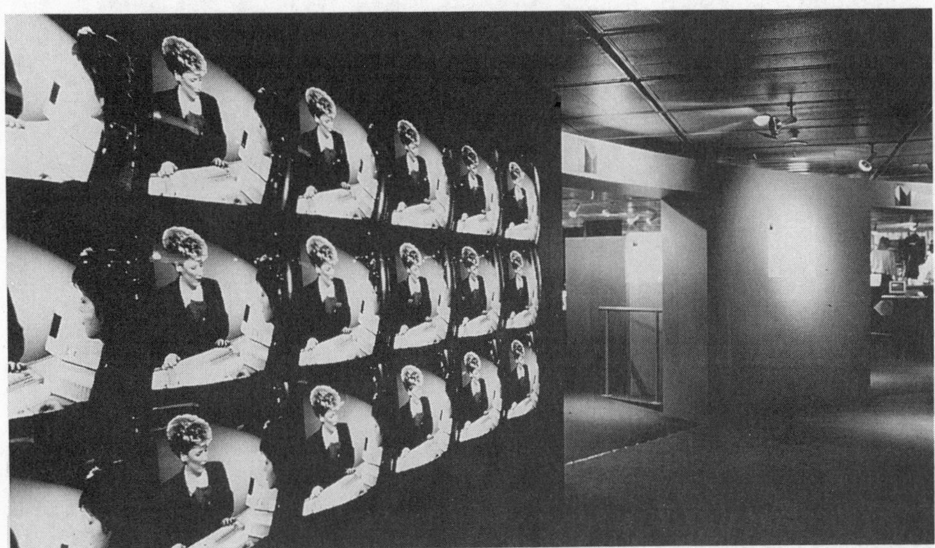

The sort of innovative use of video technology that would have been impossible 15 years ago.

HIGH-DEFINITION TELEVISION

HDTV, mentioned earlier, is still a system in flux, but much has happened in the last few years. It has begun to be used as a production tool and has grown in popularity. But there is still a battle being waged as to just which system will be chosen to transmit the HDTV signal.

RAI (Radiotelevisione Italiana) has actually been experimenting with HDTV since the early 1970s. It has produced two short subjects using the medium: *Arlecchino*, a tale about a carnival figure, and *Oniricon*, a very clever dream/murder story.

In 1988, RAI and Cinecom released the first feature ever to be produced on HDTV, *Julia and Julia*, starring Kathleen Turner, Gabriel Byrne, and Sting. Directed by Peter Del Monte and shot by Giuseppe Rotunno, the picture used the HDTV 1,125-line system. It was rough cut on a Sony ¾-inch VP5000, sent to Japan for one-inch transfer, then retransferred to 35mm Eastman negative film for distribution to theaters. The reviews, especially about the process, were interesting and diverse, to say the least. Vincent Canby in *The New York Times* reported that "high-definition tape can be transferred to film

Kathleen Turner plays Julia, a woman who finds herself in another world with a son she never knew existed, in Julia and Julia, *the first feature ever shot in HDTV. (Courtesy Cinecom and RAI Corporation)*

and look as good as anything shot on film to start with,'' while Rex Reed in the *New York Observer* thought it looked more like ''TWA travel posters shot through split-pea soup.'' Both Roger Ebert in the *New York Post* and the editors of *The New Yorker* expressed surprise at the quality of the finished product. And I loved it!

The critics were right about the tape-to-film transfer. It was generally good. Some scenics and exteriors were equal to what can be shot on 35mm, although some scenes looked hazy and others were absolutely appalling, somewhat like a VHS transfer from a pirated third-generation tape. The reds, as always in video, blossomed badly. The color just does not hold up well on tape.

Nevertheless, since *Julia and Julia* was released, the trade papers and magazines have been filled with articles about HDTV. It has become the most talked-about advance since ''the talkies.'' The incompatibility factor between it and preexisting TV systems has created a situation akin to the incompatibility of the VHS and Beta videotape formats. For the consumer, the obsolescence factor—the threat of having to get rid of current TV sets in order to make room for 1,125-line quality (currently 525 lines in the U.S.)—is a potential problem that may well slow HDTV's growth or create a booming new market in hardware.

HDTV has caused discussion and disagreement even among professionals, who realize that the innovation will again change some production techniques. But then, video has always been an industry that keeps creating new, more up-to-date, state-of-the-art technologies. David Niles of 1125 Productions calls HDTV "revolutionary." The Electronics Industries Association, on the other hand, calls it "evolutionary," comparing it to the movement from black-and-white to color TV.

The production rush has begun. The new toy is here and it's being used, long before there is a standard method of transmitting the signal—indeed, long before there is a standard signal and number of lines, not to mention screen ratio and compatibility with current TV sets.

Advertising agencies are beginning to use HDTV to produce their commercials. Can features be far behind? *Do It Up* (originally titled *Crack in the Mirror*) was the first HDTV feature produced in the U.S. Another first is the made-for-TV film *The Littlest Victims*, produced by 1125 Productions for CBS.

Is HDTV as good as its fans say? I think so. I attended a Director's Guild seminar at 1125 Productions and saw the results firsthand. David Niles, one of the pioneers in the field (who is lovingly dubbed "Captain Video"), showed some sample work as well as a portion of "The Littlest Victims." The quality is beyond comparison—as faithful in its original projection on a large screen as 35mm film. If it is controlled, and produced by experts, there is no doubt in my mind that it is the next step in video.

Niles feels that HDTV is a medium that might be compared to a new language, a new way of telling stories. As he says:

> *This is not TV. It is not video or film. It can imitate video or film, but we must look at it as totally different. It can be used to make television. But it is a new production medium, a new distribution medium.*

HDTV offers many advantages. When shooting, for example, there is no need to reload the camera as frequently as with 35mm film. The original reels are sixty-three minutes long, but a new half-inch HDTV camera can now take a ninety-minute load.

The most striking advantage in using HDTV is its potential for special effects and matting. For films that deal with stories of the future, gigantic dance

On location in Atlanta for The Littlest Victims, *CBS Movie of the Week, a television feature shot in HDTV. David Niles's 1125 Productions produced.*

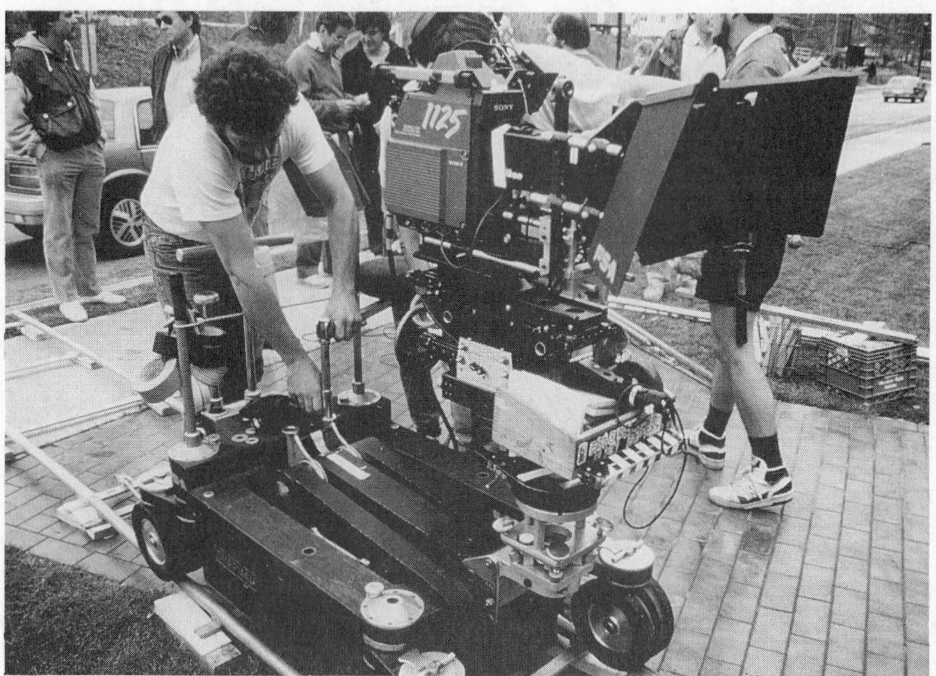

Setting a dolly shot on location in Atlanta for The Littlest Victims. *(Courtesy 1125 Productions)*

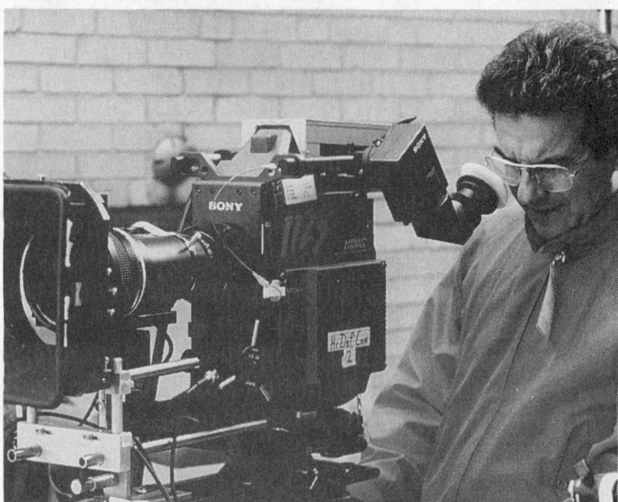

Director Peter Levin, who came from television into film, and then to HDTV. (Courtesy 1125 Productions)

Director of Photography John McPherson with a Hi-Definition camera. (Courtesy 1125 Productions)

sequences, or anything that formerly required a large and expensive studio set, the Ultimatte blending of live foreground actors or even miniatures placed on any photographic background is very impressive and the quality is totally seamless. Even when transferred to 35mm film, the special effects are breathtaking.

Will HDTV require new TV sets? There may be some laws passed that demand that the system finally chosen be compatible with current sets (as color is with black-and-white TV sets). But even if you will need a brand-new television receiver in order to get the quality of 1,125 lines (or whatever is finally decided upon), you might compare the transition with the invention of the compact disc in audio. Essentially, as David Niles puts it, CD manufacturers said, "Throw away your old, beloved record collection and you won't get any clicks anymore.'' And people did. And they will again with HDTV. The industry is betting on it.

There are just a few final points to be made about the new system. The prediction that it will lead to new kinds of programming and production might well be true. As someone at the DGA seminar said, ''Who wants to see Vanna White in High Definition?'' Somehow, the new programming will have to be suited to the quality of the new system, and if there is no improvement, what would be the reason for switching to 600 more lines on the screen?

VIDEO: A WORLD IN FLUX

Digitalization—reducing all audio, video, graphics, and computing technologies into a single one—is an innovation equal in importance to HDTV. The latest observations about HDTV now give the United States a chance to overtake the Japanese because of our know-how in computers and digital programming. The most revolutionary change to take place has been the development of two new editing systems, both based on digital technology.

Until this time, all off-line editing has been what we call *linear*, meaning that once a change was made at any point in the edit, the entire program had to be recoded and recomputed, a long, tedious, expensive job, especially for a half-hour or one-hour show. As I explained earlier in the book, what this amounts to is rerecording the entire piece every time you need to make any editing change. It's like knitting a sweater—if you want to add even one stitch anywhere, the entire sweater would have to be unraveled and redone to include it. The same would be true of removing a stitch, and the analogy applies to video editing. That is, until now. But the new AVID system (Avid Technology, Burlington, MA), and the EMC^2 (Editing Machines Corp., Washington, D.C.) have already begun to distribute their systems, both of which offer *nonlinear* editing for the first time. For the video editor this means that a change can be made at any point in the edit (as in film) and the remainder of the program will automatically adjust to the new sequence or scene.

The costs of both are rather high at this writing, but as soon as they come down somewhat, we may see yet another group of machines become instantly obsolete. For the video editor, it will be the advent of a little bit of Heaven!

If, as projected, videotape technology continues to evolve for at least the next ten or twenty years, much of what happens will affect the job market, some of it positively, some negatively. Some changes will not affect the job seeker or the ladder climber at all (a writer will still be a writer). Others will definitely affect the technician, videographer, or producer.

For the home viewer of television, even the recording of your favorite program while you're out to dinner is being made much simpler. The on-screen remote-controlled systems now in use have already replaced the awkward bar code system, once heralded as the savior for those of us who had too much trouble programming our VCRs before we left the house. All this, in the space of only two or three years.

As I've mentioned, all of the new technology may affect the job market only insofar as engineers and hardware salespeople are concerned. But, if you look at the history of the industry, *every* change filters down somewhere to the production people, the editors, the graphic designers, the directors, the scenic artists, and the special effects artists. It is, after all, the underlying qualities of creativity and visual innovation that will eventually determine the success or failure of a career in the video industry. Technology goes hand in hand with imagination and vision and artistic invention.

Are there also negatives in this growth? In a way, yes. The proliferation of production companies and postproduction companies, for example, plus the constant, almost never-ending flow of graduates, self-taught experts, and technicians in videotape has created several downturns in the field. The competition within the commercial production industry has forced many small businesses to close their doors, especially with some advertising agencies producing their own in-house work. Add to that the awesome cost of new equipment, always in demand as the technology changes, and you get some impossible financial situations for companies desperately trying to remain state-of-the-art. Even in the consumer area, no one is really sure just what the "fade rate" of videotape will be. The technology is still too new, and we have not lived enough years to prove or disprove the manufacturer's claim that the image will outlast you, your children, and your children's children. Some corporations are also building in-house facilities and staff, many of them geared to being profit centers for outside business—and thus in direct competition to the local independent producer. Others have cut back, making the role of the freelancer and the outside supplier more critical in providing professional help.

They key word for video is "change." There are projections that the entire industry will undergo major change well into the next century. And no one can really tell what is coming next. Therein lies the excitement and the potential for the people who will be pursuing their careers during those changes.

If there is a common thread in the advice given in this book, it is that it is possible to move successfully into the field of video and that each person's career path is unique. I have tried to give a balanced view of the industry, promising nothing, yet offering much in the way of encouragement as you start out or move into the field. It is an exciting field. It is, most of all, an interesting field, and those of us who have made our living in it would not change it for all the jobs on Wall Street.

Even for those of us who have been "successful," much of the success has not been financial. Rather, success has been in the area of making our lives richer; of informing us about how others live; of letting our creative juices run freely, with each and every project a new learning experience and a plunge into the unknown. For me, it has meant the ability to satisfy a deep curiosity about the world, and a chance to travel that world in more than sixty countries. It has meant having the chance to build a storehouse of knowledge about a hundred different crafts and professions without ever being bored, and meeting people along the way who have become my good friends. You'll begin to see just what I mean as you make your way into the field of video.

As an author, I must admit that it is always difficult to end a book. Have I culled every single bit of information from my files and passed it on to you? Have I told you enough? Indeed, have I told you too much? More than you want to know? Have I been fair in my analyses and my balance? And have I been wrong in my eternal optimism? Will the video industry go quietly into "middle age," as *The New York Times* has predicted? Or is my optimism correct? Will it blossom into a new "golden age," as Oliver Stone has prophesied? I'm betting on Oliver Stone. I think we ain't seen nothin' yet!

I can only wish you the best of luck!

SELECTED READING

Possibly the best way to keep up with changing video technologies is through the newsletters and magazines that are published at regular intervals. On pages 248–251 you will find a listing of the current crop. You may be sure that new ones are added every month, while some merge or disappear. Some, on the other hand, have been around a very long time (*Back Stage* and *Millimeter*, for example). Subcribe to the ones that seem to give you the information you need most.

In the section on Foundation Grants (chapter 11), you will find listings for the books and publications that deal specifically with this part of the video business. They are generally available only in foundation or public libraries. In any case, they are very expensive and go out of date quickly enough that it doesn't pay to buy them.

And finally, there are hundreds of books that any video/film producer should be reading constantly. These are the books on art, sculpture, architecture, and the museum publications that help all of us in the area of color, composition, lighting, and art history. They are as integral a part of our training and discipline as the technical knowledge about cameras, lenses, and editing computers.

The list that follows is merely a taste of what is now available.

GENERAL AND OVERVIEW BOOKS:

From Knowledge Publications, 701 Westchester Avenue, White Plains, New York 10604:

- Stokes, Judy. *The Business of Nonbroadcast Television* (1988)
- Medhoff, Norman and Tanqary, Tom. *Portable Video: ENG & EFP.* (Electronic News Gathering & Electronic Field Production.) (1986)
- Write for their *Video Bookshelf Catalog* (updated twice a year). Though you will find that some of their publications are fairly expensive, most

are written for professionals and are quite complete. You may not need to own them, but library research may help in your quest for information.

Wiese, Michael. Four books that are now being distributed in bookstores, or are available from Michael Wiese Film/Video, 3960 Laurel Canyon Boulevard, Suite 331, Studio City, CA 91604-3791 or from Butterworth Publishers (Focal Press), 80 Montvale Avenue, Stoneham, MA 02180:

- *Home Video: Producing for the Home Market* (1986)
- *The Independent Film & Videomaker's Guide* (1986)
- *Film & Video Budgets* (1984)
- *Film & Video Marketing* (1988)

London, Mel. *Getting Into Film*. Updated and revised. (New York: Ballantine, 1985). For those who might want to study the crossovers and the similarities, as well as the differences between the film and video field, both of which are beginning to blend.

Maltin, Leonard. *The Whole Film Sourcebook*. (New York: Universe Books-The New American Library, updated regularly). Though the title says ''film,'' it is invaluable to video people in determining the costs of your video project. It also contains an excellent bibliography, plus a listing of pamphlets and catalogues.

RECOMMENDED FOR BEGINNERS

Hedgecoe, John. *Complete Video Course*. (New York: Fireside/Simon & Schuster, 1989). The author made his reputation as a still photographer and has written an excellent beginner's guide that reminds the reader of the elements that go into producing a good videotape: action, composition, special effects and editing. Color photos are excellent as examples.

Moore, Frank Ledlie. *The Video Moviemaker's Handbook*. (New York: Plume/New American Library, 1989). Not as handsome a book as the previous one, but it does have some excellent information for beginners.

EDITING

Books on editing all have the same problem. They are quite complete and quite technically perfect, but the beginner might find them a bit overwhelming with detail and technology. After a few chapters, they begin to dull the senses. Then, after a few years of experience of ''hands-on'' editing, you find that you don't really need the books at all! However, these two might be good companions to keep at your side as you begin your first editing experience. They're quite complete and they've both been published recently, so "futures" are very much a part of their texts:

Browne, Steven E. *Videotape Editing: A Postproduction Primer.*(Stoneham, Mass.: Focal Press, Butterworth Publishers, 1989).

Schneider, Arthur. *Electonic Post-Production & Videotape Editing.* (Stoneham, Mass.: Focal Press, Butterworth Publishers, 1989). The author has almost forty years of experience in film and videotape editing.

FESTIVALS

Bowser, Kathryn *AVIF Guid to International Film & Video Festivals.* (FIVF—Foundation for Independent Video & Film, 625 Broadway, 9th Floor, New York, N.Y. 10012. 1988).

COLLEGES & UNIVERSITIES

American Film Institute Guide to College Courses in Film & Television. (Peterson's Guides, P. O. Box 2123, Princeton, New Jersey 08540). Updated at irregular intervals.

THE JOB HUNT

Back Stage TV & Tape Production Director. (Back Stage Publications, 330 West 42nd Street, New York, N.Y. 10036). Annual publications. Gives complete listings, with names of top executives, for production companies, advertising agencies, postproduction houses, labs, etc. One of the most helpful publications for the job seeker.

National Federation of Local Cable Programmers. (906 Pennsylvania Avenue, S.E., Washington, D.C. 20003). Has information on *Public Access* through cable stations in your area.

National Cable Television Assn. (1724 Massachusetts Ave., N.W., Washington, D.C. 20036). has two booklets that will help you in your job hunt through the cable industry. Both are updated regularly:

- *National Cable Network Directory*
- *Top 50 MSOs* (Multiple System Operators)

Media Resources Catalog. Available through the National Archives & Records Administration, National Audiovisual Center, 8700 Edgeworth Drive, Capital Heights, Maryland 20743-3701. The catalog is updated annually and gives a listing of government agencies that produce videotapes for public distribution.

INDEX

A

Abekas, 179
ACM/SIGGRAPH, 182
Actors, job of, 45
Advertising agencies
  casting files, 106–7
  cost of TV commercial, 104–5
  growth of, 103
  in-house production, 105–6
  job opportunities, 107, 109
  location scouting services, 107
  use of video, 32
Agents, use of, 264
Airvision, 190–92
AVIF Guide to International Film and Video Festivals (Bowser), 219
Akst, George, 163
All Mobile Video, 173
A.L. Williams & Associates network, 80
American Express studios, 89
American Express videos, 90
American Federation of Arts, 206
American Film Institute, seminars/workshops, 244
American Film Institute Guide to College Courses in Film and Television, 231
American Film Institute Independent Filmmaker Program, 201
Amerivan Film and Video Festival, 221–24
American Hospital Association network, 80
American Women's Economic Development Corporation, 282
Anderson, Marcia, 84
Anixter, Julie, 84, 279
  interview with, 85–87
Apogee Production, seminars/workshops, 245
Arts and Entertainment Network, 66
Art video, 198–217
  distribution, 204–12
  financial aspects, 212–13
  funding information, 201–4
  information sources for, 200–201
  interactive videos, 213–17
  public access, 209
Ashland Oil, Inc., 112
Ashley, Robert, 212
Association for Computing Machinery's Special Interest Group on Computer Graphics (ACM/SIGGRAPH), 241
  seminars/workshops, 246
Association of Independent Commercial Producers (AICP), freelance contract, 274–75
Association of Independent Video Filmmakers (AIVF), 200, 207
Audio engineer, job of, 50
Audio visual manager, job of, 41
AVID system, 294
Avon Video Communications Center,88

B

Bachner, Annette, 16
Back Stage, 220
Back State TV Film and Tape Production Directory, 36, 39
Bain, Mark, 110
Bay Area Video Coalition (BAVC), 200–201
Behind the Lens, 281
Berzok, Robert, 111
Billboard, 220
Black Film Festival, 283
Black Filmmakers Foundation, 206, 283
Black and Hispanic Images, 283
Blank, Don, 89
Blechman, R.O., 24
Blue Box Productions, 89
Blumberg, Skip, 210
Bookings, jobs related to, 186
Brakhage, Stan, 198
Broadcast Designers Association, seminars/workshops, 245
Broadcast distribution, jobs in, 185
Broadcast television, 55–63
  electronic field production, 56
  electronic news gathering, 56, 57–58
  job opportunities, 56
  local television stations, 61–62
  low-power TV stations, 62–63
  "60 Minutes," director of operations,

interview with, 58–61
use of video, 31
Brooks Brothers videos, 88
Buckley, Bill, interview with, 164–66
Burson-Marsteller, video-production, 110, 113–19
Business of Nonbroadcast Television, The (Stokes), 78, 81, 161

C

Cable television, 31
Cablevision, public relations director, interview with, 71–74
college channels, 153
growth of, 63–64, 66
job opportunities, 66
production aspects, 66–68
public access, 68–70
Cablevision, 69, 71–74
Calgary Olympics, 114
Carroll Touch Panel, 213
Carsey, Marcy, 254
Case, Don, 107
Casting Company, 106
Casting Directors Inc., 106
Casting files, advertising agencies, 106–7
Center for Media Arts, 239
Chalom, Marc, 66
Chenzera, Ayoke, 212
Chernichaw, Mark, 88
Chiani, Carol, interview with, 241–43
Chyron Corporation, 240
Cinecom, 289
Cinema 16, 198
City Market videos, 88
College applications. *See* Educational applications for video
College recruiters, 261
Color, color response of video, 24
COMMTEX, 248
Communications education
areas of interest, 232
continuing education, 235—37
corporate classes, 240
courses for video professional, 237–39
hand-on work, 233–34
lectures/seminars/workshops, 244–48
listing of schools, guide for, 231
most important schools, 229
nonprofit media centers, 239–40
postproduction courses, 240
private sector activities, 237
of professional organizations, 241
publications, 248–51
school's commitment to video, 231, 232–33
student sample videos, 234–35
technical equipment of, 231, 233
value of, 230–31
Compatibility
high-definition television, 23
worldwide video standards, 17–22
Composer, job of, 47, 52
Computer animation, job of, 47, 51–52
Computer graphics
teacher, interview with, 241–43
use of video, 34
Computer Graphics Show, seminars/workshops, 247
Contract protection, freelancers, 274–75
Coppola, Francis Ford, 10–11
Corporate classes, 240
Corporate video production
examples of, 88, 90–92
growth of, 75–80
in-house production, development of, 82, 84–87
job characteristics, 100–102
jobs in, 94–99
music videos, 171
nonbroadcast expert, interview with, 81–83
private television, 76–81, 89
teacher of, interview of, 100–102
use of video, 31
videotape production services of, 89
Cost, video tape, 15–16
Cost of Production Group, 105
Cotton Club, 10–11
Council on International Nontheatrical Events, 226
Crisis management, public relations

companies, 111–12
Cunningham, Maryce, interview with, 71–74

D

Daniel Edelman Associates, 110
D'Avino, Carmen, 198
Department of Labor, use of video, 125–28
Desktop video publishing, 196
Digital Effects, 51
Digital Post & Graphics, seminars/workshops, 245
Directing Workshop for Women, 281
Director, job of, 41
Directories, job search, 257–58
Directors Guild of America, seminars/workshops, 244–45
Directory of Internships, Work Experience Programs and On-the-Job Training Opportunities, 262
Directory of U.S. & International Festivals of Film and Video, 220
Directory of U.S. Government and Audiovisual Personnel, 258
Distribution
art videos, 204–12
broadcast distribution, 185
nonbroadcast distribution, 185–86
self-distribution, 188–90
Documentation, medical, 162–63
Domino's Pizza network, 79
Downey, Juan, 205, 212
Dreamer, Chip, 35–36
DuArt Laboratories, 202
Duplication of tape, 12–13
DuPont Corporation interactive video, 93

E

Editel, 178
Editing
costs, 26
nonlinear editing, 294
off-line editing, 25–26
on-line editing, 25–26
pitfalls related to, 25–26
sources of information on, 298–99
video tape, 12–13
Editor, job of, 48–50
Edmunds, Mimi, 58
Educational access channels, 69
Educational applications for video, 33, 151–54
cable/local TV programming, 153–54
guidance counseling, 153
instruction, 152–53
orientation, 153
recruitment, 153
Educational and Industrial Television, 94
Education Management Corporation, 237
Eisenberg, Nat, 15
Electronic Arts Intermix (EAI), 206
Electronic Cutting Room, 26, 37
Electronic field production, jobs in, 56
Electronic news gathering, jobs in, 56, 57–58
1125 Productions, 284, 291
EMC^2, 294
Empowerment Project, 210, 212
Engineer
job of, 44–45, 50–51
types of, 50–51
Equipment, rental houses, 172
Erl King, The, 214, 217
Eyepatch, in-house production, 105

F

Facets Video, 207
"Fairfield Exchange," 71
Feature films, use of video, 34
Federal Audiovisual Activity Directory, 120
Federal Communications Commission, on incompatible HDTV, 23–24
Fellows, Bruce, 28, 29
Festivals
American Film and Video Festival, 221–24
deadlines, 228
fees, 227

format required, 227
guides to, 219–20
international festivals, 226–27
ITVA Video Festival, 224
Monitor Awards, 224–26
positive aspects of, 218–19
shipping, 227–28
Sinking Creek Film/Video Festival, 224
third world festivals, 283
for video by women, 282
Film commissions, job search, 258–60
Film/Tape Production Source Book, 257
Film/Video Arts (FVA), 239, 283
Financial expert, job of, 54
First refusals, freelancers and, 274
Food Business Network, 79
Food and Drug Administration network, 79
Foundation Center, 203
Foundation Grants Index, 204
Freelancers, 273–75
cancellation problems, 274
contract protection, 274–75
first refusals and, 274
use of, 72–73
Friedman, Roberta, 199, 214, 216, 217
Funding
fund-raising, 163
sources for art video project, 210–204

G

Geographic area, video-related jobs, 37–40
Georgia Pacific studios, 89
Gillette, Frank, 213
Giraldi, Bob, 169, 171
Gofer, job of, 47
Goodman, Steve, interview with, 139–42
Government video production, 33
agencies that provide videotapes, 122–24
Department of Labor video chief, interview with, 125–28
information sources on, 120–21
police department video chief, interview with, 128–33
requests for proposals, 133–36
uses of, 125, 126
Grants Register, 204
Great Intergalactic TV Quiz Show, 92
Group W Cable, 68
Guidance counseling, use of video, 153

H

Hage, Phil, 29
Hamilton Communications, 167
Hankin, Stan, interview with, 125–58
Hanwright, Joe, 170
Harding, Kathy, 279
Harry, 179
Henninger Video, 38
Hewlett-Packard interactive video, 93
High-definition television (HDTV), 289–94
advantages of, 291, 293
development of, 289
equipment compatibility, 23
feature film for, 289–90
programming and, 294
uses of, 291
Hilleary, Duncan, 191
Hirschman, Celia, 169
Home Entertainment, 187–88
Home Video: Producing for the Home Market (Wiese), 188, 193
Home video, 33–34
airline market, 190–92
business-related issues, 189
independent producer, interview with, 193–97
international market, 189–90
self-distribution, 188–90
types of videos, 187
Hooper, Tobe, 171
Hospital Satellite Network, 83

I

IBM network, 79
Idaho Video, 35–36
Illegal copies, 192–93
anticopying systems, 193
Illigasch, Joe, interview with, 58–61

INDEX

Independent artists. *See* Art video
Independent production
  benefits for client, 142–43
  competition and, 137
  job opportunities, 143
  operation of, 138–39
  producers, interviews with, 139–42, 144–49
  rewards of business, 143
  sizes of, 138
Independent, The, 189, 201, 207, 220
Infomart, 119
Infoquest display, 93
Information sources, resources directories, 36
Information systems, use of video, 34
In-house production
  advertising agencies, 105–6
  corporations, 82, 84–87
  hospitals, 160–61
  operation of, 82, 84–87
Instant replay, 9–11
  advantages/disadvantages of, 26–28
Instant video, 187
Instruction
  medical education, 162
  use of video, 152–53
Interactive video, 17, 92–94
  examples of, 93
  growth of, 93
  uses of, 92–93
Intermedia Arts of Minnesota, 207
Intern, job of, 47
International Agency for Minority Artist Affairs, 283
International Communications Industries of Association, seminars/workshops, 248
International festivals, 226–27
International Film and Television Workshop, 239
International market, 189–90
International Production Center, 177
International Television Association (ITVA)
  activities of, 96–97
  job description guidelines, 97–99
  seminars/workshops, 245–46
  video festival, 224
Internships, 261–63
  minorities and, 262
  sources of information about, 262
Iran-Contra hearings, 187

J

Janos, Paula, 84
  interview with, 85–87
Jans, Laura, interview with, 255–57
JBM/Creamer-Boston, in-house production, 105
J.C. Penney network, 79
J.C. Penney studios, 89
Job description guidelines, ITVA, 97–99
Job interview, 267–71
  behavior during, 268–69
  follow-up to, 270–71
  preparation for, 267–68
Job search
  agent, use in, 264
  college recruiters, 261
  competition in, 253
  directories, 257–58
  film commissions, 258–60
  focus in, 254–55
  geographic area, 37–40
  internships, 261–63
  making contact, 264–65
  networking, 263–64
  resume/letter, 265–67
  sample tapes, use of, 276–78
  sources of information on, 299–300
  trade magazines/ads, 260–61
  video markets, 31–40
Jobs in video
  actors, 45
  audio visual manager, 41
  composer, 47, 52
  computer animation, 47, 51–52
  director, 41
  editor, 48–50
  engineer, 44–45, 50–51
  financial expert, 54
  gofer, 47
  intern, 47

makeup/hair stylist, 46
producer, 41
production assistant, 43–44
public relations specialist, 54
sales representative, 52–53
script supervisor, 46–47
set designers, 46
sound person, 43
special effects expert, 47–48, 51–52
technicians, 46
videographer, 42–43
voice-over narrators, 45–46
wardrobe person, 46
writer, 41–42
Johnson, Bill, interview with, 128–33
Jonas, Joan, 210
Judd Hambrick Company, 89
Julia and Julia, 34, 289, 290

K

Kasper, David, 210
Katz, Ralph, interview with, 113–17
Kavensky, kCandace, 254
Kealy, Janet, 282
Kelly & Case Casting, 107
Kimball, Jeffrey, 227
Kitchen, The, 206, 214, 217
Kleiser, Jeff, 51
Knickerbocker Film/Video Associates, 282
Kogan, Pat, interview with, 284–87

L

Law Store, 164
Legal applications for video, 163–66
growth of 164, 165
producer, interview with, 164–66
wills, 163–64
Leo Burnett-Chicago, in-house production, 105
Letter, job request, 265–66
Levi-Strauss interactive video, 93
Library management, 186
Limousine language, 217
"Littlest Victims, The," 34
Local television stations
college channels, 153–54
jobs in, 61–62
Location scouting services, advertising agencies, 107
Longo, Robert, 217
Lovinger, Jeff, 170
Lowe-Marschalk Summer Creative Internship Program, 262
Low-power television
jobs in, 63
scope of coverage, 62
Lye, Len, 198

M

McLaren, Norman 198, 199
Macrovision, 193
Maintenance engineer, job of, 50
Makeup/hair stylist, job of, 46
Malpractice cases, videos and, 163
Maltin, Leonard, 202
Markward, Frank, 177
Media Project, 207
Media Resources Catalog, 121
Medical applications for video, 80, 91, 159–63
community relations, 163
documentation, 162–63
fund-raising, 163
generic information videotapes, 161
in-house hospital video production, 160–61
malpractice cases, 163
medical education, 162
patient education, 162
pharmaceutical applications, 161
videoconferencing, 162
Merrill Lynch network 79, 111
Meyer, Peter, 282
Minorities in video, 278
and corporate video field, 101
support groups for, 283–84
Minority Intern Program, 262

Mirage, 179
Mitchell, Tony, 170
Mobile production units, 173–74
Modern Talking Pictures, 185
Monitor Awards, 224–26
MPI Home Video, 188
MTV, 171–72
Muppet Meeting Films, 91
Murphy, Brianne, 280, 281
"Music Alive," 234
Music Business Institutes, 237
Music videos
  corporate videos, 171
  growth of, 169
  MTV producer, interview with, 171–72
  types of 170–71

N

National Audiovisual Center, 121, 258
National Cable Network Directory, 70
National Television Standards Committee (NTSC), 18
Native American Screening And Video Production Workshop, 284
Neiman-Marcus videos, 88
Networking, job search, 263–64
New Day Films, 210
News 12, 64, 71
Niles, David, 291, 293
Noble, Judy, 111
Nonbroadcast distribution, jobs in, 185–86
Nonbroadcast television
  nonbroadcast expert, interview with, 81–83
  private television, 76–81, 89
  use of video, 32
Nonprofit media centers, 239–40
Nonprofit organizations
  types of, 158–59
  use of video, 157–59

O

Ogilvy & Mather, 105, 111
Optical effects, of video, 12
Orientation, use of video, 153
Outhank, Judy, 279

P

Pacific Arts Corporation, 207
Paik, Nam June, 205, 209, 210
Paintbox, 178–79
Paladin Productions, 138
Patient education, 162
Payson, John, interview with, 171–72
Pearlstein, Philip, 199
Pepperman, Richard, 163
Perkins, Michael, 191, 192
Pharmaceuticals industry videos, 91, 93, 161
Phillips Petroleum, 112
Point-of-sale videos, 90–91, 92, 93
Police department, use of video, 128–33
Porter Novelli, 110
Post: *The Magazine for Animation, Audio, Film & Video Professionals*, 176
Post Perfect, 182, 183
Postproduction, 175–82
  broadcast distribution, 185
  film/video combinations and, 176–77
  job market, 181–82
  job requirements of, 177–78, 182
  nonbroadcast distribution, 185–86
  postproduction expert, interview with, 182–84
Postproduction equipment
  Abekas, 179
  Harry, 179
  Mirage, 179
  Paintbox, 178–79
  Sunburst, 180–81
  Ultimatte, 179–80
Private television, 76–81, 89
  examples of networks, 79–80
  operation of, 76–77
  uses of, 77–78
Producer, job of, 41
Production assistant, job of, 43–44
Production companies, use of video, 32, 34
Professional organizations, courses of, 241

Prudential Insurance Company videos, 88
Public access, 68–70, 73
 rules related to, 69
Publications, video, listing of, 248–51
Public relations companies
 crisis management, 111–12
 goal of, 109
 growth of, 103–4
 job opportunities, 112–13
 video activities of, 32–33, 110–11
 video production executives, interview with, 113–19
Public relations specialist, job of, 54

Q

Quality, video versus film, 13–14
QUBE, 213

R

Rafelson, Bob, 171
RAI (Radiotelevision Italiana), 289
Recruitment, use of video, 153
Request for proposals, information requirements of, 134–36
Resume
 contents of, 266
 video resumes, 267
Roszell, Steve, 212
Royston, Curt, 209, 214

S

Sales representative, job of, 52–53
Salo, Ray, 13, 14, 37
Sample tapes, 276–78
Sant'Andrea, Jim, interview with, 117–19
Sarabia, Armand, 180
Sarnoff, Dorothy, 111
Satellite technology, 128
Sayles, John, 204
Schlott Realtors videos, 90
Schneider, Ira, 213
Schwartz, Buky, 209, 214
Screening ease, of video, 11
Script supervisor, job of, 46–47
Secret Sounds Screaming, 212
Self-distribution, 188–90, 209–10
Seminars, sources for, 244–48
Set designers, job of, 46
Sinking Creek Film/Video Festival, 224
Smith, C. Cecil, 22
Soldier's Tale, A, 24
Sony DVTR, 181
Sony Super-Beta system, 13
Sound person, job of, 43
SPAN (Spafax Airline Network), 191
Special effects expert, job of, 47–48, 51–52
Special events video
 producers, interview with, 167–69
 types of events, 166–67
Speech Dynamics, Inc., 111
Spooner, Sandy, interview with, 144–49
Standards, worldwide video standards, 17–22
Starlight Productions, 105
Stokes, Judy, 78, 81, 161
 interview with, 81–83
Stoney, George, 210
Storage of tape, 28–29
Sunburst, 180–81
Suzuki Motor Corporation, 112
SVP, 279
Swain, Philip, 80
Swift, Al, 62
System X-L, 180

T

Tasker, Jeannie, 280
Tax deduction, continuing ed courses, 236
Technicians, job of, 46
Teleconferencing, 17
Third world festivals, 283
Third World Newsreel, 207
3M Memories Technology Group Labs, 28, 29
Three-dimensional communications, 119
Top 50 MSO's, 70

Trade magazines/ads, job search, 260–61
Training, 114
  interactive videos, 92–93
Transmitter engineer, job of, 50–51
Travelers Insurance Company interactive video, 93
Trent, Barbara, 210
Trucker: The Man and His Dream, 11
Turner, Ted, 187
TV Film and Tape Production Directory, 257

U

Ultimatte, 179–80
Union Carbide, 111
Unions, 275–76
Universities, use of video, 33

V

Vagnoni, Anthony, 177
Vestron, 194, 195
Video
  books/publications related to, 297–300
  future view, 294–96
Video Bookshelf, 249
Video cassette recorders (VCRs)
  ownership of, 30
  in Soviet Union, 190
Video Central, 140, 141
Video Computer Animation Workshop, 241
Videoconferencing, 162
Video Data Bank, 189, 207, 212
Videodisc, 82
Video entrepreneur, interview with, 154–57
Video Era, 11
Video Expo, seminars/workshops, 246
Videographer, job of, 42–43
Video Legacy, Ltd., 163
Video Manager, 22
Video markets
  advertising agencies, 32
  broadcast television, 31
  cable TV, 31
  computer graphics, 34
  corporate video production, 32, 39
  educational videotapes, 33
  feature films, 34
  geographic areas and, 35–40
  government agencies, 33
  home videos, 33–34
  information systems, 34
  nonbroadcast television, 32
  production companies, 32, 34
  public relations firms, 32–33
  universities, 33
Video monitoring services, 112
Video Networks, 200
Video newsletters, 83
Video Register and Teleconferencing Resources Directory, 36
Video resumes, 267
VideoSee Saw, 214
Videotape
  advantages of, 9–17
  combined with film, 14–15
  quality, versus film, 13–14
  worldwide standards for, 17–22
Videotape recording engineer, job of, 51
Video Tape Review, 209
Video users, definition of, 78
Video Walkman, 190
Video wall, 91, 113, 114, 119
Viola, Bill, 212
Vis-Ability, 169
Visual Communications Congress, seminars/workshops, 248
Vodenos, Arna, 279
  interview with, 154–57
Vodenos Productions, 154
Vogel, Amos, 198
Voice-over narrators, job of, 45–46

W

Wang Laboratories network, 80
Wardrobe person, job of, 46
Weddings, videotaping of, 167–69
Weinbren, Grahame, 199, 214

Werner, Tom, 254
West Glen Communications, 185–86
Weynand Associates, 238
Whitewater Productions, 105
Whitney Museum, 205, 209, 214
Whole Film Sourcebook (Maltin), 202
Wiese, Michael, 188, 193
  interview with, 193–97
Wipe Cycle, 213
Wise, Howard, 210
Women in Film, 281
Women Make Movies, 207
Women in video, 278–87
  and corporate video field, 101
  festivals for, 283
  financial programs for, 280
  positive signs for, 280
  production executive, interview with, 284–87
  support groups for, 281–82
Workshops, sources for, 244–48
Worldwide Video Festival, 226
Writer, job of, 41–42

Y

Young and Rubicam, in-house production, 105

Z

Zahler, Steve, 26, 37